YOUNG ADULT
AMERICAN
CATHOLICS

YOUNG ADULT
AMERICAN
CATHOLICS

Explaining Vocation in Their Own Words

edited by Maureen K. Day

Paulist Press
New York / Mahwah, NJ

Cover image by ThamKC/Shutterstock.com
Cover design by Lightly Salted Graphics
Book design by Lynn Else

Copyright © 2018 by Maureen K. Day

Library of Congress Cataloging-in-Publication Data
Names: Day, Maureen K., editor.
Title: Young adult American Catholics : explaining vocation in their own words / edited by Maureen K. Day.
Description: New York : Paulist Press, 2018.
Identifiers: LCCN 2018000646 (print) | LCCN 2018025110 (ebook) | ISBN 9781587687648 (eBook) | ISBN 9780809153930 (pbk. : alk. paper)
Subjects: LCSH: Work—Religious aspects—Catholic Church. | Vocation—Catholic Church. | Christian life—Catholic authors. | Catholic Church—United States.
Classification: LCC BX1795.W67 (ebook) | LCC BX1795.W67 Y68 2018 (print) | DDC 282/.730842—dc23
LC record available at https://lccn.loc.gov/2018000646

ISBN 978-0-8091-5393-0 (paperback)
ISBN 978-1-58768-764-8 (e-book)

Published by Paulist Press
997 Macarthur Boulevard
Mahwah, New Jersey 07430

www.paulistpress.com

Printed and bound in the
United States of America

Contents

v

CONTENTS

Contents

CONTENTS

Contents

CONTENTS

Contents

Preface

The not-so-dirty little secret about this book—which just happens to pertain to all books—is that it is not for everyone. It is most certainly not for those who could say about American Catholicism what the doctor of *The Brothers Karamazov* renown said about humanity: the more he loves it in general, the less he loves particular individuals.[1] No, this is a book for people who care a good deal about particularity. Particular individuals, particular perspectives and life experiences, particular modes of understanding and living out a single religious tradition—nary a vague generality lies ahead for those who dive in and read the scholarly essays and personal accounts that comprise this collection.

The prospect of doing so, of course, should appeal to readers with sensibilities considerably unlike those of Dostoyevsky's doctor. More important perhaps, diving into this collection is also a good way to take some measure of what has come to be known as the "sense of the faithful," the insights and lived experience of rank-and-file Catholics that, according to long-standing Church teaching, warrants serious consideration as a source for theological reflection. Proposed reasons for why this has not always panned out to the extent, for example, enjoined by the Second Vatican Council, come from many

---

1. Fyodor Dostoyevsky, *The Brothers Karamazov*, trans. David Magarshack (New York: Penguin Classics, 1982), pt. 2, chap. 4.

directions. To these, I would add one more. Even when faced with a deep vein of insight and experience, mining is still hard work. It takes time and no small degree of effort to astutely read "the signs of the times," get the facts right, and offer thoughtful consideration to what is occurring among American Catholics or, in the case of this volume, among its subset of young adults.

Central to taking on this hard work is a commitment to honing three analytical dispositions that, in my view, are evident within the pages ahead and that I encourage readers to also deploy as they engage this collection.

The first is *Verstehen*, a practice Max Weber famously considered to be constitutive of the sociological enterprise. German for "understanding," in his distinctive usage it principally means resisting the temptation to impose one's own normative categories onto subjects' experience and thus doing one's best to understand the other on the other's own terms.[2] This sort of hermeneutical generosity is on display when this book's contributing scholars bracket whatever biases they might have and then privilege data gathering over mere presumption when addressing their respective topics. It is also reflected in the editor's wise decision to allow young adults to speak for themselves, on their own terms and in accordance with their own particular categories.

The second disposition I have in mind is what, for lack of a highfalutin sociological term, I will simply call nimbleness. Rather than relying on hidebound, black or white verities, the people in this book—scholars and young adults alike—offer reflections that, as the great G. F. W. Hegel once noted of philosophy, are painted "gray in grey."[3] Does one

---

2. See especially Max Weber, *The Methodology of the Social Sciences*, ed. Edward Shils and Henry Finch (New York: Free Press, 1949).

3. G. F. W. Hegel, *Philosophy of Right*, trans. T. M. Knox (New York: Oxford University Press, 1967, reprint 1821), 13.

hear in these pieces reflections based upon faith or reason? Both. Just as what we take to be rational is typically based on a kind of tacit fidelity to first principles (a conversation for another day), contributors here interrogate their faith commitments reflexively, with respect to what they know from both their rational faculties and the round of their everyday lives. So, are we seeing religion or spirituality at play here? Both. These young adults—even, in some ways, the marginal and former ones—interact with the objectified, institutional components of the Church while, at the very same time, doing so in terms that feel subjectively meaningful and emotionally satisfying to them. And, what of the broader tradition? Is it changing before our eyes or remaining constant? Once again, the preferred option here is for painting in grayer hues. While showing great respect for a faith that has endured for more than two millennia, they also display a keen understanding of historian Jaroslav Pelikan's distinction between tradition, the "living faith of the dead," and traditionalism's "dead faith of the living."[4] To resist carefully discerned changes, to set a faith in stone, writers for this collection seem to know, is ultimately to produce that tradition's headstone.

Inquisitiveness, our third analytical disposition, both precedes and follows the other two. In other words, one needs to be authentically inquisitive about people in order to truly listen to them on their own terms and then to avoid interpreting what they say on the basis of ham-handed, either/or taxonomies. But that is only the beginning. Beyond merely allowing people to answer our (or others') questions, being inquisitive means that we take the extra step to then question their answers. There are questions that should be asked of the analyses and reflections that appear

---

4. Jaroslav Pelikan, *The Vindication of Tradition* (New Haven: Yale University Press, 1984), 65.

throughout this compilation. Like any good book, this one is best treated, quite literally, as a conversation piece. And, like all good readers, you should consider yourself part of the conversation. Offering this very invitation, I presume, is the editor's intent in providing what I consider to be some excellent questions following each section of this book. I encourage readers to take these seriously, to think about them, and thus, along with honing a sense of *Verstehen* and interpretive nimbleness, to also exhibit the very sort of inquisitiveness that a collection like this one deserves.

To these questions, I want to add some of my own that, spurred by my own reading of the pieces that follow, may enable other readers to delve more deeply into this collection as well.

First, to what extent do the findings and analyses presented by the various contributing scholars align with the more personal reflections offered by the young adults, and in what ways might these seem at odds with one another?

Second, which dimensions of these young adults' religious lives do you suspect are what sociologists often call "lifecycle effects," and thus a function of their relative youth, versus being true "cohort effects" in that their difference from prior generations is likely to continue throughout the life course, even to when they become the age of their parents and grandparents?

Third, in what ways is this a book about distinctly American Catholics? In other words, is it possible to distinguish between when young adults engage their faith in terms authenticated by the tradition as opposed to internalizing some of what sociologist Robert Wuthnow calls the broadly salient and largely taken-for-granted "deep meanings" that define American culture?[5] For instance, some of the reflections valorizing

---

5. Robert Wuthnow, *American Mythos: Why Our Best Efforts to Be a Better Nation Fall Short* (Princeton: Princeton University Press, 2006), esp. chap. 1.

self-identity and expressivity as well as those envisioning the Church as a source of "support" for such individualized projects seem to lean in this distinctly American direction.

Last, throughout this book, to use economist Albert Hirschman's terminology, one hears plenty of "voice," people who are reflexive about the tradition, talk back to it, and are self-consciously attentive to how it does or does not make sense to them. This, as I have suggested, is important for any religious tradition and partly why this book is such a fine conversation piece. However, one hears much less from people who reflect Hirschman's other important options.[6] What of those who would fall into his "loyalty" grouping? It is doubtful that they, as the old Catholic once had it, simply "pray, pay and obey." But many of these young adult Catholics, for good or for ill, go to church on Sunday, seldom think much more about it on Monday and thereafter, and do not necessarily see their faith as something they need to address in a more intentional or even vocational manner. In short, these less vocal "loyalty" Catholics are unlike their "voice" counterparts and, yet, are just as important to this larger story. So, too, are those who "exit" and join the ranks of one of the nation's fastest growing and, with about one in ten Americans among them, largest religious designations—former Catholics. If a religious tradition is, in G. K. Chesterton's memorable words, a kind of "democracy of the dead," then it makes sense that the views of the otherwise departed should also be heard.[7] The fact that they no longer affiliate with the Church should not be taken to mean that their perspectives are irrelevant to it. Thus, in the spirit of inquisitiveness, one does well to ask how being more inclusive of those who represent the

---

6. Albert O. Hirschman, *Exit, Voice, and Loyalty: Responses to Decline in Firms, Organizations, and States* (Cambridge, MA: Harvard University Press, 1970).

7. Gilbert K. Chesterton, *Orthodoxy* (New York: John Lane, 1908), 85.

"loyalty" and "exit" options might inform, challenge, or, in any case, provide additional touches of gray to what is portrayed in the pages that follow.

As already mentioned, this book is not for everyone. Yet, for those enticed by such questions and who are indeed drawn to young adult Catholics in all their particularity, then diving in and immersing oneself in this collection is a great way to enter into an important conversation about faith and vocation within American society today.

Jerome P. Baggett, PhD, is Professor of Religion and Society at the Jesuit School of Theology of Santa Clara University and member of the Graduate Theological Union's core doctoral faculty. He is author of Sense of the Faithful: How American Catholics Live Their Faith *(Oxford University Press).*

Introduction

In October 2018, the 15th Ordinary General Assembly of the Synod of Bishops will gather in Rome to discuss "Young People, the Faith, and Vocational Discernment." The hope of this synod is to better understand the lives of today's young adults and offer them more effective pastoral care. Pope Francis expresses his affection for young adults in his 2017 "Letter of His Holiness Pope Francis to Young People on the Occasion of the Presentation of the Preparatory Document of the 15th Ordinary General Assembly of the Synod of Bishops" in writing: "I wanted you to be the centre of attention, because you are in my heart." His desire to deeply hear the insights of young adults is made explicit toward the end of the letter: "The Church also wishes to listen to your voice, your sensitivities and your faith; even your doubts and your criticism. Make your voice heard, let it resonate in communities and let it be heard by your shepherds of souls." There are many events happening to amplify young adult voices: an online survey commissioned by the Vatican available in six different languages; conferences on young adult Catholics—some conferences on young adults generally and others on specific subpopulations; books and online columns either released or in progress that feature the young adult Catholic experience. This book will help readers better understand the challenges, graces, and pastoral needs of young adults within the U.S. context. While the age range of "young adult" varies with time and place (e.g., the international survey is for those sixteen to twenty-nine years old), this book uses the range specified by the United States Conference of Catholic Bishops: nineteen to thirty-nine years old.[1]

As the publisher and author discussed the format of this book, there emerged a mutual desire for this to be both scholarly and experiential. On the one hand, to have a collection of academics discussing research on young adult Catholics would no doubt be valuable, but it risks distancing the reader from the very population studied, creating a book that speaks *about* or *for* young adult Catholics rather than *to*, *with*, or *from* them. On the other hand, a book that was rooted only in the experiential would leave the reader wondering whether or not the experiences therein are generalizable or are simply unique to that person. Recognizing that both the scholarly and the experiential are critical to the aims of the synod, this book takes a "both/and" approach. Each of the thirteen sections of this book is introduced by a scholar who has significant expertise in that specific aspect of young adult Catholic life. This scholar presents some of the latest research, offering the reader a broader context for the particular group that follows. These scholars do a fantastic job of bringing complex research to a public audience, giving the reader a very accessible summary of current and relevant academic research. Following each scholarly piece are two or more pieces written by Catholics who actually come from these populations; these experiential pieces bring the academic findings to life in a very personal way. The writers of these pieces come from a variety of backgrounds

---

1. "Youth and Young Adult Ministry," United States Conference of Catholic Bishops, accessed April 6, 2018, http://www.usccb.org/beliefs-and-teachings/who -we-teach/youth-and-young-adult-ministry.cfm.

Introduction

and experiences. Some of these experiences might resonate with those of the readers and others may seem quite foreign. But each author provides a candid window into a particular young adult's life, his or her understanding of vocation, and offers an opportunity for listening, learning, and accompaniment. There are also some questions at the end of each section to guide further reflection and discussion, making it an easy group book read. It is my hope that the reader will carefully consider both the scholarly and experiential contributions in light of these questions and find ways—at the personal level or larger—to better meet the pastoral needs of young adult Catholics striving to live their vocation.

These thirteen sections are divided into three parts. "Vocation through the Life Course," the first part, follows young adult Catholics over time, allowing a window to view the changing needs of young adults as they hit particular milestones common in young adult life. The first section within this part hears from students currently in college in a variety of contexts: Catholic colleges, private nonreligious schools, and public nonreligious schools. The second section examines the experiences of "emerging adults," single Catholics figuring out the ways their faith and life choices inform each other. The final set of voices comes from Catholic parents raising their children in an intentionally Catholic way. In examining identity and practice within the second part, the reader will discover the ways various commitments and aspects of identity—such as political ideology or ethnicity—shape understandings of religious vocation. The fourth section explores the role of vocation among Catholics who are involved in lay groups, broadly defined. Section 5 looks more deeply at the progressive/traditionalist binary that is quickly becoming quite a pastoral challenge in the U.S. Church. The next three sections look at the role of ethnicity among Latino/a, black, and Asian-Pacific Islander Catholics

xxi

who make deliberate efforts to wed their religious and ethnic identities. The ninth section looks at this same religio-identity work among LGBTQ Catholics. This part concludes with reflections from Catholics who are marginal or who have left Catholicism and what they would need to come back to or strengthen their relationship with the Church. The final part examines understandings of vocation among those directly working for the Church as priests, sisters, and lay ecclesial ministers. With the dwindling numbers of priests, it is helpful to hear the stories of those who have entered. The contributing sisters come from communities that are having varying degrees of success in attracting women to their religious communities and propose ways they could be better supported. Concluding this part, this more conventional understanding of "vocation" as ecclesial leadership will include the voices of lay ministers, many of whom feel only partially supported by the Church—understood as both institutionally and as individual Catholics in the pews—they serve. These three parts together will explore vocation from a variety of angles, collectively offering a very nuanced picture of vocation among young Catholic adults today.

One final word. Books, as a genre of communication, have their assets and liabilities. An obvious liability is that they are very one-way; clearly there are no easy opportunities for dialogue between reader and author. But this could also be an asset: the reader may want insight on being a sister, a lesbian Catholic, or a traditionalist Catholic, but they may find it difficult to make that first move to engage any person from this group. Books offer the reader the safety of anonymity, casualness, and distance. However, this more remote approach could easily allow the reader to fall into a voyeuristic mindset, reading this book for the sake of curiosity and understanding these voices as exotic or "other." I would like to propose a different lens that a reader could bring to this text: encounter. Pope Francis calls us to a "culture of encounter," which he elaborates to mean, "not just seeing, but looking; not just hearing, but listening; not just passing people by, but stopping with them; not just saying 'what a shame, poor people!'" but allowing yourself to be moved with compassion; "and then to draw near, to touch and to say: 'Do not weep' and to give at least a drop of life."[2] In this spirit of encounter, I hope that this book can act as a first encounter for the readers so that they may look, listen, draw nearer to young adults, and offer them compassionate pastoral care as modeled by the ministry of Christ.

---

2. Pope Frances quoted in "For a Culture of Encounter: Mass at Santa Marta," *L'Osservatore Romano*, no. 38, Weekly ed. (Eng.), September 13, 2016, http://www .osservatoreromano.va/en/news/culture-encounter.

PART 1

Vocation through the Life Course

A Secularizing Institution?

UNDERSTANDING THE UNDERGRADUATE EXPERIENCE

by Brian Starks

In this brief introductory essay, I detail a common yet
fundamentally flawed story of colleges and universities as
wholly secularizing institutions. In this view, colleges and
universities (especially public ones) serve as hotbeds of
contemporary religious decline. In contrast, sociological
research in the past decade has found college attendance
to be, on average, protective of religious belief and practice
among emerging adults.[1] In detailing this research, I
acknowledge an important truth in the common story of
secularization, but highlight errors and omissions that require
us to jettison this faulty narrative in search of a more accurate
account. In its place, many sociologists have described
religious life on campus as a "spiritual marketplace." While

---

1. Jeremy Uecker, Mark Regnerus, and Margaret Vaaler, "Losing My Religion:
The Social Sources of Religious Decline in Early Adulthood," *Social Forces* 85
(2007): 1667–92.

noting insights gained from this newer conceptual approach, especially with regard to research on religious organizations on campus, I end my essay by highlighting limitations and potential pitfalls with this alternative, especially when incorporating the concepts of vocation and discernment.

A FLAWED SECULARIZATION THESIS: MODERN CAMPUSES AS HOSTILE TO UNDERGRAD RELIGION

Secularization is a complicated term. I cannot explore the many, varied academic definitions of it in a brief introductory essay. Instead, I simply evoke secularization as a cultural trope of religious decline *in* and *through* higher education. According to this account, universities are modern, secularizing institutions and are therefore overwhelmingly, if not unremittingly, hostile to undergraduate religion and corrosive of religious belief.

Yet, the most comprehensive recent sociological studies, with access to the best, most representative data, have not found higher education wholly hostile to undergraduate religion. Rather, undergraduate college attendance tends to be protective of religious beliefs and practices among today's emerging adults.[2] Moreover, in a recent national survey, 80 percent of Catholic campus ministers at public, four-year institutions report a positive overall campus environment for their ministry (and 97 percent of those at Catholic institutions report similarly).[3] These are not signs of overwhelming hostility!

Not to overexaggerate the positivity toward religion on public campuses, most campus ministers at public universi-

---

2. Christian Smith, *Souls in Transition: The Religious & Spiritual Lives of Emerging Adults* (New York: Oxford University Press, 2009). See also Uecker, Regnerus, and Vaaler, "Losing My Religion."

3. Brian Starks, *The 2017 National Study of Catholic Campus Ministry: Report to USCCB* (forthcoming).

ties describe the campus environment as "somewhat positive" for their ministry, and higher education is much more comfortable with restrained, tame expressions of religiosity, than with transformative religion. Moreover, the research cited earlier indicates that higher education is protective of religious practice among emerging adults *in comparison to the alternative of not going to college.* As a longitudinal analysis of Add Health data reveals, "The assumption that the religious involvement of young people diminishes when they attend college is of course true: Sixty-four percent of those currently enrolled in a traditional four-year institution have curbed their attendance habits. Yet, 76 percent of those who *never enrolled* in college report a decline in religious service attendance."[4]

So, there is a kernel of truth here. Declines in religious attendance and, to a lesser extent, religious belief occur during the college years, but declines are larger outside of college. This suggests religious decline is due more to age or life course than to colleges and universities themselves. Indeed, life course theorists have begun to utilize the concept of emerging adulthood to discuss a new, socially constructed period in life following adolescence, when individuals begin to attenuate ties with their families of origin, but before they fully enter adulthood.

College Campuses as a Spiritual Marketplace

In our current social circumstances, colleges and universities protect religious behaviors and beliefs by facilitating opportunities for religious organizations to interact with emerging adults. Instead of seeing campuses as hostile to

---

4. Mark Regnerus and Jeremy Uecker, "How Corrosive Is College to Religious Faith and Practice?" Social Science Research Council Forum, 2, February 5, 2007, http://religion.ssrc.org/reforum/Regnerus_Uecker.pdf.

religion, this new paradigm considers campus life a spiritual marketplace where many different religious and spiritual options are made available to students.

In point of fact, U.S. college campuses are, today, home to a vast number of religious and parachurch organizations.[5] Thus, the story of campus religion is best told as one of change rather than of declension. Over time, Catholic campus ministry has experienced growth, challenge, and renewal. In 1883, the Newman movement, "one of the most popular and creative ministries of the church,"[6] began at the University of Wisconsin and soon spread nationwide.[7] In the wake of Vatican II, Catholic campus ministry gained greater momentum with the emergence of the Catholic Campus Ministry Association (CCMA), which linked (public school) Newman center chaplains with their counterparts in Catholic colleges and universities. Another landmark event, a 1985 pastoral letter by the U.S. Catholic bishops, explicitly empowered Catholic campus ministry, further solidifying the growth and vitality of CCMA as well as diocesan support for campus ministry. CCMA reached its zenith in the first half of the 1990s, as professionalization efforts culminated in a process for gaining recognition as a certified campus minister.[8] Unfortunately, by the late 1990s, financial fortunes and institutional commitments dimmed and diocesan offices of campus ministry began to experience "conflation" or the merging of their offices with other ministries. Following the sex abuse scandals in

---

5. Conrad Cherry, Betty DeBerg, and Amanda Porterfield, *Religion on Campus* (Chapel Hill, NC: University of North Carolina Press, 2001).

6. Jay Dolan, "John Whitney Evans. The Newman Movement: Roman Catholics in American Higher Education, 1883–1971," *American Historical Review* 86, no. 2 (1981): 479.

7. John Whitney Evans, *Newman Movement: Roman Catholics in American Higher Education, 1883–1971* (Notre Dame: University of Notre Dame Press, 1980).

8. Barbara McCrabb, personal correspondence with author, June 13, 2017.

the early 2000s, such constraints and challenges only deep-
ened as some dioceses were forced to declare bankruptcy.
Numerous Catholic student centers now engage in serious
fundraising efforts, with at least 15 percent employing a
full-time, dedicated development officer.[9]

An additional source of renewal for Catholic campus
ministry during this challenging time has been the emergence of religious organizations dedicated to the "New
Evangelization." As traditional campus ministers declined
from perhaps 2,200 to 2,500 in the early 2000s to about 1,500
today,[10] groups such as Evangelical Catholic, St. Paul's Outreach, and especially the Fellowship of Catholic University Students (FOCUS) have filled the gap, often recruiting
former students as campus ministers (for one- or two-year
postgraduate commitments). In the process, these groups
have retooled and revitalized Catholic campus ministry.

My 2017 study of Catholic campus ministry shows that
FOCUS missionaries are a quarter of all Catholic campus
ministers in the United States, with this group deliberately
adopting ministerial elements pioneered by Evangelical Protestant ministries. But FOCUS also cultivates an intentionally
and distinctively Catholic approach, most demonstratively
in their corporate, hierarchical understanding of the Church.
As a result, FOCUS has prospered and flourished, growing
from two missionaries on one campus in its founding year
of 1998 to over five hundred missionaries and over one hundred campuses today.

The spiritual marketplace offers a more accurate way of
thinking about college as a formative, rather than a threatening, place for student religiosity. A seven-year research project at the Higher Education Research Institute demonstrated

9. John Schmalzbauer, "Campus Religious Life in America: Revitalization and
Renewal," *Society* 50 (2013): 115–31.

10. Starks, *The 2017 National Study of Catholic Campus Ministry.*

the importance of spiritual seeking among emerging adults and found this *increased* over the course of the college experience.[11] While less threatening to religion as a whole, some religious organizations are threatened by competition within the spiritual marketplace. Conceptually, this paradigm helps us make sense of the rise and fall of various religious groups on campus without requiring overall religious "loss." Although some organizations successfully compete and thrive by providing satisfying, morally orienting religious identities to students, others deteriorate and fail. Yet the spiritual marketplace metaphor has critics, too. Christian Smith has recently opined that emerging adults are ever more successfully being socialized as consumers, rather than as moral agents or citizens,[12] and the spiritual marketplace metaphor feeds this problem by positing students as consumers of religious goods.

Vocation and the Undergraduate Experience: Discernment in a Consumerist Key?

> Vocation is fundamentally about the human person in response to God's call to love God and neighbor in building up the kingdom not in the work one does but through the work one does.[13]

Discernment and vocation, or calling, find ready acceptance amidst spiritual seekers on a college campus. But does

---

11. Alexander Astin, Helen Astin, and Jennifer Lindholm, *Cultivating the Spirit: How College Students Can Enhance Students' Inner Lives* (San Francisco: Jossey-Bass, 2011).

12. Christian Smith, Kari Christoffersen, Hilary Davidson, and Patricia Snell Herzog, *Lost in Transition* (New York: Oxford University Press, 2012).

13. G. Chamberlain, "Protestant and Catholic Meanings of Vocation: Is Business a True Calling?" in *Business as a Calling*, ed. M. Naughton and S. Rumpza, e-book, accessed April 6, 2018, https://www.stthomas.edu/media/catholicstudies/center/documents/businessasacallingpdf/06Chamberlain.pdf.

ready acceptance of these things equate to fertile ground for them? While college students often look for meaning and purpose in life, I question the depth of this search.

Some are relatively simple consumers of the religious or spiritual goods on offer. They search among various religious groups, organizations, and organized events looking for a satisfying experience. Which groups provide them greater benefits at lower costs? These students are not exactly religious free riders, but they do try out religious groups and events without necessarily trying on religious identities. Indeed, many nonidentifiers on campus fit this mold. Of course, this group is also the most likely to find other nonspiritual offers on campus (more) appealing, such as nonsupervised, drunken revelry with peers, and are the least likely to engage the religious concepts of vocation and discernment.

Beyond simple consumption, however, some college students seek a more sophisticated consumption of religious identities. Here, in order to find fulfilling relationships, college students are willing to cultivate religious or spiritual practices and beliefs that sometimes challenge their own current self-conceptions. However, in such instances, vocational discernment can be utilized in a manner similar to a "discerning" palette when someone seeks fine food. Such students are more discerning in their adoption of religious goods than the unsophisticated cafeteria Catholic, but unfortunately they are still just consuming the religious goods on offer.

Moving deeper, attention to a personal relationship with Jesus Christ, a hallmark of New Evangelization groups (though not limited to them), is beneficial for college students precisely because it goes beyond mere consumption of religious goods. It speaks directly to the notion of "vocation," or calling. In particular, Someone is calling to them, and he is calling them into deeper relationship. This can be transformational rather than consumeristic.

Similarly, an emphasis on social justice and service, a hallmark of Vatican II Catholic campus ministry (but again, not limited to this group), is beneficial precisely because it challenges a culture of consumption by emphasizing love of neighbor and provides opportunities to participate in Jesus's mission. This ministerial approach allows students to cooperate in building the kingdom through sacrifice and, ideally, by surrendering one's self. To put it simply, participation in the mission of Christ *is* vocation—building the kingdom of God is our calling.

In his addresses to the Church (and its young people), Pope Francis has consistently stressed the importance of *both* encountering Christ *and* engaging in mission. I hope Catholic college students (and those who minister to them) are listening, because these are two crucial elements for challenging a religious consumerism that currently threatens college campuses. The undergraduate years are not solely about seeking, but also about building—building a relationship with Christ and building the kingdom of God… and the two go hand in hand!

Brian Starks, PhD, is Associate Professor of Sociology at Kennesaw State University. Brian's research explores the impact of religion on parental values, politics, generosity, and more, with a special focus on Catholic identity. He is currently finalizing an edited book on parishes that emerged from a collaborative effort to revitalize parish studies, and he is the principal investigator for The 2017 National Study of Catholic Campus Ministry in collaboration with the USCCB's Secretariat on Catholic Education. He previously directed the Catholic Social and Pastoral Research Initiative at the University of Notre Dame.

Fearless

by Claire Dixon

My fears are different now. My fear is not a fear *of* my future. Not a fear of missing my path or displeasing God. It is a fear of wonder, of wisdom, of knowing that God *is* my future. I am more afraid of losing God than finding him in my future. "Reverential fear" is what they call it. He has made me fearless.

Growing up, the idea of vocation would make me anxious. I knew that we were each called down a specific path, whether that be marriage, religious life, or single life. I was fearful of my call, mostly because I did not know what it was. I saw my future through a lens of dread and despair. Like many, I had an unexplainable fear of my future, the unknown.

All I could focus on was the present. I had goals and aspirations, mostly motivated by what I wanted to achieve. In the middle of high school, I decided to work toward earning my Gold Award in Girl Scouting. My project was focused on young mothers who attended pregnancy classes at a small pro-life clinic. I saw my passion in helping the mothers and their children—helping them understand that they were loved and supported. In my pursuit of gathering funds for my project, I wandered to the small Catholic Church five minutes down the road from me. My family and I attended a parish twenty minutes in the opposite direction. I had emailed the youth minister, asking him if I could attend one of the youth group meetings to ask for support of my project. I went and I stayed.

I kept coming back. Three months later, the youth minister asked if I would join the group to their annual trip to Arizona for a Steubenville conference. I begged my mom to let me go. After she met with him, she complied. I went, not knowing what to expect. Little did I know that my simple understanding of my faith and my fears would be turned upside down.

That weekend, I fell in love. Seeing people just like me fall to the floor in adoration, hearing speakers talk about their faith journeys and feeling the Holy Spirit completely flood and overflow in my heart—how could I not fall in love? It shook my world. It rattled my fears. Near the closing remarks of the conference, the celebrating priest invited those to the front who were considering a religious vocation. Other young women who ran up to the front did not go unseen. My heart longed for what they had. They had no fear of the future—of what Christ called them to. I sat, antsy in my seat. "All those ladies who want to give their lives to Christ. Who want to fall in love with him, dedicate their lives to him. Come to the front." My heart shook, and I felt my fears cave in upon themselves. I did not know if I was called to the religious life, but I did know that I wanted my life dedicated to Christ. I stood up and ran to the front.

It is here that a crucial shift took place. A shift that too many teens and young adults do not experience. It was when my fear shifted from the mixed fear of displeasing God and losing my call, filial and servile fear, to wonder, curiosity, astonishment. I knew wherever he would lead me, whatever my future held, would be wonderful, it would be what my heart was made for. I knew God would be within me and he would *be* my future. That was my discovery and my promise.

As an undergraduate student, I am constantly faced with the expectation of the medal of success, money, fame—internships, awards, job offers, honor roll—all are such "real" ideals of success. I was expected to know what I wanted to do with my life since day one of freshman year. But, the reality was that I did not know my major, my dream job, or even my vocation. I just knew that I wanted to follow Christ... whatever that meant. I will not lie; it is difficult navigating the world as a young adult. I always feel pulled in so many different directions: stability, success, simplicity. It was not until very recently that I heard my call. It was a broad, simple answer to a big, bold question. I am called to be a warrior.

Why a warrior? It seems as if I am already on the front lines. I have my armor and my weapon; my armor is love and my weapon is the message of the Gospel. I have been called to fight. Fight for the souls of this campus, fight for the right representation of our beautiful Church, fight for the love of all God's creation. It was not a battle I entered knowingly, but a battle that I believe we are all called to fight in. We are called in different ways. Although we each have different gifts, we are under one Church and one God. Our fight is a peaceful one. Our fight is full of love; our fight is spreading love.

As a part of being called to be a warrior, I see myself being called as a defender and a missionary. I know that God is speaking to me in gentle ways to bear his face to each and every individual that I meet. I know that he wants me to bring him to the most despairing parts of this campus—to those who feel alone, unworthy, used, compromised, those in the hookup culture, the parties steeped in alcohol, drugs, and the false notion of sexuality. I know there is the possibility of hope. My job is to plant the seeds. My heart breaks for those who do not know the utter joy that he gives or the infinite love that fills the hole in each of our hearts. He has called me to bring him to them. He has known that this is what my heart was made for. My heart was made to fight.

It does not end here. What I have learned is that God reveals his plan to us bit by bit. He used my past, my passions, and the people in my life to guide me to where he intended me to be. I could not have gotten here alone, and I continue to not be able to live this calling on my own. It is difficult, exhausting even. I lean on prayer, on the Church, and on the wonderful friendships that I have made. It is so joyful to know that I have companions on my faith journey. We hold each other up and encourage each other to keep going. God is going to call us to do some crazy things, and my friends support me through it all.

I do not know where God will lead me next. As St. Pope John Paul II said in a homily on April 26, 1997, "Life with Christ is a wonderful adventure." It sure is! He has led me to Arizona, then to Santa Clara, CA; Poland; Rome; San Antonio, TX; Washington, DC, and now this summer to Georgia. It is so full of wonder and joy. I have discovered that God only wants *for* us. He wants the best for us; he wants to make our hearts full. That is what vocation is. It cannot be mistaken for an end goal or a position. It is a mission. It is having the faith that where he will take you will be what you were made for. Sometimes it is challenging; it requires surrender and trust. I remember that more than anything, God *wants* me, he *loves* me, and he is *using* me to build up his Kingdom. I know that following him will bring me the most joyous life, one that I could not have ever imagined.

Looking back, in some ways I wish that vocation was presented to me more broadly. I remember learning about the three paths back in eighth grade. Eighth-grade me was not thinking about marriage, I was thinking about my science project due Friday. I have seen several of my friends, anxious with the idea of vocation, wishing that they knew right *now* what their vocation was. We are oh-so-pressured to *know* what we want to do that we barely have the time or space to *not know*. There is no space for surrender, no space for trust. No room for discovery or reflection. Our lives are so loud that even if God is speaking to us, he gets drowned out.

The Church is working, but we need more. We need more formation and more direction. In a time marked by relativistic thinking, we young Catholics need strength and direction in our faith now more than ever. Where learning happens—in confirmation programs and on college campuses—there also needs to be the presence of the Church, for that is the presence of the Holy Spirit.

Our parishes need to make more of an effort to reach out to our youth, whether that be through youth ministry, confirmation classes, service opportunities, or fun events. I firmly believe that providing a space and an opportunity for young adults to dive deeper into their faith is crucial for the Church. In my experience, the high school confirmation classes in our parishes focus on meeting requirements. I envision confirmation preparation to be a transformative journey of maturing in one's faith. Unfortunately, this is rarely the case.

As an undergraduate student, I feel that I lack proper intellectual formation, even though I attend a Catholic university. I wish that I could be given the resources to dive deeper into the knowledge of my faith so that I can not only understand it, but defend it. I especially desire to be trained in Pope John Paul II's *Theology of the Body*, as many progressive themes seem to be attacking the Church's view on sexuality, gender, family, and marriage. I long to be able to answer the call to be a warrior with a full and open heart. I long to be filled with the knowledge of Church teaching and opportunities to exercise my passions and to discover more. I thirst and I long, and I know others do too.

Claire Dixon is a twenty-year-old, second-year student at Santa Clara University. Born in Southern California, Claire has attended Catholic school throughout her whole life and considers her faith to be of utmost priority. This summer, Claire will be a missionary in Georgia through Life Teen, a Catholic organization ministering to middle school and high school teens.

Vocation in Action

DISCOVERING IDENTITY THROUGH RELATIONSHIP

by Jack Turney

My faith has given me strength and hope in my vocational discernment. I was raised as a Catholic and attended Catholic schools in every stage of my education. I used to think that being Catholic was about going to Mass, receiving the sacraments, participating in Church life as an altar server or minister, and just trying to be a good person. This worked for me as a kid, and I owe a lot of who I am to my parents and the Church. As I grew older, however, I started to feel like my faith was asking more of me. The theology classes I took in high school and college radically shifted my ideas of what it means to be Catholic. Simply attending Mass and a few mandated service events was not enough. There are numerous examples in the Bible of Jesus, his disciples, or other people going out and *doing*. Great saints and Church leaders were always *living* their faith. How could I emulate them?

Part of the answer to this question came to me last summer in the form of a phrase. It was "Listen to your heartsong," and was on an art card that my mentor had given me. This is a phrase that poetically defines "vocation" for me. It is a constant reminder to listen to the voice within ourselves, whether we want to name that our conscience or our soul or something else. To me, that voice is a constant thought. I devote much emotional and mental energy to meditating on what my "heartsong" is telling me. Sometimes it whispers, sometimes it shouts; yet it never really stops. Figuring out my heartsong defines my day-to-day activity in the same ways that breathing air and drinking water do. It is second nature, oftentimes done unconsciously, yet always happening. To clarify and specify what "vocation" is for me, I want to use *identity* and *relationship* as themes to ground my vocation in concrete terms.

Identity and relationship go hand in hand for me. It's hard to define myself without identifying my relationships to others. I am a student, a facilitator, a peer, a friend, a student leader, and so on. All of these designations connote deep and meaningful interactions with others. Some of the more memorable college experiences I've had, from conferences and retreats to conversations in class, have all come as a result of partnership and collaboration with those around me. Part of my vocational discernment, then, has been to ask myself where I can bring the most joy and love to those around me. There are two experiences that have helped me discern where I can bring that joy and light to others.

In the spring of my junior year, I facilitated an immersion trip for my fellow University of San Diego (USD) students in Tijuana for a week. In addition to entering into a relationship with various communities in Tijuana, there was a small group component to the trip. I facilitated a small group with four USD students, and we dealt with questions of immersion, accompaniment, and transborder relationships. One student struggled deeply with being in Tijuana; she struggled to find meaning in simply "being with" the community when there was so much suffering and injustice. This is an incredibly valid and appropriate question that I don't think is asked enough in the United States. Yet our point in being there was not to "solve problems." It was simply to be with, to stand with another in order to see what they see. This is a critical step to take if we are ever to "solve the problem" of immigration, economic oppression, and social injustice. This experience of walking with one of my peers as we figured out what it meant to "be with" was not pretty. It was not neat, it was not straightforward, and it sure wasn't easy. Yet, by the end of our time in Tijuana, my small group was left better prepared and more informed as to how they might be propo nents of change in the world. The beauty of this memory is that I was challenged to grow, just as much as I challenged my peer to embrace a different perspective.

My second experience came through a summer work/ immersion experience. I was fortunate enough to spend a summer living and working in the Alameda/Oakland area of Northern California as a MICAH (Mulvaney Immersion Communities for Action and Humility) Fellow. I was exposed to gross societal inequities and social problems that I had never heard of. Yet I also learned how to live in community with formerly homeless neighbors, and connect with them even though I was an "outsider." I went to Christian evangelical services and saw firsthand just how much religion played a role in their lives. I was able to spend quality time with my neighbors and share stories about life, identity, and our journeys. I heard about how kids were affected at school just because they were from a low-income family, and how families were experiencing the difficulties of an absent parent or mental illness in the family. This was a messy experience, but it gave me insight into a world that was vastly different from my own. I realized I had privileges other people couldn't dream of, and that I needed to do more to change the system we live in so that marginalized people can live life *from birth* free from discrimination and oppression in whatever forms these may take. Our society has marginalized many populations, and these individuals' human dignity and societal contributions are intentionally ignored. My vocation means living out my faith in a way that radically subverts the dominant power structures in society. I believe that my faith is asking me to transform the status quo in a way that emphasizes wholeness. Too many people are excluded from participation or meaningful positions in society; are we not a universal Church? Jesus's ministry was centered around making society better and welcoming people who had been excluded from mainstream society back into the fold. Matthew 25:40, Galatians 3:28, and Luke 17:11–14 all demonstrate that interpreting the Bible from a paradigm of, "What does it tell us about how to make the lives of others better?" invites genuine action.

These two instances are just a couple of many formative experiences in college. They are important for me because I was able to help make a difference in someone else's life, and also understand a different way of thinking. I experienced a fiery kind of passion, the kind that can only be forged in relationship with another. I need that. It will never be enough for me to sit at a desk and convince myself that I am doing all I can with my life. My ultimate concern, my heartsong, whatever you may wish to call it, can only be fulfilled when I am in meaningful relationship with others. When I think of vocation, I do not think of just a career. I think of communal, mutually beneficial relationships. I will be asking the question of how to live out my vocation for years to come. However, my answer right now is to work for systemic change and to engage in meaningful relationships with those around me.

Finally, I want to say that I have been fortunate enough to have multiple circles of support during my college career. From academic professors to staff members, each of these mentors has helped me actualize my potential and discern my vocation. Primarily, the staff members of University Ministry and the Mulvaney Center at USD have been instrumental throughout my college career. They have supported me in struggling through deep questions of faith, accompaniment, service, presence, intentionality, social justice, and love. The Catholic Church as well, through both my local parish in Orange County and USD, has been invaluable in guiding me on my path to becoming my full self. I hope to continue the relationships that I have developed with those mentors, whether they are priests, professors, or lay ministers. However, I understand that as I go forward I need to provide the same sort of mentorship to younger people in my community, particularly the Church community. I would like to see current ministers supported in their work and a stronger invitation from the Church to invite young adults (seniors in high school or older) to participate in Church life more regularly. I think that instead of placing an emphasis on participation in Mass by young people, an emphasis on participation in community would be invaluable in terms of deepening their faith lives. Without the opportunities that I have been given, I would not be who I am today. I hope that the Church continues to provide support and love to its members, and thinks about how it can radically serve those on the margins and provide its members with what they need. For young people, this can be a difficult task, but I believe that if we are given the power to enact change and take more responsibility for our formation in the Church, Catholic youth can become an unstoppable force for transformative change in the world. As we go forward, I hope that our Catholic communities can "listen to their heartsongs" in order to fulfill every person's vocational need and make our world a more loving and joyful place.

Jack Turney is a twenty-two-year-old senior at the University of San Diego. Jack was baptized and confirmed in the Catholic faith and has attended Catholic schools his entire life. He cares deeply about right relationships, understanding through difference, loving and respecting others, embracing change, and spreading joy.

God in the Fabric of Our Lives

A Tapestry of Faith

by M. Nick Rogers

"Be still, and know that I am God!" (Ps 46:10). We live in *medias res* and so in the middle of things we find ourselves. Our material lives are woven together by layers of threading that overlap and cross, yet all of these layers in their totality fail, in a holistic sense, to convey the deepest nature of personhood. Yet, when God calls us, he calls us in our wholeness. Pulling on any one observable thread that weaves through the fabric of one's life inevitably reveals the stunning complexity of the material with which we are made. God observes and comprehends all of the threads within us, and he sees the beautiful textile we can become as they fall into place. He supplies the fabric, the tools, and the vision. Like a patient teacher, he guides us as we weave the threads of our lives. Sometimes he places thread down that we knew not of before, but he knew we would need it all the same. The fabric he wants to weave is beautiful beyond comprehension; we need only discern his gentle instructions.

Artistry is a beautiful gift, and I find that the image of woven fabric helps convey the belief in a creator God whose creation is now. I grew up in a Catholic family, went to Mass weekly, participated in the sacraments, and attended Catholic school. Not until a series of blessed events unfolded did I begin to notice a pattern emerging in the threads God had placed before me. The family serves as the bedrock of society and, crucially, the foundation of God's kingdom on earth. We often take our families for granted and usually without perception. But the family is a blessed entity, and it exists—like the people it includes—beyond mere physical, material terms and requires nurturing, prayer, and respect.

My parents did the best they could to present these values to my sister and me, and so I feel blessed to have grown up experiencing the love and joy of familial relationship. Yet my parents divorced during my sophomore year of high school. A crucial foundation of my life was, in the end, not a foundation at all. Something changed—many things changed. But something essential to the way I understood the world changed. A rupture in the way I identified myself and reconciled my life with the lives of others started to cut into my faith. How could it be, as we Catholics profess, that married persons experience inseparable union while my own Catholic parents do not? A disruption in the fabric that composed my life had reverberating effects, some of which I have felt and resolved and others I have yet to recognize and address. Yet all the while, God was most certainly at work within me. I did not realize it at the time, but my quest for healing was also a quest for God, who is the source of all healing.

"Fight the good fight of the faith" (1 Tim 6:12). If the threads that make up our lives come from God, we can understand what he is saying by closely observing them. In the last two years since starting college, I have been overwhelmed by the ways God has revealed himself to me. It began with my commitment to him. During my freshmen year of college, I took up an active practice in my faith. I no longer exercised my beliefs out of pure duty, but out of joy. I came to discover that through my parents' divorce—an experience truly uncomfortable and undesirable that I would wish for no person—God enkindled within me a fire of devotion and faith.

The Church's defense of the family, a unit that in popular culture has come under attack from almost every angle, particularly resonated with me. The fact that the family is such an essential component in Catholic theology, combined with my personal experience of this, ignited a desire to develop my faith and understanding of the Church. While this type of intellectual formation led me into a deeper relationship with Christ, it also allowed him to communicate with me. The family became something I took an active role in caring for—it became something I wanted to defend and revere.

God speaks to us through joy, hope, and life; for me, these avenues are synonymous with family. My vocation to more deeply understand the role of the family in God's kingdom comes at a pivotal time in my life. As a college student, I am beginning to refine my goals, discern my career, and develop a path of growth that will take me well into adulthood. God's timing—the way he has spoken to me—has greatly altered and reordered the values I hold. My career, my interests, my missions—I must organize each around the family.

I have imagined the process of discerning one's vocation like approaching the same object from two sides: the present and the future. To ask, "What is God calling me to do today?" differs in approach from asking, "Who is God calling me to become tomorrow? And in five years from now?" These questions are not discrete inquiries; they, like the elaborate threads of our lives, overlap and interweave.

The layers of thread that God desires for me to weave today will not mar the completeness of the tapestry he intends for me to complete in my future. Then, finally, sometimes God desires for us to just *choose*. In a special way, our choice—our free will—is what he uses to make beautiful his artistic creation. Recognizing that in his image I am not a predetermined slave, but a humble servant, reminds me that God desires relationship; it is a relationship he is calling me to through family.

"Take the helmet of salvation, and the sword of the Spirit, which is the word of God" (Eph 6:17). The Church requires unity; only through a persistent and unified front can she attract and form students. Moreover, congregants and leaders must acknowledge that there exists a serious and pervasive faith crisis on college campuses. A Pew Research study in 2009, for example, found that 80 percent of those who leave the faith do so by twenty-three years old. Worse, what the data does not capture are the prevailing sentiments of undergraduates. Though colleges vary widely, a "work hard, party hard" mentality often prevails. One must accede to the reality of a faith crisis in order to appropriately minister to the undergraduate youth. Further, the Church must be a yardstick of quality. Take Aristotle's bent-stick metaphor: When a stick is contorted, to right its crookedness an agent must bend it further back in the opposing direction. The Church must be such an agent of correction.

On college campuses, our Church must work to foster the essence of new life and redemption that Christ embodies. Opportunities for the Church to elucidate God's truths pervade our culture, yet too often among undergraduates, her teachings remain unheard. In a world of academia where success and failure frequently appear gamified, where rules can feel cold and arbitrary and grades govern personage, the Church must remind students that there is *meaning* and *significance* to their work and lives. It must remind students that their work is a project—part of their vocation—for serving the kingdom of God on earth. The Church must foster faith on campuses in such a way as to orient students toward the ultimate ground of meaning and purpose: Jesus Christ. Spiritual experience must mark the process of learning, for where the mind engages the world with the gift of reason, there too must Christ's Church be present. For this reason, opportunities for theological studies ought to be a hallmark of Catholic universities.

Catholics on college campuses must constantly avoid spurious displays of faith that at best somewhat mischaracterize and at worst wholeheartedly contradict Catholic teaching. Catholic schools must embrace Catholic teaching, even on complex issues like the pro-life movement. They ought to be wary of falling into complacency with congenial dissenters who do not have Rome's best interests at heart, for "well meant are the wounds a friend inflicts, / but profuse are the kisses of an enemy" (Prov 27:6). The Church needs soldiers on campuses throughout the world, especially in the United States. Young men, in particular, often either forget or fail to recognize that the world is a spiritual battlefield in need of warriors.

The type of presence necessary to effect change in our society must connect, on some level, with intellectual formation. For example, Pope John Paul II established the Institute for Studies on Marriage and the Family and expounded the Church's teachings through *Theology of the Body*. College students need exposure to these projects. With exposure and guidance, the Church, through her Catholic institutions, must warmly guide her children as they weave the fabric of their lives.

Nick Rogers, twenty, is a student at Santa Clara University, studying economics, philosophy, and computer science. He grew up in Los Angeles, where he attended Loyola High School. In his free time, Nick enjoys writing short essays, building computer programs, praying, and walking around the beautiful gardens of Mission Santa Clara.

The Value of Opportunity and Authentic Relationships

by Megan Siroky

I was raised Catholic in a loving, supportive family by parents who were deeply grounded in their shared Catholic faith and values. Throughout my childhood, these admirable parents taught me and my three younger siblings to be polite, kind, determined, patient, and Christlike. They continually emphasized that God and family come first. I would watch my father leave and come home from work each day, telling our family all about it at dinner each night. He showed me the value of hard work, responsibility, and leadership. Meanwhile, my mother served our family tirelessly as a stay-at-home mom, taking us to and from school and making sure we were always healthy, fed, clothed, and loved. Through their actions and strong commitment to one another, my parents impressed upon me the blessing of marriage, education, and having a fruitful career. They guided me toward a life that would emulate the one they gave me. Therefore, I grew up never doubting that I would eventually be college educated, have a job that I love, get married, and raise my own family.

These decisions were set in my mind before attending college; however, I had never thought about them as a vocational discernment. For a long time, I honestly thought vocation was solely for those wishing to enter the priesthood because one of the prayers of the faithful at my parish Mass was always, "...for the vocation of the priesthood and religious life." I did not know the term applied to me until much later.

The discernment of my vocation really began when I went to a Catholic high school, although I did not think of it as discernment. I recall being encouraged to attend a highly acclaimed university and get a job that would benefit me financially. At the time, I enjoyed many subjects, but not one gave me great joy. Thus, I had no idea what career I wanted, but I definitely knew I did not want to be a doctor, lawyer, or businesswoman, which are jobs that traditionally make the most money. So, I ultimately chose a college that would give me a liberal arts education and the opportunity to discover what I love to do most. I entered the University of San Diego in the fall of 2013 and attended a retreat sponsored by University Ministry; this immediately gave me a sense of belonging, comfort, and joy. I knew I had made the right decision. College life was not easy, though, and I was constantly strained by the difficulty of classes, living away from home, finding where I fit in, and avoiding destructive behavior. I found myself moving further away from my faith, as I did not make the time for my relationship with God in my daily life. I ultimately found solace at the end of my freshman year when I reconnected with my Catholic faith as a part of a servant-leader group, where I became a mentor to first-year students and liturgical minister at Mass. It gave me the chance to feel God's presence in my life through prayer and spiritual reflection. Through my experiences of faith formation and immersion in various communities, I developed relationships grounded in Catholic values that shaped my life in positive ways.

I entered sophomore year with the intention of pursuing a degree in architecture and environmental studies because I was told that my artistic talent and mathematical ability would make me a skilled architect, and I agreed that it would be a good fit. I was also very interested in caring for the planet, and I thought that obtaining both degrees would help me jumpstart a career in the sustainable building industry. My classes fulfilled my interests and I thought this was a beneficial career path for me. However, by Christmas, I began thinking a lot more about my choice before declaring the majors. Sitting in prayer one night, I felt in my heart that this did not actually suit me—I encountered a conflict in what I thought my future held and what God was actually calling me to do.

Hoping that it would help me in the discernment process, I attended a retreat for sophomores the following January. This retreat weekend was pivotal; it allowed me the chance to intentionally reflect on the meaning of vocation for the first time. A speaker talked about the definition of *vocation* according to Frederick Buechner: "The place God calls you to is the place where your deep gladness and the world's deep hunger meet." Before the retreat, I had not understood why I no longer felt called to architecture, but I realized here that it was God telling me that the place I was at was not what the world needed or where God needed me. The retreat led me to consider more options based on my interests, my personality, and my past experiences in order to find my calling toward something more meaningful. The Church had been encouraging me all along to serve God and my brothers and sisters, but I did not know where my joy united with my gifts and the opportunity to serve. It all came quite suddenly when I felt God calling me to become a teacher. I remembered my love for children, connecting with their joy and innocence. I wanted a workplace where something new would happen every day, where I was not confined to an office space, and where I could be creative. In this discernment process, I understood the need for education, just as it had been given me, as a foundation for the pursuit of a happy, successful life. I became passionate about education, especially when I had the chance to share my newfound vocation with loved ones, who met me with incredible support and interest.

I have learned even more since then about the meaning of vocation in the context of theological anthropology, or the study of the human being in light of faith. In a Catholic theology class I took one semester, we discussed questions like these: What is the purpose of a person? What is our motivation? Does God have a plan for our life? Of course, one could go on forever in a conversation on this topic, but the main point I took away was that I'll best find myself when I give myself to others in service. Jesus leads by example in this way—serving those most in need. I believe God calls me to serve his children through teaching. I am still learning about myself and my vocation, and I think my undergraduate experience has provided many opportunities for me to prayerfully discern God's call, whether it was a class lecture, a homily at Mass, or a conversation with a friend. I do not yet know my vocation to live a married or consecrated life, but I understand the importance of having an open heart and mind in this matter, and to similarly discern in the way I have done for my career choice.

Being an undergraduate is a crucial period of individual growth, and intentionally discerning my vocation has been a significant part of both my spiritual and intellectual development. I regard the Church's support as essential in my endeavor to live out God's calling for me successfully. First,

I think it is necessary to understand that each of us has a unique vocation that deserves support in a variety of forms. Since we are all called to life with Christ in different ways, young people need to feel respected and acknowledged as contributing members to the Body of Christ. Throughout my career as a student at a Catholic university, I have had the privilege of building relationships with like-minded students, professors, pastoral counselors, and priests. They offered me quality time to reflect on my faith and lived experiences, and how to further grow in my spiritual life. For Catholic undergraduates and young people who have not had this opportunity, it is especially important for the Church to reach out and provide support in the discernment process by having dioceses offer and promote the use of pastoral counseling, young adult groups, and vocational workshops or retreats.

I have noted that I consider strong, compassionate relationships to be formative in the pursuit of my vocation. I appreciate it most when people actively listen, give me guidance in making decisions, and share in my joy. Spiritual direction, career counseling, and advising are indispensable resources that help me feel grounded. The opportunities I have been privileged with have helped me to grow in countless ways, especially the love and support of being surrounded by a community that recognizes the value in each person and lifts one another up. Therefore, I would encourage Catholic and other religious universities to direct funding toward career development resources, marriage and religious life seminars, and other programs that guide future growth and provide a supportive community.

As a member of the Church, I have grown immensely in knowledge and in faith by forming relationships with leaders, peers, and mentors who challenge me to reflect on my identity, purpose, understanding of the world, and much more. For instance, priests and lay ministers should allow students to discover these perspectives by asking probing questions instead of sharing personal opinions or definite answers. To me, being a Catholic undergraduate has meant not knowing all the answers, but remaining open to learning and discovering through experiences that are outside of my comfort zone.

Megan Siroky is a twenty-two-year-old undergraduate student at the University of San Diego, working toward a bachelor's degree in liberal studies. The faith community at her institution has shaped her life tremendously as she has been involved in university ministry by serving at Mass, participating in immersion trips, and attending/leading retreats.

Seeking a Challenge

VOCATIONAL DISCERNMENT
IN AN AGE OF COMFORT

by Frederick Ley

I have been Catholic my whole life. I went to Catholic school
from kindergarten through high school and have actively
participated in the University of Southern California (USC)
Caruso Catholic Center all four years as an undergraduate.
My strong devotion to my faith started early, for throughout
my parents' divorce, I looked to my faith as a source of
stability and support. In high school, I mostly engaged my
faith through Sunday Mass and religion class along with
nightly prayer, but I also took on some leadership roles. I
attended two retreats my freshman and junior years, and led
each of them in the subsequent sophomore and senior years.
After confirmation, I became a lector and a eucharistic
minister, and I was engaged in religious leadership at my
high school, primarily in the form of planning and organizing
on-campus Masses. During this time, I would also dabble
in service. However, while I understood that service is
important, I struggled to consistently engage due to a lack of
personal connection to the ministries.

VOCATION THROUGH THE LIFE COURSE

One of my first actions at USC was to become involved with Catholic life on campus. Indeed, visiting the newly opened Catholic center on my college tour strongly influenced my decision to attend USC, so participation in the community was an early priority and would turn out to radically influence my time as an undergraduate. I started by getting trained as a liturgical minister, signing up for a Bible study, and getting to know fellow students and administrators. The following semester, I went on a mission trip to Puerto Rico. While I was somewhat disappointed in the amount of service I did on the trip, I grew very close to some fellow students, and the Catholic center consequently became my primary community. During my sophomore year, I served as the liturgy chair of the student leadership organization. I also continued to participate in Bible study—eventually leading my own—participated in some all-night adoration services, attended my first daily Mass, and was trained as a sacristan. In my junior year, I continued my leadership through the Pastoral Council.

I also attended the spring retreat my junior year, and on that retreat I decided, and explicitly stated in a letter to Jesus, that my life is his. Coming back from that retreat, I started attending Mass five days a week and praying a Holy Hour on a regular basis. Within a few weeks, one of my friends invited me into a spiritual accompaniment relationship with him in which we would meet once a week to pray and study. I increased the amount of spiritual reading I did, including reading from either the Bible or the *Catechism* every day. I also began to feel my love for the poor finally growing. This past year, I led the fall retreat and invited another student to join me in spiritual accompaniment. I also increased my participation in the corporal works of mercy. I led a Bible study that sought to understand the way in which our faith bolsters our service and our service actualizes our faith. I now regularly visit the Los Angeles Catholic Worker to make and serve food on Skid Row and, most significantly, have begun engaging in juvenile detention ministry.

Juvenile detention ministry has completely changed my life; my first visit to juvenile hall completely stupefied me. I was profoundly moved by the sorrows that had plagued the lives of these young men and how desperately they were searching for a glimmer of light, and I decided I needed to spend as much time there as I could. I knew this was a place that needed Christ, and that somehow I was called to do whatever I could to bring him there. I prepared one young man for his first communion and confirmation, and was his sponsor. I am the godfather of another young man whom I have been visiting. Finally, I followed up with one young man after he was released on probation, and he is now a dear friend whom I see and talk with regularly as he strives to reform his life. Working with young men has shed so much light on what the Gospel means and who Christ is.

Now, as I am graduating from USC, I am faced with the question of what my vocation is. I wonder how I will continue to serve the Lord in a new place and in a new way, especially as I accepted an offer to work as an engineer at Microsoft before I even considered my vocation. I think of my relationship with Christ as having four main components: faith, intellect, service, and evangelization. The former two are ways in which I develop my understanding of who I am, who I am called to be, and who God is. The latter two are the ways in which these questions and answers manifest in my actions and in my impact on the world. My vocation—lay or religious, married or single, professional or volunteer— sits in between these two groups. If my faith and intellect are the bedrock of my relationship with Christ, my vocation is the soil that nourishes the fruit-bearing tree; my vocation is the substrate, the medium on which my visible life as a son of God rests and grows as supported by the foundation of my interior life. In other words, my vocation is something that facilitates, augments, and empowers my ability to realize God's kingdom on earth as determined by my personal discernment by way of prayer and study.

As of right now, I am signed to work with Microsoft after I graduate, and while I did not have this understanding of my vocation back then, this newer understanding has certainly shaped the way I am preparing for my new job and the way that I see my career progressing. The importance of my spiritual life has played a strong role in where I live up in Washington; I have researched local parishes as much as I have apartments and houses for rent. I have considered how my work schedule will integrate with my prayer schedule and how I can make space for daily Mass and frequent adoration as well as Bible studies and other ways to continue to strengthen my faith. I have made connections in Washington relating to detention ministry opportunities and, in the longer term, I have considered whether I would move back to Los Angeles to continue with the work that has influenced me so greatly. I have started thinking about people I know up in Washington who are strong in their faith and can continue to guide me, particularly through rigorous study and reading. I have wondered how various choices of neighborhoods will affect my ability to reach, and therefore evangelize, my peers. Such are the questions that now guide my transition process more than any question of logistics, entertainment, or socializing.

In considering all this, one of the greatest concerns I have is that I will fall away from all of the dedication and good habits I have developed. I think the most helpful thing the Church could do is to challenge me. It can ask me hard questions and hold me to a standard worthy of the call of the gospel. I believe this is the most effective way to occasion growth, yet it is a quality astonishingly absent in many parishes and faith communities. One of the most influential homilies I heard at USC was at the beginning of freshman year. In effect, the priest explained to the congregation, "All of you, especially you freshmen, should bless your food before every meal. It is quick and easy, at no cost to you, and I can guarantee that no one around you will take offense. You may even inspire some people. And most importantly, it will please the Lord. So what's stopping you?" In fact, I had stopped blessing my food out of timidity, and, faced with this simple and sound challenge, I began to again. This single act inspired a pattern of increasing boldness that enabled so much more growth in my faith.

Unfortunately, so few of the homilies I have heard since then, in any parish I have attended, have really pushed me. More often than not, they skirt the difficult theological questions and fall back on a trite message of, "Remember you are loved." Yes, this is an important message, but it can lead to complacence. It doesn't cause any introspection; it doesn't invite a transformation of heart. A person will most often walk out of these homilies the same as they went in, no closer to emulating Christ. The pastoral nature of the Church has exchanged an approach that moves parishioners closer to the uncomfortable, difficult, radical truth of Christ for one of comfort, avoiding anything offensive or difficult. Even a call to "give everything to Christ," while challenging in some sense, is too vague to be meaningful. What I think the Church needs is to incite action and impart deeper truth. I want the Church to ask me when was the last time I went to confession. I want the Church to ask me when was the last time I performed a corporal work of mercy. I want the Church to remind me that nothing, not a career, or hobby, or even family, is more important than our Lord because his generosity is the only reason I exist at all, and prayer should therefore be our highest priority. I want the Church to make me wonder whether my prayer is genuine. I want the Church to remind me that Christ's love, as modeled by so many saints, was radical, impractical, and sacrificial and that to love another person truly and completely hardly leaves any room for self-preservation or pragmatism. I want the priest in his homilies to teach me how to pray, to lead me in a meditation, to open my eyes to the splendor of the Lord. I want the priest to form my conscience and discuss difficult questions of morality and encourage me to adhere to what the Church has to say, even if it makes me uncomfortable. We Christians are not even entitled to our own lives if the Lord asks for them. Why should we feel entitled to our comfort?

Furthermore, this lukewarm preaching, this lukewarm culture, is an important reason why Church numbers have declined. Young people today want substance. A culture of beauty or one that emphasizes pastoral accompaniment is certainly good, but it can so often be hollow. In a generation that is almost nauseatingly concerned with whether it is "making an impact," in which each person is so fanatically obsessed with their own personal efficacy, the Church needs to extend a call to action. It needs to illustrate that Christ's Word and love are revolutionary, and that the greatest impact we can possibly have as young people is by honestly and faithfully following him.

Rick Ley is a twenty-one-year-old recent graduate of the University of Southern California with a degree in computer engineering and computer science. He grew up in San Francisco and Napa, California. He will be moving to Seattle in August to begin work at Microsoft as a software engineer.

Learning to Shut Up and Listen to God

A How-To Guide

by Rachel Takacs

Much of my life is spent worrying. I'm consumed constantly with the weight of the world, and at times the pressure of it all can feel as if my rib cage is going to collapse in on itself. The stress of the unknown, the ambiguity that entails this life, is something that I assume many college undergraduates—and really people in general—experience. Plan everything in my life for the foreseeable future? I barely know what I am going to eat for lunch, let alone what I want to do for the rest of my life! This pressure can be even greater when religion is thrown into the mix. It is believed that we all have a purpose in this life, a reason that we were brought into this world. There is a greater plan curated by God that we are supposed to follow. A vocation exists in this life that I must discern so that I may live according to God's will. What if I choose the wrong vocation? What if I lose my way? What if I can't hear his voice? What if I don't like the path he has laid before me? The "what ifs" can eat you whole if you let them. Luckily, I found a way to ease this constant worry and discern my path in life.

In some ways, my stress was eased when I entered college; in other ways, it was made much worse. College is a huge step in one's life, and from the moment you enroll, you are expected to pick a major. This major is supposed to be connected to your future career and provide you with the necessary tools to excel. At the age of eighteen, I didn't feel prepared to make a decision like that. I had no life experience, I had never traveled, I was barely legal, and I was intended to decide a future for myself? Underprepared and overwhelmed, I sent myself into a tailspin of overthinking. I rushed to take online vocational quizzes; according to the internet, I was designed to work in about seventy different fields. My confusion was greater than ever before; I had no direction. I was a sheep separated from my shepherd. I was lost in the woods with no compass. I was tired and scared.

One night it got particularly overwhelming. I had just finished my first year of college and I had no more knowledge about my future than I had a year prior. Seated at my dorm-room desk, in the most uncomfortable chair, I cried. I held my head in my hands and let the sobs shake my body. Desperately, I looked around my room, searching for something that could help me. My eyes landed on a beaded item beside my bed. I crossed the small room quickly and grabbed it into my shaking hands. Clutching the rosary to my chest, I tentatively did the sign of the cross. I would love to say that the clouds parted, the angels sung from above, and I received a message from the Lord. I wish it would have been that easy. I did, however, receive some clarity that night: if I wanted to find my vocation, if I wanted to do God's will, I had to communicate with him.

Born and raised in the Catholic Church, I never thought much about my own faith. I believed what the Catholic

Church taught, I attended Mass on Sundays and on holy days of obligation; I did what I was "supposed" to do. In reality, I wasn't doing anything. I had no conviction or fire. I was simply going through the motions without any feeling at all. The complacency of my spiritual life was the root of my anxiety. Being stubborn and prideful, I naively believed that I could attain the map of my future all by myself. I was incredibly wrong. I began to work prayer back into my daily life, and instead of begging God for answers or clarity—as I had in the past—I asked him to help me trust.

I was praying constantly, but I was still struggling. My mind was incessantly churning, my words and thoughts dominating the space. For a long time, whenever I would pray it would be a monologue. I would talk and talk, and never let the Lord get a word in edgewise. I would yammer on, feel a little better, and end my prayer. Yet I still felt as though I was missing something. I could tell I wasn't trusting God fully—I had full faith in his *existence* while I withheld faith in his *guidance*.

With the guilt of this lack of trust in his guidance weighing me down, I went to confession. Finally, the Lord could speak to me. That day, God reassured me he forgave me and he used the priest as a vessel for his love. He expressed to me that I needed to be quiet. I needed to stop saying everything all the time; I needed to listen. As my penance, I was instructed to go into adoration and sit in silent prayer. I did as I was told and, initially, it was extremely hard. All that kept running through my mind was, "This is ridiculous. How is God intended to know what is going on in my life if I don't talk? He hasn't said anything to me yet, how is this going to work?" After some time, my mind began to slow, my breathing evened, and I finally stopped talking. The silence consumed me, but not in a negative or scary way. It enveloped me like a warm blanket; God was holding me in his arms.

All this time when I had been talking over him, I was fighting against him. I was fighting against the feeling of total trust. I kept him at an arm's distance because I didn't want to get hurt or be let down. I could feel his presence surrounding me, closing in on every one of my senses. Before this moment, I was like a puppy who had escaped from the yard, running down the street away from my owner, running out of fear, fun, and familiarity. I had spent my whole life running; this was the first moment I had stopped. There he was, in his infinite love and compassion, waiting for me. He held onto me, finally able to show me love.

Overcome by warmth, tears streamed down my face, but not from fear or sadness. I was joyful, it was like the sun breaking after a week full of rain. It was hope, it was joy, it was the unfathomable love of God. A love that isn't jealous or discriminatory. A love that knows no bounds, for it is unconditional and eternal. The answer to my vocation was revealed to me that day in adoration. Love. Love is my vocation, love is my future, love is my life. No matter what I do or where I go, if I'm acting with love then I am doing God's will.

I try not to talk so much anymore. For I realize now that the Lord knows my heart because he is my heart. In the silence of my prayer, he is able to reach me. To speak to me, he doesn't use verbal language. He doesn't tell me what I need to do. Instead, he loves me, holds me, and forgives me. In those moments of unconditional love, he teaches me more than any verbal instruction could. Through his love to me I can constantly learn how to love with the same intensity.

We were created out of love. God sent his only son to die on the cross because he loves us. The acts and works that I do are only meaningful if they are done with love. In this life we become so bogged down, obsessed with the material, the mundane, the flesh. Our souls are more than that. We are more than materialistic possessions and pleasures of the flesh. We are made for something much greater: love. Young adults face a fast-paced world in which we are constantly talking through posts, tweets, and more. The most valuable spiritual transition I made in my young adult life was to stop talking so much and start listening more. It would be so helpful for the Church to invite young adults to engage in the rich contemplative traditions of the Church. Through retreats, *lectio divina*, special prayer groups, and more, young adults will have increased opportunities to *listen*.

It would be wonderful to say that my life was all sunshine and roses from that point on. Horrible things have happened to me since that moment of clarity, and the truth is that throughout my life I will experience more sadness and turmoil. Thankfully, there is goodness. Happiness does exist, for joy can be found in the light of a new day. There is both beauty and sadness to be found in the reality that nothing lasts forever in this life. All things will change, but one constant does exist—the love of God. In the darkness of life, trust in the Lord and love God and one another. In the light of life, trust in the Lord and love God and one another. It is easier said than done. I still find my mind racing, I still feel anxious and scared, and I'm still unsure of what lies ahead. The difference between me now and me when I was crying in my dorm room is that I have tasted the love of the Lord. Do not be concerned or scared of the ambiguity of this life. Embrace all that is unknown and terrifying. Every moment of every day, try and love with just a fraction of the intensity that God loves us. If you walk in that love, devote your life and soul to that love, you will be living out God's will. I know absolutely nothing. My lack of knowledge no longer scares me, for I know I have God's love. I trust in him and I know he will bring me home.

Rachel Takacs is a twenty-year-old college student at Kennesaw State University. She is about to enter her third year at KSU, and her major is sociology with a concentration in cultural studies. She was raised in the Catholic faith and attempts to remain active through KSU's on-campus Catholic ministry.

On the Undergraduate Catholic Experience

ENCOUNTER IN THE GROTTO

by Madeline Lewis

As I write this piece on what it is like to be a Catholic undergraduate student, I have approximately ten days, twelve hours, and nine minutes until I can no longer count myself an expert on the subject. On a soon-to-come Sunday, on what I hope will be a warm spring day, I will graduate from the University of Notre Dame. Here I am, curious about this ending that seems quite capable of grabbing everyone's attention, wondering just exactly what it will mean to end my time as an undergraduate Catholic. What comes to mind is a favorite storytelling technique from a favorite professor for any writer looking for an ending: *the ending is usually hidden in the beginning.*

The beginning, my very first night at college, was, as beginnings are often wont to be, particularly messy: a story involving candlelight, wandering, and a very unfortunate lack of tissues.

When I arrived at Notre Dame on an especially hot August day in 2013, I brought with me a framed photo of my

47

dog, a small wooden crucifix, a meticulously picked-out comforter set, and a brand-new Notre Dame sweatshirt. I also brought a tightly packed bundle of questions tucked inside me like clothes stuffed messily into a too-small suitcase: Will I find friends? Will I find things to do on the weekends that don't involve copious amounts of alcohol, loud music, and bad decisions? Will I be able to keep up in my classes? Will I ever stop feeling alone? Will I be accepted?

My first evening at Notre Dame, having carefully unpacked all of my things out of my suitcases and into my dorm room, I was left with this tangle of questions. Hence, we come to my story. It was around midnight, and from what I could tell, my entire dorm had emptied out in an exodus to dorm parties. I found myself alone, wandering around at night on a campus unfamiliar to me. Sniffles were coming on strongly as I walked down an empty quad sidewalk staring at the ground with a heart that began to feel emptied out of all hope. I had only been on campus for a day and already felt like lugging my metaphorical suitcase full of questions safely back home.

I shriveled up onto a bench under a tall tree, trying to shield my puffy eyes with my hand as groups of upperclassmen walked by in clusters, laughing and catching up about summer vacation adventures. I fumbled for my phone in my pocket and dialed a familiar number.

My mother answered immediately, although it was way past her bedtime, and just hearing her sleepy voice made my tears start up all over again. It was not my most articulate moment, and the words bubbled out of my mouth in teary skips of breath:

"Please come pick me up. Please come bring me home."

I repeated these sentences over and over again, and after each time, they were met with the most gentle "no" from my mother. I tried my best bargaining strategies: I helpfully suggested that, if she would only come pick me up, I would enroll in online classes the very next day, learning whatever those things are that turn high school graduates into smart college students from the comfort of my own room at home. My mother gently refused this brilliant idea. She told me to stay, to sleep, and to call her in the morning. For some reason, which I can only now name as some sort of small and persistent grace at work that evening, I didn't head back to my unfamiliar dorm bed after I hung up the phone. Instead, I continued to wander, sniffling awkwardly, trying to regulate my jerky breaths with the beat of my steps on the sidewalk—completely missing the fact that I had some-how made my way to one of the most famous parts of Notre Dame's campus.

Somehow, in my numb wandering and teary sniffling, I had ended up at the grotto.

The loud music that had blasted from buildings sud-denly felt very far away, and despite the loud insecurity blasting from my heart and the incessant feeling that I didn't belong, I tumbled into a place of quiet. It was here, in the quiet glow of candles, and in the quietness of prayer, that I began to really, really cry. And I mean, really, really cry—like snot-all-over-my-face kind of cry. Once my emotional crisis really got up and running, I began to have all sorts of crazy "good" ideas: maybe I could transfer! Tomorrow! Or actually convince my family to let me take those online classes from home! Even better, I could just skip college altogether! It was abundantly clear, after all, that college life was certainly not for me.

But then, something happened to me that I will never forget. Not in ten days, twelve hours, and nine minutes, and not in all the days, hours, and minutes to come. Suddenly, I felt someone touch my shoulder.

The hand stayed there for a few seconds.

I didn't look up, seeing as my face was completely covered with the aforementioned snot. I never saw this person's face, I never said thank you, and I never got to ask permission to include this gesture in this piece. In fact, that grace-filled human will never even know that it was his or her tender touch that made me stay, that handed me a different question, hopeful instead of insecure: What if this scary, scary place could become a home?

This was the beginning: the tender and anonymous touch on my shoulder, one messy, grace-filled night. There have certainly been many more of those nights. And by the persistent grace of God, nearly nine hundred nights later, this place has become the place I call home. Finding home here at college has always been inextricably wound with the pattern of vocational discernment: both professional and relational, both glimmering moments of hope and shadowy pauses of doubt. It has been the place where I have felt God's tender touch nudging me to pick up an unexpected elective, or to striking up a surprising conversation with a boy after class. These little nudges have come to light as the grace-filled beginnings of some of the most wonderful adventures: I now know that unexpected elective as the very subject I'll spend years more pursuing in graduate school next year, and I now know that boy as the man I'll marry on an August afternoon a year from now.

My junior year, at the beginning of the second semester, I decided to visit the grotto each night before bed. The beginning of living into this promise was also the beginning of growing especially acquainted with a particularly South Bend brand of cold. Biting, snow-flurried winds made waves on the back of my thick parka as I shuffled down the dark path from my dorm into the glowing flickers of the grotto. I remember how warm the candle would be on my bare palms, and I would make my prayers as I cupped the candle in my hands. It was like that every night: back and forth, from my dorm to the grotto, treading the dark path, but arriving and resting in the candlelight. All of the vocational discernment that happened during my time as an undergraduate was like that, too. There have been shadowy sidewalks and moments of cupping the light. There have been wonderings about whether I will be strong enough, or creative enough, or loving enough to do the work that God has set before me, and wonders of strength, creativity, and love poured into my cupped hands. This has always been the pattern: My soul traveling the snowy path, yet finding home in the candlelit cave.

I have not had to make this movement alone. One of the most wondrous things about the undergraduate experience is the chance to live into this pattern with friends and mentors in abundance. In shadowy moments of doubt, they are the ones who have walked me closer to light. On a cold February morning, when past heartbreak eclipsed my vision of the great gift of the relationship that had come into my life, my roommate sat on my dorm room bed with me, holding my hand and speaking words of comfort. And throughout my undergraduate experience, whenever I doubted that my love of words could ever bear real fruit, it seemed that a bearer of light was always at the next curve of the nighttime sidewalk: the professors who wrote affirmations in the margins of my papers, who asked me to write articles and stories and poems, who created spaces for me to use my greatest gift for the good of the Church on blogs, in classrooms, and in warm, light-filled chapels.

My hope for the Church is that she may continue to walk this same pattern with undergraduates in the fold of her mantle: those of us who are still new to the lifelong movement between uncertainty and hope. As college students, we will always have a great need in our heart for reminders that we are made strong, creative, and loving when we bring our cupped hands to the Church. We will have a great need for light bearers: for those older than us who can spot our gifts shining and create spaces for them to glow bright enough for us to realize they are really there. We will have a great need for company as we walk each night from our dorms to the grotto, for someone to chat softly with us along the walk, and perhaps to remind us that we haven't got too far to go before we catch sight of a candle, flickering with all its might. And, just maybe, if you catch us on a particular kind of messy, grace-filled night, we'll need a tender touch on the shoulder—a nudge that brings us home.

Madeline Lewis is twenty-two years old and a soon-to-be graduate of the University of Notre Dame with a bachelor of arts in English and theology. Her next step will be moving to Ohio to pursue a master of fine arts in poetry at Miami University. She thinks a lot about the way that God draws us to him through the small details of the everyday world, and how our own storytelling reflects and reveals the ever unfolding narrative of God's grace at work in our world.

Questions

1. Dr. Brian Starks states in his précis that "Pope Francis has consistently stressed the importance of *both* encountering Christ *and* engaging in mission....The undergraduate years are not solely about seeking, but also about building—building a relationship with Christ and building the Kingdom of God...and the two go hand in hand!" However, despite the mutuality he advocates, many programs geared for undergraduates emphasize one or the other; some of the essays here, likewise, do not convey a balance of these two aspects of discipleship. To what extent do you agree that this balance is important, and in what ways should we rethink undergraduate ministry to ensure this?

2. What are some of the challenges that undergraduates discuss in their essays? In what ways can families, parishes, and dioceses better support them in these years?

3. Looking for deeper meaning, challenge, growth, and interpersonal connections was a recurring theme in many of these essays. How can your parish offer support to local campuses and even older high school students in satisfying these longings in meaningful ways?

Emerging Adult Catholics and Parish Engagement

by Kathleen Garces-Foley

One of the curious things about being a young adult today is the strong impression—among them and by outsider observers—that they are not really adults yet. They have reached legal adulthood, but most will not reach the traditional markers of adulthood—a long-term job, marriage, and parenthood—until their late twenties or early thirties. According to a 2011 report from the Pew Research Center, the average age of first marriage in the United States has reached 27 for women and 29 for men, compared to 20.3 and 22.8 in 1970. The age of first parenthood has similarly risen, but parenthood and marriage have become untethered as an increasing number of children are born to unmarried parents. There are several cultural factors behind the postponement of marriage and parenthood. Chief among them is the shift from a manufacturing economy to a service economy, which requires education beyond high school in order to secure stable, well-paid employment. Prolonged education and weak job opportunities are the main reasons for the postponement of marriage and parenthood. National statistics mask the major differences in life trajectory among those who have some college and those who have no college. Sixty-two percent of women with a high school education or less have their first child before age twenty-five, compared with only 26 percent of women who have a bachelor's degree.[1] Access to reliable birth control and career aspirations of women are also important factors in decisions to postpone marriage and parenthood.

What are we to make of this prolonged time period between finishing high school and entering the stable adult roles of marriage, parenting, and a long-term job? Psychologist Jeffrey Arnett argues that this is a new stage of life, which he calls "emerging adulthood," is distinct from adolescence and adulthood.[2] Emerging adulthood is a period of identity exploration as individuals learn about themselves through education, working, and developing relationships. It is a time of a great deal of instability that can be both exciting and stressful. Compared to eighteen- to twenty-nine-year-olds of past generations, emerging adults experience unprecedented freedom to focus on themselves as they figure out who they are and what they want in life before entering a long-term career, marriage, and parenthood. During emerging adulthood, they may have multiple romantic relationships and many cohabitate. Parents with financial means enable emerging adulthood by providing financial and other support to their adult children. More than one in three of eighteen- to twenty-nine-year-olds live in a parent's

---

1. Gretchen Livingston, "For Most Highly Educated Women, Motherhood Doesn't Start until the 30s," *Pew Research Center*, January 15, 2015, http://www.pewresearch.org/fact-tank/2015/01/15/for-most-highly-educated-women-motherhood-doesnt-start-until-the-30s/.

2. Jeffrey Jensen Arnett, *Emerging Adulthood: The Winding Road from the Late Teens through the Twenties* (New York: Oxford University Press, 2014).

home.[3] Emerging adulthood is not unique to the United States; the globalization of the world economy pushes young people worldwide, who aspire to stable employment, into postsecondary education while postponing marriage and parenthood. These major cultural changes inevitably affect the religious lives of emerging adults. Setting aside the evaluative question of whether the phenomenon of emerging adulthood is a positive or negative development, this essay seeks to explain the experiences of U.S. Catholics who are experiencing emerging adulthood.

Two national studies provide a valuable overview of Catholic young people. The Pew's 2014 American Religious Landscape Report reveals that 17 percent of adult Roman Catholics are between the ages of eighteen and twenty-nine years.[4] This group is equally divided into men and women and very diverse ethnically: 44 percent identify as Hispanic/Latino and 44 percent identify as white. Twenty-three percent of eighteen- to twenty-nine-year-old Catholics are immigrants, and 26 percent are children of immigrants. Most eighteen- to twenty-nine-year-old Catholics appear to fit into the emerging adulthood stage: only 16 percent are married, 22 percent have children, and roughly half have some college education. In terms of their religious lives, 47 percent say religion is very or somewhat important to them, and 78 percent say they attend church on a weekly (28 percent) or monthly (50 percent) basis. The National Study of Youth and Religion has surveyed a representative sample of Catholics three times as they aged between thirteen and twenty-three

---

3. Richard Fry, "A Rising Share of Young Adults Live in Their Parents' Home: A Record 21.6 Million in 2012," *Pew Research Center*, August 1, 2013, http://www.pewsocialtrends.org/2013/08/01/a-rising-share-of-young-adults-live-in-their-parents-home/.

4. "Religious Landscape Study," *Pew Research Center*, accessed April 9, 2018, http://www.pewforum.org/religious-landscape-study/.

years.[5] It finds that Catholics ages eighteen to twenty-three are very much like Catholic young people of recent generations in terms of their attitudes, beliefs, and behaviors. The only major difference is a significant decline in Mass attendance. This study reveals a strong correlation between faith formation in childhood and adolescence and the religious beliefs and practices of eighteen- to twenty-three-year-old Catholics. Somewhat surprisingly, attending Catholic high school has little independent influence on the religiosity of eighteen- to twenty-three-year-olds. Committed Catholic parents are the most powerful force shaping the religious lives of Catholic young people.

National surveys provide a big picture overview, but to understand how emerging adult Catholics are engaging with the Church, we need to look at what's happening at the local level of parishes. According to the Pew survey, three-fourths of eighteen- to twenty-nine-year-olds reported that they attend Mass at least monthly, but it is obvious to those in the pews that far fewer are actively engaged in parish communities. In their 1996 national plan for young adult ministry, the U.S. bishops urged parishes to be more welcoming of young adults, which it defined very broadly to include eighteen- to thirty-nine-year-olds.[6] One way to welcome them is to develop young adult ministry (hereafter, YAM) in the parishes to facilitate the formation of relationships with peers and provide age-appropriate spiritual support. Not surprisingly, larger parishes have an easier time forming and sustaining these groups, which are largely, if not completely,

---

5. Christian Smith, Kyle Longest, Jonathan Hill, and Kari Christoffersen, *Young Catholic America: Emerging Adults In, Out of, and Gone from the Church* (New York: Oxford University Press, 2014), 265.

6. A separate model of young adult ministry exists for Hispanic Catholics in the United States. *Pastoral Juvenil Hispana* has roots in Latin America and combines older youth and young adult ministry for ages sixteen to thirty, according to the Instituto Fe y Vida.

dependent on the volunteer efforts of young adults. In the Washington, DC, region, where I have focused my research, YAM groups offer opportunities for spiritual reflection, service, and socializing, which are frequently combined. For example, several parishes in the D.C. area offer monthly or quarterly evening events that include praise singing, eucharistic adoration, opportunity for confession, and socializing afterward at a nearby pub. Smaller numbers gather for spiritual reflection, such as Bible study groups, and service activities, such as feeding the homeless. YAM activities are advertised through social media including Twitter, but more commonly, information is shared through email announcements and Facebook pages. Facebook event posts play an important role for newcomers to the parish, as it allows them to see how large an event is going to be and whether those planning to attend (as indicated on Facebook) look like potential friends. One of the issues they consider is age; as noted earlier young adult ministry can draw those between eighteen and thirty-nine years of age, but emerging adults are looking for peers within a much narrower age range. Parishes friendly to emerging adults are known through word of mouth and can become magnet parishes, drawing emerging adults from the area. The success of magnet parishes makes it difficult for other parishes to sustain the critical mass needed to support their own YAM groups.

What are emerging adult Catholics looking for in a parish? Not surprisingly, this diverse group seeks many different things in a parish, but the overwhelming answer we hear in interviews is that they want to form relationships with other Catholics "like them." By this they mean peers experiencing the challenges and excitement of emerging adulthood. At this stage of life, most aren't looking to get married, and for this reason, they steer clear of "singles" events. They look for parishes that have friendly, welcoming, vibrant young adult communities and engage in a process of "parish shopping" to find a good fit. Few emerging adults pay attention to parish boundaries or norms of parish registration. Instead, they rely on word of mouth and the Internet, starting first with the parish website. While finding peers is their top priority, the culture of the parish, set by the pastor, is also important. Some emerging adults look for priests who are faithful to the magisterium, while a large number want an inclusive pastor who is nonjudgmental. In their parish search, emerging adults also pay attention to the worship experience, particularly the quality and style of the liturgical music and preaching. While they seek out these aspects, some emerging adults are not searching for a parish home. Instead they are "plugged into" multiple parishes, allowing themselves more options for attending Sunday Mass and young adult events that fit into their hectic and often unpredictable lives. This practice, which I call "parish hopping," is aided by diocesan young adult ministry programming that encourages emerging adults to connect across parish lines.

Large, urban dioceses have paid staff to support young adult ministry on a larger scale than the parish groups. For example, in Washington, DC, a monthly parish "holy happy hour" draws thirty to fifty emerging adults, while the diocese's Theology on Tap events will attract four times as many. Theology on Tap is offered by many dioceses in the United States. As the name suggests, it combines theological reflection and beer by hosting speakers at a local pub. The informal bar atmosphere provides an easy entrée for Catholics new to the area or returning to the Church. In addition to hosting large events, diocesan staff support parish young adult groups by sharing information across the region through social media. Using their regional reach via e-mail lists, and Twitter and Facebook followers, the diocesan YAM office helps draw to parish events the critical mass of Catholic peers that emerging adults are seeking. As noted earlier, the successful creation of region-wide emerging adult networks does undermine the traditional norms of parish membership. While not inevitable, it is likely that most emerging adult Catholics involved in YAM will eventually marry and have children, settling into a parish home that is family focused.

Kathleen Garces-Foley, PhD, is Professor of Religious Studies in the department of theology and religious studies at Marymount University in Arlington, Virginia. Her research focuses on religion and culture in the contemporary United States, with special interest in race, immigration, young adults, and end-of-life care. She is currently coauthoring a book on the religious and spiritual lives of American twentysomethings. She is the author of Crossing the Ethnic Divide: The Multiethnic Church on a Mission, *and editor of* Death and Religion in a Changing World.

Overcoming Fear and Emerging into Adult Faith

by Teresia McCarthy

I'm the youngest of twelve, and I was raised in an Eastern Catholic Rite in which my father was a priest. Growing up, most Sundays we would celebrate Mass in my house. On the other days of the week, my mother took us to Roman Catholic Rite Masses. My mother often lifted me up high to kiss the feet of the statue of the Blessed Virgin Mary at the end of Mass when I was very young. Now, at thirty-two years old, I'm driving home from the Berkshires where I now live and I see the Virgin Mary statue propped on a hill overlooking the turnpike. She still watches over me. She has held my hand and guided me through the toughest of times in life, and she has helped me to realize that through the mud, flowers can grow. This "mud" is symbolic of the issues I've struggled with in this life, from depression and anxiety to addiction.

Each vocation in my life has been like a flower. It comes and goes with time and always a new flower emerges in place of the one that has died. My vocation, like these flowers, has changed multiple times throughout the years. Many times, in my life, I felt lost because I was so unsure of where I was supposed to be and what my purpose was. My miraculous recovery from a Tylenol overdose is what led to the canonization of St. Edith Stein. I often thought when I was young that because of this miracle, I was supposed to do something great in this world. After all, *she* did! I was named after the name she took upon entering religious life. She was martyred and interceded for me; it made sense—from a certain perspective—that God expected great things from me, too. Because I never saw this "great thing" in my life, I felt like a failure, causing me to struggle with depression and anxiety for many years. I believe now my vocation is not one obvious thing, but that I have been called to do many things and it is in *how* I do them that they become my calling. I've worked as a paramedic, with computers, as a swim instructor, in a battered women's shelter, and as a sales associate selling beauty products. They were all flowers that I have learned from. And like the wind blows the seeds of the dandelion to new places, so have these jobs brought me to new destinations in life.

I've always prayed to do God's will. Though sometimes I feel I go against what I should be doing, I believe God never gives up on me and works with the situations I sometimes get myself into. When I feel I've lost my way with God, I call upon Mary to bring me back to her son. My vocation is about always doing the next right thing and being caring to others. It is to try the very best that I can with what is given to me in any given moment. I strive for this. I pray to the Mother Mary to hold my hand and guide me to God's will. Life can sometimes be disappointing, and things that at first appear to be God's will turn out not to be: jobs don't work out, relationships fail, people you care about get sick, you get sick. It has all happened to me and it's hard to stay the course of life without some kind of faith in God's plan. It is in this process of failing and losing things, though, that I've discovered in me the quiet power of resilience. With each trial of life and faith, this resilience grows. I, therefore, know now that God has given me these trials not to bring me down, but to build me up.

As I've grown into my adulthood, I've been disappointed and saddened at times as well as encouraged and empowered by this vocation. All flowers start as seeds. My faith was but a seed when I was younger. Being the youngest of twelve children, I more often than not depended on the strength of the faith of those who were older than me. I asked them to pray for me. I asked them what was right and wrong. I asked them to tell me about God and the Bible. And I followed somewhat blindly into what I was told, how I was to behave, and what I was supposed to believe in. I had to learn in my own time what truly moved me and brought me closer to God. I'm much older now and know that I cannot waste my brief time on this earth contemplating anymore on sin and despair. I despaired for so many years, focusing on what I was doing wrong in this life instead of what was right. This led to even more despair and caused me to neglect the good qualities that God had blessed me with. It made it impossible to nourish the life of God within me and to thus emit that love out to others and the world. I've learned to accept my downfalls and believe in the power of God's mercy to allow me to grow from them, like the daffodil that emerges from the ground at the end of winter and beginning of spring. It does not let the nearby patches of old snow hold it back from the sun. So, too, I will not let my sins of the past hold me from the light of God's love and forgiveness that he offers me today.

I'm now in church, kneeling before the blessed Virgin Mary. Praying to find another job, for my relationship with my boyfriend, and for the gifts of the Holy Spirit. Her feet are raised too high above me to kiss them like I did when I was a child. I'm no longer small enough to be lifted up, and my mother, who is now wheelchair ridden, is too frail to help. I know Mary is there, not because of the statue, but because I feel today the presence of God in me and my connection to all the saints in heaven and all the life on earth. I have just received communion and am now in communion with all that is God and from God. I know that God has not given me a *future* in this broken world to look forward to, but has given me a *now* to live in and to live in with love. This is the gift of vocation: the ability to live in love in the moment God has given to us. That "now" moment and every moment is a new beginning, a new chance to bring God's love into the world. Beginning right here, right now.

My hope from the Church, as to help me in my vocations, is that we focus more on the inclusion of others. I believe it can do this by providing more education and focus on how we all, in this life, have the Spirit of God in us. It would be great to see more Catholic, faith-based support groups for diseases, such as addiction and depression. It doesn't take a statistic for us to know that many in our world struggle with these things. It would be good for those facing a challenge of this kind to know that just because we struggle with disease doesn't mean we are more separated from God. In fact, we are closer to his loving Spirit because we are in need of it. Jesus's words are a beautiful reminder of this, "Blessed are the poor in spirit, for theirs is the kingdom of heaven" (Matt 5:3).

Teresia Benedicta McCarthy is a thirty-two-year-old woman living in Lee, Massachusetts. She is an Eastern Rite Catholic who currently works as an advocate in a women's shelter.

Faith in Action

by Deborah Francisco

After I graduated from college, I worked for several years as a youth minister, hoping to share the joy of faith I had experienced as a teenager. During that period, I had been inspired by Ignatian spirituality practices of discernment, which helped me recognize that we have been created with wonderful gifts and we are meant to use them to the best of our ability. We are called to not only cultivate our faith and prayer life but to put it into action in the world. St. Ignatius believed that the world was our monastery and that we are called to serve those most in need by becoming the contemplative in action. That phrase burned inside of me: *contemplative in action.* As much as I loved my job, I still felt like I was being called to something more. This question continually filled my mind: What did it mean to live in solidarity with the world, with the poor and vulnerable? I didn't really know. I needed to see firsthand what it was like for those living in a developing country, and I felt that God was calling me to live my faith in action out in the world. I eventually discerned that my vocation—who God was calling me to be and how I could become the best version of myself—was to serve abroad, and after a year of waiting, I was finally accepted into the Peace Corps.

I was sent to the Philippines and worked on several community outreach projects, including a music program for youth. During my time there, all the things that I was passionate about—serving others, music, advocating for social justice, learning about new cultures—came together, and my work became a synthesis of everything that I loved and could do well. It had been an opportunity to use all my skills and passions in a way that was both challenging and fulfilling. It was exactly what I had needed, and somehow God knew that. I finally realized why I had been called to that journey in the first place.

However, encountering destitute poverty for the first time, I felt crippled by my own sense of helplessness. I'd cry out to God, "Why do you let this happen? Why don't people do anything about this?" It was then that I saw a great need for more education in the United States on issues happening in the world. I saw a great need for initiating more efforts to alleviate poverty, challenge unjust social structures, and stand in solidarity with our brothers and sisters who live in difficult conditions. I saw a great need for more participation from Christians to take action on these issues, to make service and justice a regular part of our faith lives. In my time abroad, it had never been more clear that God was calling us to become his hands and feet, to be the face of Christ to others, and to recognize the face of Christ in those around us. That experience of service in the world has transformed my life. It has informed the lifestyle I choose to live, the way I act toward others, the friends I make, and the career path that I seek today.

As a kid, I learned in faith formation classes that Jesus loved the poor and outcast, and that we must help others in need. I participated in many service experiences, but with the view that it was a nice thing to do. *Charity*. We are often led to believe that acts of charity—serving at a soup kitchen, giving money to the poor—are enough. But without justice—asking why these issues exist in the first place and working for change—charity will never be enough. One thing that I missed in all my religious education classes and youth group involvement was that our very identity as Catholics is *integrally* tied to justice work. Social justice is not just one of many things we can do as Catholics; it is central to the very core of our faith. I felt as if I had to discover that on my own, through my experience abroad, through further studies, through conversations with those who had walked a similar path. The one thing that keeps coming back to me is *why did I not know this sooner?* How could such a beautiful part of our faith be kept hidden from me for so long? Catholic social teaching (CST) is often referred to as the "Church's best kept secret." Why are we not sharing this rich collection of teachings to all the faithful, especially to young Catholics?

Many of my peers have left their faith because they care deeply about social justice issues like poverty, immigration, and protection of the environment, and they do not believe, or perhaps know, that the Church cares deeply about those issues as well. As I learned more about CST and that working for justice is a central tenet within our Catholic faith, I discovered that God was calling me and all of the members of the Body of Christ to reach out to those most in need, to stand in solidarity with the poor and vulnerable, to live out the gospel teachings of Jesus. Young adults want to make a difference in the world, and if they knew what the Church teaches on the current social issues, I believe they would draw closer to the Church. Young adults want a real and lived faith, one that challenges them to go beyond themselves in service to those most in need. If the Church can learn to infuse CST into the life of parishes and schools—including faith formation programs, parish service projects, community events, the liturgy, and prayer—we will draw more young people into the community of faith, young people who are inspired to give, to serve, and to participate in bringing about the kingdom of God here on earth.

Young adults are also searching for a faith community that welcomes all people, no matter who they are, where they come from, or where they are at in their faith journey. It is in living together as one community that we experience God's grace, love, and mercy. Young adult programs that emphasize a personal faith over participation in the collective life of the community will only perpetuate individualism and teach young adults to remain inside themselves instead of living out their faith in the world. If we are to teach young adults to follow the gospel, the Church must create more opportunities for young adults to not only encounter the poor and marginalized, but understand the responsibility required of all Christians to work together for a more just world. Creating programs and opportunities that integrate mercy, justice, and community life with faith would resonate with an entire population of emerging adults who are yearning for "something more."

Today, my Catholic faith is not just focused on going to Mass and praying. Those things, although essential and necessary to our faith, are not enough if we are trying to emulate the gospel teachings to feed the hungry, clothe the naked, welcome the stranger, and to love our neighbor. As Catholics, our faith and identity are integrally tied to justice. I hope that the Church will make CST more of a priority in all the different aspects of parish life. We need to teach young adult Catholics, and the generation that comes after us, that our faith is one that requires courage and commitment; it is a faith that is challenging, a faith that requires us to go beyond our comfort zone, perhaps even to go beyond country borders in order to reach out to those most in need. CST helps us to recognize the face of Christ in each person that lives in this world.

We are all born with unique gifts and talents that make each of us who we are, instilled with the capacity for greatness, to become more fully that person we are meant to be is our vocation and lifelong journey. Ignatius's idea of becoming the contemplative in action inspired me to grow deeper in my faith. As I grew more aware of the needs of others in this world, serving abroad was the way that I felt called to live out my faith in action. Not everyone is called to spend years serving abroad, but we are all called to work for justice, to follow wholeheartedly the gospel teachings in order to further the mission of the Church.

Deborah Francisco, MTS, age thirty-two, has worked in youth ministry and community development for over ten years. She served three years in the Philippines as a Peace Corps Volunteer (2011–14), working on youth and family outreach programs. Deborah recently received a master of theological studies from the Franciscan School of Theology.

Vocational Discernment in Twenty-First-Century California

by Dominic Borchers

The journey to finding one's vocation can seem overwhelming at times. This is especially true for the last few generations. In the past few decades, the world has turned its back on everything connected with religion and has embraced immoralities we cannot commit and ideologies that we cannot follow; the enthusiasm that accompanies such sin can lead one to despair. God is good, however, and his ways are not our ways. Trying to discern one's vocation in this day and age, then, has an added level of difficulty for young adults such as myself. Not only do we struggle to open our minds and hearts to hear the Lord call each of us to our particular holiness, but we must also battle to suppress the cacophony that the world is shouting, tempting us to follow them down their path of pleasure, self-interest, and ultimately self-destruction. The Church, perhaps more than ever before, ought to do her best to help me and my fellow young adults to answer this most important question of what our vocation is, or at least give us ample opportunity and resources to help and guide us along our paths.

I am a cradle Catholic; I was born into a Catholic family and have been blessed to have two devout parents who are both supreme examples of the pursuit of holiness and a holy marriage. My upbringing has given me a strong foundation and a frame for discerning my vocation. Just this past year, I graduated from one of the few truly Catholic colleges remaining in America with a bachelor of arts in theology. After some discernment, I decided to pursue a dream of owning my own restaurant, and acquired a job at a nearby establishment. It took a week before I was splashed in the face with the cold fact that I did not share a reality with my coworkers. Far from it. Most of the conversations seemed to steer with alarming speed into immoral conversation—usually regarding alcohol, crazy parties, drugs, and sex, to be blunt. Work quickly became a cross in that way, for I had to constantly be on guard against such conversations that were sometimes an occasion of sin. Thankfully, my coworkers quickly picked up that I was not interested and, indeed, was opposed to such conversation, and they avoided discussing these things around me. Sometimes, a few of them would ask why I reacted the way I did, which offered a wonderful opportunity for evangelization, and was an incredible grace and blessing amid the less positive parts of the job.

Even before my experience in the restaurant, I was very aware that the culture that Catholic young adults live in departs significantly from Catholic values. I am invited every once in a while to join my coworkers for activities, but I am often extremely loath to accept the invitations. More often than not, I go along just to keep an eye on people and not to enjoy myself. These outings are not a pleasurable experience for me because their idea of having fun is quite distant from what I would consider as fun. For example, once they invited me to go out drinking and smoke marijuana. Such an outing I knew would be fraught with uncomfortable situations and occasions of sin. I would much rather spend time with friends simply hanging out and catching up or doing some other activity—such as bowling, hiking, or road tripping—since this gives ample opportunity for healthy discussions and wonderful memories. Everyday life does not provide much vocational fodder for young graduates who are earnest about their faith. Despite several wonderful qualities of the people I work with—a sense of care for one another, friendliness, pride in their craft—there are several negative traits that are contrary to God. They are clearly coworkers and not peers in the more meaningful ways. I could not, for example, ask my fellow workers for guidance; they would be at a loss as to what I was asking for, perhaps even be outright scornful.

How can the Church help me and help us? In light of all this, the first thing I would ask of the Church to help me in my vocational discernment is for there to be more Catholic young adult groups. It would be invaluable, I feel, to have a group that I can hang out with, if you will, a group with whom I would not have to be constantly on guard or ill at ease. When I am with coworkers outside of work, it is difficult to enjoy myself when their idea of fun is usually not only far from what I would think of as enjoyable but rather borderline, if not outright, sinful. Since I attended a college on the East Coast and now live on the West Coast, I also do not have a plethora of friends nearby, especially friends who share my beliefs and morals. Not only would young adult groups be welcome on a social level, but also spiritually and perhaps even vocationally. Having friends of the same beliefs who can encourage me in my daily endeavor to draw closer to the Lord and give a kind of good and wholesome "peer pressure" would greatly help in my discernment, rather than those at work who present peer pressure of an entirely different kind. Also, if I am called to the vocation of marriage, young adult groups seem like a fitting place for future spouses to meet. Nowadays, it is difficult and even risky to go on dates and, frankly, it can sometimes be disheartening. A Catholic young adult group, however, would be much more ideal because the people there, just by showing up, demonstrate that they are of the same or similar mind as you.

When these young adults meet, it seems like a perfect place to speak and focus on vocations, which is my second request of the Church. This can be done in many ways, whether it be in talks, events, seminars, or inviting religious to socialize. The talks could be given by a variety of people to give a greater knowledge to the youth of the diversity of vocations. The talks could be given by a couple speaking on or taking questions about marriage, a priest discussing the priesthood, or a religious describing what it is like to be a brother or sister. Nowadays, this exposure to vocations in religious life is especially critical as there is so little contact with them on an everyday basis. Because of this near invisibility, it is rather difficult for Catholics, or anyone for that matter, to get to know religious and to understand their particular way of life. Such a gathering of young adults seeking clarity in their personal vocations is a prime forum for promoting inquiries to religious life.

I feel I would not be a good Catholic if I did not request that there be more availability of the sacraments. Thanks be to God, there is a very decent selection of daily Masses to attend in the Diocese of Oakland, so in this regard there is no need for an increase in availability. Perhaps the most needed is the sacrament of reconciliation. It seems there are only confession times during the weekend, almost exclusively on Saturday, and perhaps one other day during the week. I know that the harvest is great and the laborers are few, but if each church within a deanery chose a different day of the week besides Saturday to hear confessions, I feel this would be tremendously helpful in the discernment of my vocation. How can I hear the Lord if I, God forbid, have been cut from his graces by a grave sin, and yet have to bend my schedule at work more often than not to find time to receive God's forgiveness? Saturdays are work days for many people in restaurants and other businesses.

One final request I would ask of the Church is that there be a greater availability of the blessed sacrament for adoration. Is there any better way for us to get to know Jesus than by spending at least one hour with him as often as we can? And I know that getting to know Jesus better will also clarify my vocation. Thankfully, there are several churches that offer adoration, but sometimes these opportunities are few and far between, both in time and distance. Those who have a full schedule, which is quite common among young adults today, can sometimes find it difficult to spend even an hour with the Lord.

I hope these words will help the Church discover the best way to assist me and my fellow young adults as we discern our vocations. Know that I am eternally thankful for your effort in doing so, and may God bless you in your endeavor!

Dominic Borchers is twenty-three years old. He comes from a devoutly Catholic family and is the third of eight children. Borchers was born in the Midwest, but has lived in California for the past twelve years. As a recent graduate of Christendom College, majoring in theology and minoring in philosophy, he is actively pursuing his vocation in the food industry.

Breaking in New Shoes

IMAGINING A MORE INCLUSIVE CHURCH

by Anthony Ferrari

As a student of theology, I am no stranger to the images and metaphors that we use to talk about God. We encounter God the Father, the Mother, the Spirit, the Judge, the Shepherd, the Creator, the Redeemer, and many other images of God. However, I want to propose another notion of God. What about God the Shoemaker? I cannot claim this speck of theological wisdom as my own. My godmother first introduced me to God the Shoemaker during my adolescence. At this stage in my life, I find myself trying to fit into categories, labels, and rules that others prescribed to me. In a letter, my godmother warned how the labels and categories that we hold onto can become tight like a pair of old shoes. She recounted that she had worn many different "shoes" during her life, and she revealed that whenever they became too tight, God would throw her another pair of shoes. This is the perfect advice for someone who is experiencing the physical, spiritual, and emotional growing pains of young adulthood. I would be wise to keep my godmother's advice in mind: God is moving me toward a special discipleship.

As a young person who contends with the ebb and flow of life, I am constantly on the lookout for the next pair of shoes that God will throw my way. Currently, I feel God calling me to be a leader in the creation of a more inclusive Catholic Church. I hope to pursue this end as a religious educator. In this spirit, I feel that the Church would also be wise to think of God as a shoemaker. I sense serious growing pains in our Church as it changes in ways that we cannot imagine. Yet I also fear that some of our rules and practices are limiting us like a pair of old shoes. We ought to pay more attention to the cries of those who suffer in the midst of our growing pains. These cries are coming from inside and outside of the Roman Catholic Church—they come from women, the poor, people of color, gays and lesbians, religious minorities, the disabled, and many other individuals. It is high time that the Church doors are flung fully open in gentle welcome to all God's people.

I offer this invitation and critique in the wake of my own growing pains. I recognize my status as a white male, and I am becoming more aware of the privileges that I am afforded with this identity. As someone who will someday become a wrinkly, old, Italian guy, I feel emboldened to say, there are too many of us in the Vatican! I want a more diverse Church! My experience teaching high school reinforces my longing for a more inclusive and diverse Church. In the classroom, I often became frustrated with my students when they made comments like, "Mr. Ferrari, you look like Jesus." In fairness, many of the artistic representations of Jesus do look like me: a young, fair-skinned, bearded man with brown hair. I also happened to be the person that most frequently discussed Jesus with them. Nevertheless, in the event of being physically compared to Jesus, I reminded the class that the historical Jesus was a Semitic Jew who lived in first-century

Palestine, an ethnic and cultural background quite different from my own.

On one particular occasion, I had a memorable experience while walking home from a day of teaching at this high school. As I crossed the street toward my house, I spotted an African American man pushing a shopping cart on the other side of the street. I saw the contents of the shopping cart: some food, another pair of clothes, a blanket, a radio, and a few other knickknacks. I was aware that this man was likely experiencing homelessness, and I understood that the contents of the shopping cart could be his only possessions. As I approached the man, he turned and shouted, "Hey! You look like Jesus." My stomach sank. As I looked him in the eyes, I felt a sense of sadness welling up inside of me. Stunned, I could not produce anything encouraging or clever in response. I froze in the middle of the crosswalk and stood there as he proceeded toward the other side of the street. I could not help but ask myself, why am I the one who looks like Jesus? Aren't we all part of the Body of Christ? It certainly didn't feel that way. It felt like our community had forgotten that he, too, is part of the Body of Christ. Still, these questions have not left me. I want a do-over. I want to go back to that moment at the crosswalk. I want to wait in anticipation of his remark, "Hey! You look like Jesus." And then I want to turn to him and joyfully yell back, "So do you!"

On another occasion, I had a similar experience of revelatory dismay while in San Salvador for the beatification of Monseñor Oscar Romero. Witnessing the beatification ceremony was one of the most beautiful experiences of my life. I have fond memories of waking up at dawn to celebrate the life of Romero with more than two hundred thousand other people. I remember marching toward the plaza with masses of laypeople, religious women and men, and priests. It was a sight to behold. Romero's face was on every building and

T-shirt in sight. It seemed that the crowd could not go five minutes without shouting, "*¡Viva Romero!*" and the accompanying response, "*¡Que viva!*" There was even a solar halo that appeared around the sun in the moment that the relics were brought out for veneration. I could not believe what I had witnessed.

After the ceremony, I exclaimed my joy in witnessing such a wonderful moment. This bliss continued until I spoke with a friend who expressed some disappointment. She reminded me that the altar was surrounded by hundreds of priests who sat comfortably in a sort of VIP section. Meanwhile laypersons stood behind them, sometimes fainting in the heat. Even the Sisters of the Divine Providence, who had worked tirelessly to preserve Romero's household and belongings, were not included in the ceremony. This was not an appropriate celebration for an archbishop who was so committed to the lives of his flock—a man who was beloved by mothers and grandmothers, an advocate for the poor, a person who chose to live on the nuns' property instead of in the bishop's residence. Romero was a priest who, in the words of Pope Francis, lived with the smell of the sheep. Why did his beatification ceremony push these sheep so far away? And why had I not realized this during the ceremony? I do not want to disparage a beautiful day where so many people came to celebrate the life of a wonderful man. I will always think fondly of my time at the beatification. But looking back on my experience, it seems obvious to me where Romero's spirit was during the ceremony. It was not amongst the crowd of priests that surrounded the altar. Instead, the spirit of Romero was with the women and men who baked in the sun on that morning, some fainting in the heat, all hoping to celebrate the hope and joy that Monseñor Romero had brought into their lives.

These experiences have helped me to develop a greater

awareness of those being pushed to the margins in our Church and our world. I do not pretend to be innocent of the biases and partialities that are typical of the Roman Catholic Church. I have been involved in Catholic education, as a student and teacher, for almost twenty years. My life is deeply intertwined with that of the Church. The anxiety that I feel regarding the growing pains of our Church has drawn me deeper into prayer. I often choose to practice Ignatian contemplation, in which I place myself in the scenes of gospel stories. I feel that God continues to call me toward the story of Zacchaeus, a wealthy tax collector who climbs a tree in hopes of catching a glimpse of Jesus. I am struck by the way that Jesus instructs Zacchaeus to "hurry and come down; for I must stay at your house today" (Luke 19:5). I think that Zacchaeus correctly recognizes Jesus's instruction as an invitation into downward mobility. After all, Zacchaeus responds to this instruction with a promise to give up half of his possessions and to repay those whom he had cheated. I see so much of myself in Zaccheus. I try to seek God in all aspects of my life. Yet I sometimes forget that I need to come down from the tree before I can walk with Jesus. In this way, I believe that I, myself, and many others in the Church ought to come down from the tree of power and privilege. I know that this is good news because Jesus is waiting for us at the bottom. And I think that God the Shoemaker is waiting for us too, except God might be holding orthopedics, high heels, or working boots. After all, we have a lot of work to do. This work should include taking the question of women's ordination seriously, preparing ministers to reflect theologically on issues of race, and continuing to empower marginalized communities to advocate for themselves. I hope to bring the dream of a more inclusive Church to the centerfold of my ministry. In this respect, I feel God calling me toward a vocation as a religious educator. Inevitably, there will be growing pains and maybe even some discomfort as we continue on this journey. Yet we cannot ignore the vision of the gospel, in which Jesus walks with those on the margins and welcomes everyone to the eucharistic table.

Anthony Ferrari is a twenty-four-year-old student pursuing a master of theological studies at the Jesuit School of Theology of Santa Clara University. A San Francisco Bay Area native, Anthony attended Santa Clara University and Bellarmine College Preparatory. He hopes to pursue a career as a Catholic educator.

Living in Grace

EMERGING ADULTS COHABITATING

by Taneisha Figueroa and Austin Rodrigues

Taneisha: I come from a religiously relaxed family. My parents were raised Catholic, which in their case meant they knew a great deal about Catholic traditions and the Bible but felt no strong connection to Catholicism. My mom would take me to catechism classes every Tuesday when I was in second grade, and we'd go to Easter and Christmas Mass as a family. I have good memories of the Church as a child: donating toys and diapers to orphaned babies in Puerto Rico, donating clothes and food to the homeless of Las Vegas, and going to the Kairos retreat in high school. As an adolescent, I didn't understand much about my religion, but I did know God was ever-loving and accepting. My parents and family taught me the importance of humility and giving back to the world with small deeds, like smiling at others, and big deeds, like helping a person in need.

While in Catholic high school, I took many religion classes, including Catholic vocation, which was too strict and, at times, sexist. For example, the priest told us that men and women are meant to have children, but the priest got angry when we asked about women who didn't want to become mothers. This then led to a heated argument about whether same-sex families should adopt children. Our Catholic teachers silenced us students by saying, "That is just the way things were and are; it's the natural way." I was turned off by those teachings, but I still continued with my faith and good morals.

Austin: My parents got divorced when I was four years old. As a religious person, my mom sought guidance from God because she felt that the Church was the only place where she felt comfortable and not broken. My dad was very upset about the divorce, but he did not fall back on his religious background; instead he kept himself busy with work. Little did I know that this divorce between my religious mother and my religiously indifferent father would change the way that I viewed both religion and love.

Fast forward twenty years and I am in a steady three-year relationship, and I find myself thinking about what comes next. I was raised a Christian, but I am not rigid when it comes to how much I let religion affect my life. I trace this back to my mom's pious and steadfast devotion to God and her sincere prayers for him to save my parents' marriage; God either could not or chose not to. This was a critical revelation. No matter how much you pray to God or go to church in this world, you need to create your own destiny and be the captain of your own life. I do believe that God is there, but I know that he only helps people who help themselves.

Taneisha: We met our sophomore year at Santa Clara University. Initially, we were friends and then quickly realized how much we had in common and how easy it was to be our truest selves with each other. Three-and-a-half years later, we are very in love and living together. But it has taken a lot of advice from family, friends, professors, and God to get us to where we are today.

Very early on in our relationship Austin suffered with some depression, and we went to God for guidance. We went to Mass at the Santa Clara mission and listened to the homily like our life depended on it. On our way to and during Mass, we were at ease; singing the songs helped put us at peace. There was faith and clarity! It was a very scary time for both of us when Austin went home to Hawaii to get better, and I was left brokenhearted. Time passed and we took good care of each other along with concerned doctors, family, and God. We never gave up on each other, even when it was difficult. A few years later, before we graduated, we took a religion class called "Theology of Marriage" that changed my understanding of the Church and of relationships. Our professor, Dr. Day, made so much sense to me! She used simple analogies to dig into the deep questions we faced as graduating seniors.

I used what I learned from this class during our difficult first months living together. We balanced jobs, chores, and personal space while still making room for quality time. So many times I would feel Austin took for granted all the planning I did for our dates, the cleaning, the cooking. He would feel I was nagging too much and he felt unappreciated. Living together tested our relationship's patience and limits. There was an instant while reevaluating our priorities and figuring out ways to improve our shortcomings where we asked one another if we were even meant for each other. And I remembered what Dr. Day said, "There isn't a 'perfect partner,' but there are people willing to work with you for a happier and healthier relationship." Austin and I are vastly different, and we are learning so much about each other and our relationship. But one thing is certain: we will always work together because we know that a relationship is always changing and it needs constant maintenance. Dr. Day's teachings were and are a blessing. We want each other's happiness more than anything! This happiness includes splitting housework equally: dishes, trash, vacuum, laundry, cooking, and so forth. It includes broadening our horizons when it comes to free time. One day we will do candlelight bedtime yoga and the next we will watch a sci-fi movie. This happiness includes knowing that when we get married, there will be a standard of feminism in all aspects of our relationship, from ambitious careers to pregnancy to raising children. We will do things equally and we will do things together. We've found that together we are happier and stronger.

Austin: As mentioned ealier, I do not have the strongest vocation, stemming from my Christian roots, but I do know that if I ever need to turn to God, he is there. I do, however, have another vocation, and that is with Taneisha. Our relationship is the most important thing to me, and I want to take the next step of marriage with her eventually.

I view marriage as a sacred bond between two people who love each other very much. To be able to get there, though, the couple must have a lot of experience with each other and know what they want in life. My biggest fear is ending up like my parents even though I vowed when I was much younger that I would never let that happen. With the uncertainty of life and rising divorce rates, the one thing that puts me at ease is that Taneisha and I know we will do anything and everything we can to work things out together. Since Taneisha and I started living together, we know far more about each other than we could have discovered otherwise. All the fights that we have gotten into about a messy house or someone not helping out were only possible because we lived together, spending time together in the mundane, beyond the specialness of date nights. These arguments have only made us stronger together, and I know that if we keep learning about each other, loving each other in the tough times, and inspiring growth in the other's weaknesses, then we will have a happy marriage.

My vocation to Taneisha is more than just making our relationship work. It is a promise that no matter what, I will put her above all else. Seeing the smile on her beautiful face not only lights up the room but makes my heart skip a beat. I may sound like I have this all down pat with my appreciation of her and our desire to put the other first, but the truth is I am still working on this and I have a long way to go. There are still times where I think about myself first, even if in the smallest ways. It is not easy to put someone above yourself. If you don't put your significant other first, then your relationship will never last. There is a huge amount of trust and faith that goes into this. If all goes as planned, your significant other will be putting you first as well and therefore you will be taken care of. It is a circle that can either be vicious or reflect the pure love and joy of Christian living. Although Taneisha and I have been together for over three years, we still have yet to perfect this circle. Even if it might never be perfect, we will never stop trying.

Together: We miss going to the 9:00 p.m. student Masses at the mission of our undergraduate. No matter how busy you got or how badly you procrastinated, there was no excuse to miss that 9:00 p.m. Mass! And, importantly, you didn't want to miss it. You walked in and you saw people your own age who were going through the same things as you. Homilies would tie in the Scripture passages to the anticipation of going home for the holidays or the angst of finals; they were, in a word, relevant. As emerging adults cohabitating together it would be nice to see more church communities focus on people like us. Often the Church focuses on married people, young families, and elders. The struggles and joys of these populations are not the same as ours. We want our experiences—the joys and hopes, the pains and sorrows—to be recognized and affirmed or supported within our parish. We'd like to think that we are good, religious people who live a good and healthy life in the eyes of God. We pray every night and say three things we are grateful for from the day. Our religious roots have instilled in us solid morals that enable us to have a prosperous relationship with each other and our families. But young, single adults are neglected by the Church. We would like to see churches have homilies about young love, work, community, and so on—to preach on what is relevant to our lives.

Also, not only do we feel that much of what happens in church is not for "us," but we feel that much of what makes us "us" is not celebrated in Church. We are young, educated professionals whose lives and experiences are very different from our parents' and grandparents' worlds. While a number of experiences shaped the Catholicism of past generations—the Cold War, the pill, Vietnam, *Roe v. Wade*, Central America— new events shape ours. These include climate change, gender equality, ethnic diversity, same-sex relationships, later marriage, and many others. Speak to us about the world we live in, a world that shapes us and that we shape in turn. Give us wisdom and responsibility to make the best choices. Invite us in so that we feel accepted and a part of the Church with our "liberal" ideas of cohabitating and feminism. There should be more churches opening their doors and perspectives to the new generation. We are loving and respectful of traditions. It is hard having just us two with no family close by. We want nothing more than to find a community where we can trust and grow closer to each other and to God.

Taneisha Figueroa, twenty-two, graduated from Santa Clara University in 2016 with a bachelor of arts in communications and a minor in theatre. She's been living in California for the past five years, learning and creating art and film. Family is the most important part of her life. Her mom and dad are her moon and stars. Taneisha wishes to travel, give love, and illuminate Hollywood with her truth!

Austin Rodrigues, twenty-three, was born and raised on the island of Oahu, Hawaii, and was very excited to move to California. After getting a great education at Santa Clara University and earning a degree in civil engineering, he is ready to build a new world for everyone to live in. This is all possible with the love and support of his family and friends.

A Hampered Horizon

THE COMPETING DEMANDS OF DATING, CAREERS, AND FAITH

by Michelle Fat and Sam Varney

Growing pains. As twenty-two-year-old recent college graduates navigating the "real world," stability is lacking and exploration is in full force. After a postgraduation three-week "summer break" together, I (Michelle) began dental school and I (Sam) started a job in biotechnology while preparing my application for medical school. After dental school, I (Michelle) will only be licensed to practice in California, and will need to look for work within the state. With the uncertainty of medical school admissions, my (Sam's) future is stuck in a temporary limbo. The commitment from our three-and-a-half year relationship together and the strength of our love for each other allows us to remain at peace with the instability surrounding us.

Marriage is a foreseeable element of our future when looking out onto a flat horizon, but with dental and medical school added into the mix, the straight line to marriage is filled with mountains and crisscrossing paths that hinder our once-clear view. Our vocational draw toward the healthcare field conflicts with our parallel calling to begin the journey of raising a family, when we have little ability to plan even a year into the future. With no guarantee of being in the same state a year from now, we look to the Church for assistance in resolving the contradictory pulls between the sacrament of marriage and individual careers in healthcare.

Both dental and medical programs are demanding on the whole of a person and require personal sacrifices in exchange for effective training. This, too often, materializes in reduced time spent together building our relationship and even less time to regularly attend Mass. In what little free time we have, we must choose between spending it on building our spiritual connection as partners and fulfilling our obligations to the Church. Ultimately, we as young adults need a Mass that gives praise to God while simultaneously providing us with opportunities for our relationship to grow stronger.

Our Jesuit university provided a multitude of readily available ways for us to delve into our personal understandings of the Church that were likewise relevant for our stage in life. The "real world," in contrast, lacks such opportunities. Though in different majors, we made a concerted effort to take one class together before graduation: Theology of Marriage. As a couple, we developed a large part of our relationship's foundation through the course's integration of theology with the challenges of young professionalism into a single forum. One of our deepest and most fundamental discussions as a couple stemmed directly from an in-class discussion surrounding our generation's tendency to put off marriage until well into our thirties. While on a late walk after studying that night, we found ourselves reflecting on the arguments our peers had made both in favor of and against marrying so late. Hesitantly, we began to nudge each other to reveal each other's opinions on the matter.

Slowly, we brushed away the sand covering our real positions and our personal hopes of when we would marry; we differed by at least ten years. My (Michelle's) parents married in their mid-twenties, while my (Sam's) parents married in their mid-thirties, with each of us expecting to follow our parents' footsteps. As the hours passed into the night, we parsed our reasoning and began formulating our mutual goal as a couple. Without the discussion that day in class, we very likely would have put off addressing these disparate plans until well too late in our relationship, with feelings of hurt and, from my (Michelle's) perspective, the idea that marriage was being delayed.

After fleshing out each of our concerns surrounding marriage, we resolved our different visions through extended conversations and garnering further understanding about the other person's perspective. We now see ourselves marrying around our late twenties, but out in the working world. Currently, we struggle to find similar opportunities for faith discussion that so easily integrate and resonate with our stage in life. Compared with the many opportunities to explore the general teachings of the Church, like Mass and Bible study, there is a relative dearth of opportunities that focus on the application of these teachings to our specific challenges as a young, professional couple. We acutely need long-term, intimate forums consisting of other young, devout couples in which we can explore strategies for resolving the common conflicts that we face between our faith, society, and professional pursuits. Similar to our Theology of Marriage course, such forums would be most impactful with the inclusion of an experienced and broadly informed person or couple. This latter serves to organize and guide the discussions, while offering an outside perspective through examples from their own long-term relationship. Such forums provide us with material and perspectives that nucleate further discussions critical for our mutual discernment of a strong, unified direction for our relationship.

The Church played a central role in our childhoods. Growing up, both of our families instilled Catholic values in us through regular Mass attendance and life lessons at home. We identified as Catholics and lived our lives with constant reflection upon the value system we derived from Scripture and parish life. Our identity as Catholics was central to our self-concept. After graduating from college and entering a phase of life that is filled with self-motivated mindsets that are irrelevant or even discouraging toward our religiosity, we feel a growing disconnect from the Church. The fading presence of the institutional Church in our lives is further diluted by the largely secular work and social circles in which we find ourselves. The existence of religion outside of the university often feels more like an unspoken undercurrent rather than an easily accessible, open forum. It is hard for us to come across peers who openly discuss attending church, let alone other couples who are open about their faith, whatever it may be.

The Church fails to support us in a personal manner during our critical period of transition into the working world, and we see this as an opportunity for pastoral change on an institutional level. Even while the institutionalized version of Church is lacking in our lives, we have experienced an increase in our practice of the "domestic church" that serves to fill in that void. The Bible itself does not call for any central, institutional Church. Rather, it offers a value system and patterns of behavior as examples to follow. As a young couple in the modern era, we find solace in our personalized version of the domestic church in which we constantly reaffirm our values and challenge each other to act upon our moral compass regardless of what is happening around us.

We feel most connected with the Church when we are able to apply its teachings in a context relevant to our own.

Interestingly, this rekindling of our dedication to the Church is not solely confined to interactions with other Catholic couples or peers. In reality, we feel a rejuvenated connection after interacting with peers who are strongly dedicated to any religion. Through my (Michelle's) dental school, we became acquaintances with several Mormon couples who delayed attending dental school in order to explore their faith and establish a family; something unthinkable to most others in our social circles. I (Michelle) delved into a deep discussion with one Mormon husband who described traveling on his mission trip and marrying his wife soon after as the path that best fit his priorities in life. The couple now has two children and plans on having more before he finishes dental school, while his wife stays home to raise them. Despite this being an unlikely route for us, as we are both pursuing professional degrees, it is nonetheless a breath of fresh air to know that other couples have found a harmony between their domestic and professional vocations that is supported by their church. Witnessing the faith of others reminds us of all that our faith gives us. It stokes the embers of our spirituality and reignites our desire to discern our path following the love and stability that lie at the core of the Church.

Despite the need for it, there is a void of community amongst young adults within the Catholic Church. This need is especially acute for those of us in relationships facing the pressures of a nonreligious society. Considering the vacuum that the Church leaves for emerging adults like us, we propose the development of small faith groups that are comprised of young Catholics in similar life stages. We felt the support of the Church during our childhood years, and we've witnessed the support that it gave our parents and other married couples. In contrast, we see a lack of formal support and even a tangible uneasiness toward young, unmarried couples who are pursuing individual careers as opposed to those focused on marriage. Small group gatherings of young Catholics in our age group, including couples, will stimulate connections that allow its members to feel at home within the Church. Such meetings will fill the voids left by both society and the Church by simultaneously acting as social events, prayer groups, and platforms for relevant, faith-based discussion between peers. This will help young adults like ourselves to really integrate our faith with our vocation and other commitments, rather than having to compartmentalize our faith into a Sunday activity. Opportunities like these will help to reaffirm the personal connection and dedication to our faith by developing a community that young adults can turn to and rely on when the greater society challenges it.

The Theology of Marriage course mentioned earlier facilitated our exploration of the many facets of marriage through the lenses of both theological teachings and societal trends. The in-class discussions with our peers served as the catalyst that encouraged us, as a couple, to each bring our theological beliefs into the sphere of our relationship, allowing us to begin merging and reconciling our beliefs early on. These in-class discussions also gave us specific points to address when discussing the topics outside of class, in the context of our own relationship. We often stayed up late into the night discussing an argument made by one of our peers in class, exploring our individual reactions and delving deeper when our reactions diverged from each other. In contrast, we currently are unable to discover a forum like this outside of our university. Only occasionally do we find topics that we relate to as a couple in the homily during Sunday Mass. There are many other young couples in church each Sunday, but each is separated into the groups with which they attend church. What we need, as young couples, is an intimate forum in which we can use other peer couples as sounding boards to help us negotiate the common barriers we face.

Michelle Fat and Sam Varney are twenty-two-year-old recent college graduates from Santa Clara University who have been dating for three years. Michelle is currently enrolled at the University of the Pacific Dugoni School of Dentistry, following in the footsteps of her parents, who met as students in the same program. Sam is working as an engineer in biotech, and will also be following in the footsteps of his parents when he applies to medical school later this summer. When they can find time to themselves, Michelle and Sam enjoy maximizing their time outdoors. They like to hike in Marin County year round and are avid skiers during the winter months.

Questions

1. As Dr. Kathleen Garces-Foley points out, emerging adulthood is a relatively new life phase, a decade or so of exploration and uncertainty. How does this compare to your own coming of age?

2. Two of these essays came from dating couples, both of which lamented the lack of personal relevance in the vast majority of parish programming. An important corrective would be to have events, speakers, retreats, social media outreach, and so on that are explicitly meant for young adults. What are the resources your parish or deanery might offer to become more innovative and welcoming of emerging adults?

3. These essays demonstrated a very large diversity of young adult needs. When was the last time your parish held a focus group to hear the needs of the unmarried adults in the community (if "never," hold one!)? What are some of the steps you take in meeting these needs that can incorporate spirituality, relationship, and service (these themes are common to many of the essays here)?

Recreating the Domestic Church

YOUNG ADULT CATHOLIC PARENTS

by Mary Ellen Konieczny

In cultures across the globe, each successive generation is challenged by the task of parenting. All parents face the fearsome privilege of providing protection, nurture, and constant love for a child, but each generation also faces unique challenges. This is certainly true in the United States today, where millennials (born roughly between the early 1980s and 2004[1]) are now marrying and starting families of their own. They join their Generation X predecessors (born between 1965 and 1984[2]), many of whom are just moving out of young adulthood while parenting children. By contrast with those who came before them, these young adults embark on the journey of parenting

---

1. Different surveys and generational analyses mark the start of the millennial generation anywhere from 1980 through 1984.

2. Dates from George Masnick, Harvard Joint Center for Housing Studies, as quoted in Philip Bump, "Here Is When Each Generation Begins and Ends, According to Facts," *The Atlantic*, March 25, 2014, https://www.theatlantic.com/national/archive/2014/03/here-is-when-each-generation-begins-and-ends-according-to-facts/359589/.

children in a quickly globalizing world, seemingly rent with economic and cultural instability, and filled with rapid change.

What does the Catholic Church offer to these young adults as they face the challenges of parenting in today's world? What do today's young adults desire from the Church as they form families and raise children?

The essays that follow reveal that young adult Catholic parents clearly find profound meaning in parenting. Many, though perhaps not all, of the challenges they write about will be familiar to older generations. Significantly, these writers are knowledgeable about, and treasure, the Catholic tradition. They are engaged in parish life, even if they sometimes find themselves frustrated by their local parish's imperfections. But in their relationship to the Church, they are not typical of their peers. Social science research tells us that millennial and Generation X young adults who were raised Catholic, though often spiritual seekers, tend to be less connected to the Catholic Church and less knowledgeable about Catholicism than their parents' and grandparents' generations.[3]

It is precisely because these writers are involved with Catholicism that they have much to teach the Church about how to incorporate and best serve millennial and Gen X parents. No less important, their words also offer their peers who are less connected to the Church an "in the trenches" perspective on what Catholic tradition and parishes have to offer them as they go about the manifold, exhausting, and often daunting tasks of parenting.

Because these writers are part of a relatively small group of highly committed, young adult Catholics, I contextualize their essays for readers by painting a general portrait of Catholic young adult parents and their millennial and Gen X peers. This is important for two reasons. First, it allows

---

3. William V. D'Antonio, Michele Dillon, and Mary L. Gautier, *American Catholics in Transition* (New York: Rowman & Littlefield, 2013).

readers to place these essays in the context of the larger population of young adult Catholic parents. And second, even if the authors of these essays are not "average" young adult Catholics, they have been shaped by the same social worlds as their generational peers; they may be different from them in terms of religious practice—and several other characteristics—but similar in some of the ways they live, work, socialize, and raise their children.

I invite readers to think about how these essays reflect the experiences of peers who are both more and less like them—not only how they mirror the experiences of other young adult Catholics who indeed *are* integrated into parish life, but also how they might help us to understand the challenges of Catholic parents who may not feel as comfortable or unequivocally committed as they do. Although millennial and Gen X young adults are often wary of religious institutions, these generations show strong impulses as spiritual seekers, and a desire to be people who are authentic and faithful to what they believe.

Young Adult Catholics: Diverse and Institutionally Detached

To understand how young adult Catholic parents are navigating their world, it is important to know who they are as members of their generations.

First, they are demographically diverse. The Pew Research Center has characterized the millennial generation as "the most racially diverse generation in American history."[4] A 2014 CARA poll, administered to parents aged twenty-five

---

4. Pew Research Center, "Millennials in Adulthood: Detached from Institutions, Networked with Friends," March 7, 2014, http://www.pewsocialtrends.org/2014/03/07/millennials-in-adulthood/.

to forty-five who had at least one minor child living at home, shows that U.S. Catholic families are more diverse ethnically and racially than the overall Catholic population, which is now about 32 percent Hispanic. Catholic parents today are majority nonwhite and Hispanic: the CARA study finds that 54 percent of Catholic parents are Hispanic, with 40 percent white, non-Hispanic, and 6 percent of other races and ethnic groups.[5] Despite Hispanics' new majority status, finding and lifting up their voices is a struggle for the U.S. Church, a reality regrettably reflected in these essays and an area where the Church needs to do better.

Second, young adults, especially millennials, are also characterized as distrustful and independent of many of American society's foundational institutions, including religious institutions; 29 percent of millennials are religiously unaffiliated. However, trust in institutions—including the government, educational, and religious institutions—has been declining generally among Americans over the last half century.[6] In this respect, then, young adults serve as something of a window on social changes in the United States overall. Pew describes them as "relatively unattached to organized politics and religion, linked by social media, burdened by debt, distrustful of people, in no rush to marry"— but also, and perhaps surprisingly, "optimistic about the future."[7]

---

5. Mark M. Gray, "The Catholic Family: 21st Century Challenges in the United States," CARA survey, June 2015, https://cara.georgetown.edu/staff/webpages/CatholicFamilyResearch.pdf. Computing from the 2014 date of the CARA survey, these respondents were born between 1969 and 1989—encompassing younger Gen Xers and the older portion of the millennial generation, who are now in their thirties.

6. Pew Research Center, "Millennials in Adulthood: Detached from Institutions, Networked with Friends," March 7, 2014, http://www.pewsocialtrends.org/2014/03/07/millennials-in-adulthood/.

7. Pew Research Center, "Millennials in Adulthood."

This mix of distrust and optimism is evident in young adults' marriage rates and reasons for remaining single. In 2014, only 26 percent of millennials were married—but three-quarters of those who were unmarried wanted to marry. They just felt they were not in an economic position to do so, an understandable concern given rapidly changing economic conditions in the United States today. Elizabeth Tenety explains how her generation's experiences bear on decisions to delay marriage and attitudes toward religion, saying, "Millennials are often critiqued for delaying or devaluing marriage, but for many, that attitude comes from a place of deep pain: older Millennials are children of peak divorce in the late 1970s and early 1980s....This generation was born into a world where the central family unit's status was uncertain."[8]

Tenety goes on to say that world events contributed to millennials' feelings of uncertainty, from President Clinton's impeachment over the Monica Lewinsky affair, to 9/11 and the priest sexual abuse scandal in the Catholic Church. Given the national environment in which they came of age, it should be no surprise that contemporary young adult Catholics are less institutionally connected to the Church than previous generations.

Young Adult Catholic Parents: Institutionally Independent and Spiritually Anchored

Racial and ethnic diversity, institutional detachment, and attitudinal differences are not the only kinds of distinctiveness found among today's young adult Catholic parents.

---

8. Elizabeth Tenety, "Not Right or Left, Wrong or Right: Millennial Catholics and the Age of Mercy," in *Polarization in the US Catholic Church: Naming the Wounds, Beginning to Heal*, ed. Mary Ellen Konieczny, Charles C. Camosy, Tricia C. Bruce (Collegeville, MN: Liturgical Press, 2016), 115.

Like American families generally, on average Catholic families have two children at home. Similarly, Catholic families are also increasingly diverse in the forms they take, although they are more likely to look like a "traditional" nuclear family—a heterosexual married couple with minor children—than those in American society as a whole. Seventy-nine percent of young adult Catholic parents are married, 76 percent of them to a Catholic spouse. Sixteen percent of Catholic parents are single; although a large majority of these single parents, about four fifths of them, report that they live with a partner. Only 4 percent are divorced.[9]

When it comes to institutional religious practices, Catholic families are similar to U.S. Catholics in general in some important respects, but different in others. They tend to be less embedded in Catholic institutions and traditions than previous generations; only 8 percent of parents have children enrolled in a Catholic school, and only 32 percent have children enrolled in Catholic religious education programs. Although most Catholic parents say that it is "very important" that their children celebrate their first communion (66 percent), and confirmation (61 percent), these are lower percentages than in previous generations.[10] About 22 percent of Catholic parents attend Mass weekly, similar to Catholics overall (24 percent). But parents attend Mass at least monthly at a higher rate: 53 percent of Catholic parents attend Mass at least once a month, compared with 43 percent of Catholics overall.[11] Other studies have shown that the busyness of family life often means that family members, especially mothers, attend religious services less often than

9. Gray, "The Catholic Family."

10. Mark M. Gray, "Practice of Faith in the Catholic Family," CARA survey, August 2015, 1–2, http://stage.hcfm.org/AboutUs/~/media/Files/HCFM/PDFs/HCFM-CARA%20Third%20Special%20Report.pdf.

11. Gray, "Practice of Faith," 12–19.

other congregants.[12] These relatively low rates of institutional connection and practice, then, are understandable. But they also show a striking commitment of many Catholic parents' efforts to retain a connection to the Church in the midst of their numerous responsibilities.

Perhaps most significant, young adult Catholic parents find spirituality and prayer to be quite important in their lives. Almost three-quarters (71 percent) of Catholic parents see prayer as essential to their faith. Most parents say they pray alone (76 percent), although many do pray together outside of Mass, most often before meals. In fact, millennials are more likely to say they pray at family gatherings (31 percent) than previous generations. Young adult parents say that what they pray for most is the well-being of their family; 83 percent do this always or most of the time when they pray. Altogether, more than half (53 percent) pray with the Scriptures, Catholic devotionals or prayer books, and/or the Liturgy of the Hours.[13]

An Invitation

Today's young adult Catholic parents, although often at a distance from their Catholic parishes, have not forsaken belief and have rich prayer lives that keep them connected to the Catholic tradition. The essays that follow reflect the longing for, and practice of, a connection with the spiritual life that most young adult parents share, as well as an invitation to all young adult Catholic parents. These writers' essays invite other young adult parents—some close to the Church, others more distant—to join them in their faith journeys in

---

12. Penny Edgell, *Religion and Family in a Changing Society* (Princeton, NJ: Princeton University Press, 2005).

13. Gray, "Practice of Faith," 12–19.

ways that allow them to find support for their parenting not only among their peers, but also from a Church that, while it may sometimes struggle to know how to best reach them, has many gifts to give.

Mary Ellen Konieczny, PhD, is Associate Professor of Sociology and Henkels Family Collegiate Chair at the University of Notre Dame. She is the author of The Spirit's Tether: Family, Work and Religion among American Catholics *(Oxford University Press, 2013). Mary Ellen and her husband, Chris Chwedyk, have two millennial generation sons who one day hope to marry.*

Growing in Vocation, Shrinking in the Church

by Justin Combs, with Monet Combs

When I was on a weekend retreat for young adult Catholics in the mountains of Julian, California, I discovered my vocation. It was Lent of 2012 and I was preparing to receive the sacraments of baptism, confirmation, and communion at the upcoming Easter Vigil. Over the previous year I had heard a number of RCIA speakers and homilists discuss the importance of stewardship and finding one's vocation. I was plowing full steam ahead toward my initiation and took what I was learning about being a part of the Church very seriously. I offered my time and talent by signing up to play guitar in the parish choir six months before my initiation; now, the weekend before the Easter Vigil, I had discovered my vocation.

On the last day of this Lenten retreat, I wandered off by myself into the woods with a copy of the New Testament. I let the book fall open to a random spot and began to read. "We know that all things work together for good for those who love God" (Rom 8:28). This passage indicated to me that it was time to propose to my longtime girlfriend. In our final sharing session for the retreat, I told my small group that I was ready for marriage. To say that the young adults were surprised at my words is an understatement; perhaps I was just ahead of the curve! Yet, when I reflect on that experience today, the other young adults' reaction to me getting married in my early twenties is somewhat troubling. Fast forward five years: Today, I am a young adult Catholic, my vocation is marriage and family life, and I am a proud husband and father. Why the objection to marrying young?

The Church and her ministers consistently teach the importance of finding one's vocation. Yet, as my wife and I have found our vocation and are bearing the full fruits of it, we can find no prominent ministry that is tailored to our spiritual needs as a young and budding family. While the young adult ministry at my parish is well-known throughout the diocese and has an inviting atmosphere that is spiritually rich, since becoming a husband and father in my twenties, I have found the parish's young adult ministry to be less and less relevant to my spiritual needs. Our parish has a ministry for just about every age group: a twenties and thirties group, a thirties and forties group, and others. But my wife and I do not feel that we fit into any of these ministries. Being married and parents in our twenties has put us in a sort of "no man's land" at our parish. At our parish's young adult Bible study, my wife and I find that we can hardly relate with others there. Sure, we're all Catholic and somewhere between the ages of twenty and thirty-five, but our life situations are drastically different from the large majority of those in this ministry. So now I ask myself, "Where is the young-adult-married-with-children ministry?"

The lack of ministerial support for young families does not seem to stop there. In our experience, the Church seems to hold up an ideal of family life. Though now that we have met that ideal as a family, it almost feels as if we have been given a ribbon for finishing the race, but we know that faith is a lifelong journey, ongoing and never finished. Although I feel blessed to be part of a parish that strives to connect all of its members with Christ in one way or another, I feel that my young family is falling through the cracks. To make this point clear I'd like to share a few experiences my wife and I have had since being married and becoming parents.

I went through a full year of preparation to receive the sacraments of initiation. My wife and I went to Pre-Cana, a handful of meetings with our parish's deacon, and a weekend Engaged Encounter over the course of nine months, preparing for the sacrament of marriage. In stark contrast, we had one meeting with a parish minister and an evening of orientation to prepare for our daughter's baptism. Sadly, the amount of time and contact we have with our parish outside of Mass has gradually diminished even while we live and express our vocation of marriage in fuller ways. Our marriage and Catholicity would be so much more integrated if we had the active, visible, and committed support of our parish.

After our wedding, we went from ongoing marriage preparation and support to none. As most married couples know, the first year can be trying at times; this was especially evident in our experience. As my Catholic faith grew and I became more involved in our parish, my wife felt left in the dust, believing that my commitment to the Church outweighed my commitment to our relationship. This was a time when we needed counseling and the Church to help us find balance within our marriage. But support after the sacrament of marriage is something that is not built into the structures of marriage preparation; there is no post-Cana support. If the frequency with which we met with clergy to prepare us for marriage continued after the exchange of our vows, this storm may have been easier to manage. But no such system is explicitly in place. While we were able to weather this storm, and came out of it stronger as a couple, my wife and I were still left to struggle on our own.

And as soon as we resolved one challenge, it seemed like another appeared. Upon bringing our baby to Mass for the first time, my wife found no comfortable, peaceful place where she could breastfeed our newborn daughter. She instead found that the "mother's room" had unsupportive seating for breastfeeding mothers, was full of screaming toddlers, and was an area of high foot traffic. All of this made it impossible to nurse. And while my wife would have loved to breastfeed in the pews, our daughter experienced latching issues for the first few months of her life, which often resulted in minutes of crying while attempting to nurse. Feeling that she had no easy place to breastfeed at our parish, my wife opted to nurse our daughter in the car. She subsequently was not comfortable coming to Mass for months.

Despite these experiences, I still have a strong faith and love being a part of the Catholic Church. I also want to serve the Church more, but I need to be realistic. Since becoming a father I have had to scale back my involvement in Church ministries because now my most important ministry is to my family. At times, I start to feel alienated because I cannot do as much around the parish as I used to. Also, other men in their twenties do not necessarily want to converse with a guy who has a baby on his hip. On the other hand, most of the other guys with babies on their hips are in their forties and are engineers or architects, while I'm in my twenties, a barista, and just completing my graduate studies. While we can connect on the level of being Catholic fathers, our life experiences are otherwise too different. Furthermore, chatting with other parents and parishioners for ten minutes after Mass does not satisfy our needs to connect with others on a spiritual level who are in the same social location as my wife and I. Additionally, as a husband and father, I feel it is no longer appropriate to leave my family on a weekday evening to attend the young adult Bible studies. And while my wife and I may have attended together in the past, I do not think many would be happy with us if we brought our baby along to any parish events besides Mass or movie nights during the summer. My wife and I would so much enjoy going out with other Catholics our age for "Theology on Tap," but the last time I checked, it's illegal to bring a baby into a bar. So even beyond the lack of ministries focused on young adult Catholic married couples and parents, the logistical resources, like daycare or babysitting, aren't even provided by our parish.

Our family feels that it has truly taken to heart what the Church teaches about finding one's vocation and living it. We have given our time, talent, and the little treasure we can spare. We are not seeking a prize or a pat on the back; we are seeking support from the Church that we love. We received so much support before the reception of sacraments, but now our budding family receives hardly any ecclesial support, even while we feel the greatest need for this at present. On harder days, I feel like the Church is becoming much like our fellow brothers and sisters who only come to Mass on Christmas and Easter. Every time we seek a sacrament, the Church is there, ready and willing; yet it is virtually absent—outside of Mass—for us in-between these sacramental milestones.

What would be ideal for our young family is a ministry that gathers families like ours together in Christian fellowship, a place where we can share the joys and struggles of married life and parenthood in the context of our faith. Likewise helpful would be a sort of mentoring ministry, where young couples are paired with other young married couples. This would allow people like my wife and I to be of service to other young couples while we show them that it is possible to find and live your vocation at a young age. Although young adult ministries do a lot of good, our experiences demonstrate that they are geared toward single people without children. As much as those involved in these ministries are committed to the teachings of the Church, our own experience of neglect demonstrates that these same people do not take vocation seriously. If young married couples, young parents, young priests, and young religious were more visible within our young adult communities, then perhaps more young Catholics would feel supported in discovering their vocations earlier in life.

Justin, MTS, and Monet Combs met in 2008 while they were both attending San Diego State University. At the time of this writing they are both twenty-nine years old, have been married for three-and-a-half years, and have a beautiful one-year-old daughter. Justin and Monet's experiences in the Church have been largely positive, though recently they have become somewhat bittersweet. Justin earned his master of theological studies from the Franciscan School of Theology.

Praising God with Full Hearts

by Peter and Claire Hansen

God calls us to trust and praise. Attending Mass at Mission Santa Clara challenges us to look to God with trust and not be afraid when difficulties obscure our chosen path. With the community we lift our voices in song to praise God who is present and walking with us in our daily experiences. These two thoughts together express what keeps us coming back to church each week. Attending church prompts us to grow in our trust of God. This is not something we can fully appreciate until deeply challenged; in order to move through the difficulties we face, we must trust God, even when we do not see how we will make it through the experience. Church helps us to pause, reflect, and recognize where God is present in our daily experiences and give thanks for the many blessings we would not otherwise recognize.

When we first began talking about having children, Claire thought that it would be a simple matter to "conceive and bear a child," and she was far more worried about our financial future. Because we live in Silicon Valley, she felt we should own a home before having children. The security of home ownership and the stability of a mortgage seemed like the responsible thing to do in the wild housing market in which we live. We saved for two years and eventually bought a two-bedroom condominium. After this we began actively trying for a child, which turned out to be more of a challenge than we expected. For several years, we watched many of our friends become parents once or twice over as we continued to try for our first. At one point, we decided not to pursue having our own child and began the process of open adoption. We were with a great adoption agency for over two years, but with so many parents trying to adopt and fewer babies being put up for adoption, an open adoption never materialized. Amazingly though, we were finally able to give birth to a son, whom we named Paul; he is a light in our lives and the best part of each day. We love to watch him crawl around the house, picking things up and babbling as he goes. Seeing him joyfully clap his hands as we read his favorite books over and over gives us the energy to keep reading. We share this because throughout the ups and downs of trying to become parents, Claire felt unsure of where God was leading and wondered if maybe we were not being called to be parents. She remembers breaking down in tears while listening to the gospel during Advent when the angel tells Mary that "nothing will be impossible for God." Peter was the one who trusted that God's call to us was to have a family, though we did not know how that would come to be. Peter's faithfulness to the path ahead was a firm foundation in our marriage during these difficult times.

Paul's arrival was celebrated by many, especially Claire's mom, who had been living with cancer for two years and was focused on surviving long enough to see Claire become a mother. After Paul was born, her goal became living long enough to see him baptized into the Church. Because we attend weekly liturgy at Mission Santa Clara, which is not a parish, we began making plans for Paul's baptism. Despite his living a good distance in Los Angeles, our close Jesuit friend agreed to travel north to perform the baptism. Claire asked a local parish if we could hold a private baptism there. They allowed us the use of the church with a $500 donation, and we asked if our friend could come up to perform the sacrament. We filled out forms to indicate we were planning on a full Mass and we gave everyone the date. Peter's parents flew down from Oregon and Claire's family came from Illinois. We rented the parish hall for a reception after the baptism and $600 dollars later we had the key and the use of the facility. Claire was shocked at how expensive the baptism had become, but also realized that being a Catholic was an important part of her life and her family's life. We also felt that Paul's baptism was a needed joyful event in the midst of the sadness of saying goodbye to Claire's mom. Claire also wondered if the prices were higher because we live in Silicon Valley, where so many people have large amounts of disposable income. A paralegal and a campus minister do not share in quite so much wealth, but we still felt it was worth the cost for Paul's baptism to be celebrated with our family and friends. On the weekend itself, we set up the hall, picked up the cake, decorations, and flowers, and arrived at the church with full hearts. Fr. Mark began the liturgy, and friends and family members proclaimed the chosen readings. When it was time, Mark brought us forward and called Paul's godparents, Claire's parents, and my parents to surround us. Looking over at her mom, Claire was struck again by how much her mother had sacrificed so that she could be present to see this moment. Her mother prayed each day for our special intentions and her faith in her daughter was a gift that Claire will always be grateful for.

However, when it came to the liturgy of the Eucharist, there were no gifts of bread and wine to bring up. An older lady had opened the church for us, and had remained in the assembly. She was a volunteer sacristan who set up the necessary supplies for the baptism, but she had not put out the bread and wine. When Fr. Mark asked her about it, she refused to get them. Fr. Mark, ever gracious and resourceful, had the congregation gather around the altar to pray an Our Father as a way of concluding the ceremony. We were upset, not that the bread and wine had been mistakenly omitted, but that the parish's representative would not make the effort needed to retrieve them. Paul had been baptized, which is what we came to do, but the lack of hospitality left us angry and disheartened. Claire called the parish the following week to tell them what happened. The office manager said, "Oh, sorry," and that was all. Because we are committed, lifelong practicing Catholics, the Church will never lose us. However, many people who seek baptism for their children are not necessarily so convicted. A similar experience might turn a young family away from a parish.

Thankfully we attend weekly liturgy with a wonderful community at Mission Santa Clara. This community celebrated with us as we prepared for Paul's arrival, and has not blinked an eye as Paul has fussed his way through Mass. Claire recalls one particular Sunday when Paul was talkative during the homily and a gentleman in front of us leaned back and said, "Better to have him fuss in church than fuss at home." That sense of welcome and acceptance has made us feel wanted in the community. The people who sit in our section all smile and wink at Paul on their way to communion and always come over to greet him after Mass.

There are several qualities of the Mass at Mission Santa Clara that help us praise God with full hearts. We love that the whole community sings during Mass and that so many people participate as eucharistic ministers, lectors, greeters, and choir members. There is a sense of "fully conscious and active participation" of all who are gathered for worship

(*Sacrosanctum Concilium* 14). We also love how full the church is. It is rare to sit next to an open seat; instead, one is usually surrounded with many others who are there to worship. This feeling of a great crowd reminds Claire of the crowds who followed Jesus during his public ministry. We like the variety of causes the collection supports. For example, three Sundays a month are devoted to the maintenance of the Mission, the needs of the local parish, and the campus ministry programs at Santa Clara University. But the fourth Sunday is typically a social ministry, such as Jesuit Refugee Service, Catholic Charities, or the local Catholic Worker community. We also love the rotation of Jesuit presiders because we hear homilies from a variety of perspectives. Also, the weekly rotation of about a dozen priests seems to take the communal focus off of the personality of the priest.

As much as we love Mission Santa Clara, at times we wonder if we should join a parish. We would like Paul to attend catechesis classes and a middle school and high school youth group. These were powerful experiences for Claire's faith formation, and we'd like Paul to experience them as well. At some future point, we will probably join a parish. We hope to find one that takes as much joy in the liturgy and in supporting one another as does the community at Mission Santa Clara. In the meantime, we will continue to lift up our voices in praise and to grow in our ability to look to God with trust.

Peter, MDiv, and Claire, MDiv, Hansen live in San Jose, California. Peter is forty-eight, Claire is thirty-eight, and their son, Paul, is one year old. They attend weekly liturgy at Mission Santa Clara on the campus of Santa Clara University. Claire is a campus minister at a Catholic high school for girls, and Peter is a paralegal at a law firm.

Working Together for the Kingdom

A Young Mother's Experience

by Naomi Hoipkemier

At twenty-five years old, I was at a crossroads. Three of the past five years had been spent pouring my energy out to children at an orphanage in rural Honduras. The experience left me sure that I was called to be a missionary wherever I went and in whatever I did. But what should that be? What does being a missionary look like when the foreign places and tongues are stripped away? The romance of giving my life to God as a sister sang to me. Yet I had also met a man whose romance sang to me. I sought counsel from a religious sister who told me a lie. She said my state didn't matter—if I chose to be single, to be in a lesbian relationship, to get married, to enter religious life—God would love me no matter what path I chose. Now that last part is true. God loves. He cannot but love. But it *does* matter! The path we choose does matter. And some lead more directly to sanctity than others. To leaders and mentors in the Church, I would say, tell our discerning youth the truth about vocation. We are meant to be in communion; we are meant to be in community. Single life and same-sex relationships do not draw us to God in the same way that religious life and married life do. Now that I am in the midst of married life, bearing and raising children, I feel in my bones how special this relationship of marriage is, and how no amount of loving feelings in same-sex relationships, or fruitful projects undertaken together, can replace the amazing joy and responsibility of cooperating in God's creative power through marriage. The culture is full of lies about what marriage is. We need the Church to proclaim the truth, and to do it boldly.

By and by, the troubadour of my heart asked me to marry him. And I said yes. Then we wondered what to do next. Engagement seemed like a time for continued discernment, but none of the offerings we saw seemed comprehensive enough. We decided to use every tool available, all at the same time. We read books together with titles like, *How to Avoid Marrying a Jerk*. We went on an Engaged Encounter retreat. We met with the transitional deacon at our parish. We asked a mentor couple at our parish to meet with us one-on-one and discuss John Paul II's writings on marriage. We also took a daylong retreat to write our vows together—we didn't know at the time that writing your own wedding vows is not actually allowed. The vows we composed included all the usual "for better and for worse," and added, "I will encourage you in holiness and work beside you for the Kingdom of God." This reflected the deeper reason behind the yes in my soul, the reason this was more than just a surface attraction, a youthful infatuation. I could hear God saying in prayer that this relationship was to be my path to holiness. This was and is how he wants to sanctify me. Does every engaged couple need to do so many different kinds of discernment activities? No. But is every couple called to build the kingdom of God together? Yes. Alongside the pastoral desire to make marriage

116

accessible and not burdensome should also be avenues for deepening discernment for those couples who seek them. An effective way to strengthen young marriages would be parish programs that form continuing relationships between mentor couples and engaged couples. This could include preparation, but also carry over through the first years of marriage. Mentor couples with a real relationship can give couples help and advice where they need it most.

Now my wonderful husband and I have five little ones. They are our labor and our joy, and we feel heavily the responsibility of being their first and primary educators in the faith. In this task, I am constantly trying to keep ahead of their questions by educating myself. "Momma, why did they kill Jesus?" "When we get to heaven, will we all live in the same house?" Every parent knows that the youngest children ask the toughest questions. They usually direct these questions to the people they spend the most time with and trust with all their heart: their mothers and fathers. These are the people who need to have those deepest truths of the faith in hand. We cannot forget the importance of adult faith formation in the parish. Most young Catholic parents went through their own faith formation at a time when the theology was a bit light. When my oldest (twin boys) were two, I started training for the Catechesis of the Good Shepherd—to be a catechist to the youngest children in our parish, ages three to six. My formation course was deep and incisive, full of insights into the Eucharist, the kingdom of God, and the person of Jesus Christ. It gave me formation so that I could be the leaven that lifts up the children and the parish as a whole. And it is absolutely beautiful in practice! When thinking of children's formation, parishes should not neglect the formation of the parents.

We teach our children at home. As a Montessori-trained educator, this comes naturally to me. I also seem to be part of a nationwide phenomenon. More and more parents are choosing to educate their children at home. Everyone has their own reasons. For us, some factors include natural inclination, desire to give the children freedom to have a childhood, financial considerations, the appeal of family unity, and a touch of snobbery that I, as their mother, can give them a better education than another teacher could. Homeschooling families can be a great asset to a parish. They have the time and flexibility to be involved in the liturgical year in a unique and beautiful way. Our local homeschool group participates in the parish May processions, Candlemas, and All Saints gatherings. They can also be seen as a threat—especially to parishes with a school attached. I cannot speak to the current or future situation of Catholic schools. Much good has been and still is done by them. But they are not the only way. Parishes should be open to welcome families that are choosing to school at home. Perhaps there are spaces that could be made available for homeschool events. Perhaps school sports or extracurriculars could be open to all parish children. And perhaps it is time for the parish to focus more on living the liturgical year.

When our twins were followed shortly by another boy, we needed some time before being ready to be open to another life. As though it were a secret, I came by word of mouth to hear about the Creighton model of natural family planning. We had taken the diocesan classes on the sympto-thermal method, but found it cumbersome. The Creighton classes at the nearby Catholic hospital were not covered by our insurance (though a steady supply of birth control pills would have been free!), and were expensive for a young family trying to make ends meet on a graduate school stipend. It should be a priority of Catholic hospitals to help couples seeking to live out the Church's teaching on sexuality. Creighton seems to be the best model out there—medically respected, easy to use, and scientifically tested. It can be very successful at achieving as well as avoiding conception. Parishes should include information about natural family planning in the bulletin, on the boards at the back of church, and so forth. This treasure should not be a secret. We need more doctors and nurses who can teach and use the Creighton model of fertility care.

This spring we bought a pop-up camper to tow behind our family minivan for a summer road trip. As a trial run, we headed to the local beach campground. I had visions of time in nature, and the foretaste of heaven that we were about to give to the children. We proceeded to have the grumpiest twenty-four hours of camping known to man. As we unpacked upon our return home, my husband realized, "When was the last time we went to confession?" Longer than usual. If we can't even handle a camping trip when we're off our spiritual game, what happens when a real crisis comes? What my family needs most is Jesus at the heart of our home. During challenging times the death of a parent, the birth of a child with a disability, a change of career, camping, the list goes on— we especially need Jesus at the center. The Church can help us with this by keeping him at the heart of the Church. Both literally—with tabernacles in the center of the church and offerings of eucharistic adoration (twenty-four hours a day if possible)—and figuratively—by centering homilies on Jesus, making sure parish events are all centered on Jesus, offering frequent opportunities to meet him in the confessional, and daily Mass times that make sense for people's schedules. Our parishes need a Jesus-centered vision for what makes a good parish.

"My soul proclaims the greatness of the Lord" along with Mary's own Magnificat. The vocation I have been given is a beautiful one: the sacrifices I am called to make have shining children's faces attached to them, and I pull my yoke alongside a faithful man. The Lord is present to me in our relationship, and in the children with which he has blessed us. It is an exciting time to be a Catholic mother. Never have so many resources for personal growth in faith been available. The resources for Catholic homeschooling are also abundant. And though we suffer from the mobility of our culture, people are waking up more and more to the importance of community as we raise our children. As I build up my own family, I know that I am playing my own small part in building the kingdom of God.

Naomi Hoipkemier is a thirty-four-year-old cradle Catholic originally from Ventura, California. She is currently living out her vocation to marriage with her husband, Mark, in South Bend, Indiana. Together they care for five children, six chickens, and a rabbit.

Catholic Life with Kids

by Caleb and Sheila McKinley

Our alarm sounds before six o'clock most days, and we are up to get our wide-eyed two-year-old (his nickname is Bamm-bamm!) out of bed to start the day. The seven- and five-year-olds are still sound asleep, thank goodness! But our light sleeper doesn't give us much opportunity to contain the chaos of raising three children. Our days are packed full of scraped knees, playing and laughing, fighting, school lessons (our older two children are in a part-time charter/homeschool program), errands, cooking, some tidying up, bathing, TV time/mommy break time, and maybe, on a good day, the toddler will take a nice long nap! By the time the kids are tucked in bed, we both jump on our computers and get to work or collapse in exhaustion. I (Caleb) have just started my own business and also handle our finances, while I (Sheila) work part-time from our home office. So, most nights we are working away while the dishes pile up and the same clean clothes remain unfolded in the laundry bin. It's physically exhausting, but we remember to count our blessings, work hard, and trust in God's strength to see us through!

What brought us together over twelve years ago and led us to marriage was our Catholic faith. We both went through a process of discerning our vocation to marriage, and even though we contemplated alternatives, God's will was clearly revealed to us when we met each other. Because our faith was of such great importance to us, we knew we would openly accept the gift of children. We also knew our faith would allow us to have a lasting and fulfilling marriage. Our Catholic marriage preparation emphasized the point that the most important relationship is the marriage and the kids come second. What a challenge that can be, ten years into our marriage and three kids later. We do everything we can to cherish our marriage, our friendship, and the many things that brought us together. Our kids see Dad being a gentleman and opening the car door for Mom, they see Dad dance with Mom in-between flipping pancakes on Sunday morning, and they see us embrace after a long day of not seeing each other. Of course, they also see the arguments and doors slam when disagreements happen. But we don't let those not-so-holy moments go to waste, as we teach them about forgiveness and humility.

We have found that there are four key aspects of living out our vocation as parents and bringing our own children into a deeper love of Jesus, our faith, and our world: community, service, prayer, and the sacraments. These are all hallmarks of raising our kids in a Catholic home and training them in the faith. And none of them can be fully experienced or done well apart from the support of our Church.

Community sets the stage for living out our vocation as Catholic parents. We need one another. We need support and friendship. We need the example and wisdom of older couples who have raised their kids in the faith. We need friends who are single to share in their faith journey. We need couples who are going through the same types of struggles and joys of raising children.

We are blessed to have a thriving community in our parish with many families who are wholly committed to serving both inside and outside the parish. Unfortunately, we are painfully aware that many Catholic families do not find such a welcoming, supportive community in their parishes. In order to build strong Catholic families we must have parish communities that strengthen parents in their vocation through programs *and* relationships. The families we have met in our parish are some of the most loving, joyful, faithful, and humble servants, and they inspire us in many ways to be better stewards of all the gifts we have been given.

We find that in many ways our family's service stems from our community, which not only includes our church, but also those in our neighborhood, at the park, and other activities. It is important that our children learn to be friends with new people of diverse cultures and faith backgrounds. We don't want them to only serve those with whom they are comfortable; we want them to see that every person matters, and to reach out to those who are marginalized. Our most recent idea was to set up a playgroup at the nearby nursing home facility. This would be a way to bring some love to the residents, many of whom are lonely or forgotten, and joy to all of the children as they experience service!

Within the domestic church of our family, we teach our children how to serve each other, take responsibility with chores, and contribute in our home running smoothly. In this way, they learn to see that they have an active role to play in our community. They see the needs within our parish community come to life when a family is suffering either physically or financially, and they see how we respond. They see the dinners we make for families who just had a baby and need an extra hand in the kitchen. They are quick to make a card for a friend or someone they don't even know who is lonely or sick. They see us leave on Sunday nights to teach confirmation, which we are only able to do because our parish provides free babysitters who come to our house while we teach.

Most recently, our children saw how our community supported us when we had our fourth miscarriage. We are blessed to have an amazing support system with our parish Moms and Kids group, and these families have helped us heal. Many parishes are without this kind of support. More needs to be available to those suffering from miscarriages and fertility issues, as well as to those who are foster or adoptive parents.

These are just some of the small ways we can teach our kids how to serve. It's a process that will take time. Just like any form of training, you can't expect them to climb high mountains overnight. As adults, we are still trying to figure out how to best serve, on a local and global level, when we have so many demands and tasks we are juggling. How do we prioritize? How do we learn to sacrifice so that our budget can look a little different and allow for more to be spent on those in our world who need it most? We are surrounded by a selfish, consumerist culture and it very subtly sucks us in. In raising a family that is countercultural, we need our Church to provide a hedge against the prevailing winds of our world.

Our prayer life plays a huge role in bringing our service to life! There is nothing like the sweet little prayers said *out of the mouth of babes*, when our two-year-old hears a siren and runs up to us saying, "Hail Mary, Mommy! Hail Mary!" It's very apparent how close Jesus is to our children and that he wants to remain in their hearts as they journey into adulthood. We only have a limited time to guide and teach them the beauty of a prayer life connected to Christ. Before we leave our house for the day, we've made it a habit to gather and pray the morning offering, the Hail Mary, and ask some of the saints to pray for us. At night, we pray with our children, ask for their prayer requests, and sing them hymns. Though they may be too young to understand the words to some of the prayers, we also make time for more informal praying throughout the day.

The source and summit of Catholic prayer life is the Mass. Something that drew us to our parish was the support to young families and the many childcare opportunities they have available. Mass has never been so peaceful as when our two-year-old is in the church nursery. Of course, this isn't going to work for all families, but we have found it to be a blessing and a break for more contemplative prayer time at Mass. That break gives us the strength to continue walking in prayer throughout the week. A parish must make the Mass a welcome, inviting experience for parents and young children, whether they offer childcare or just some smiles and helping hands to parents during Mass.

An active prayer life allows us to experience the sacraments in a deeper way. For a family, the sacraments of initiation—baptism, holy communion, and confirmation— are the greatest touchstones for living out our vocation. Our Church can support parents by elevating the sacraments in all of their beauty so that our children see how special and vital they are. Gathering children around the baptismal font so they have front row seats, being fully present to the Eucharist, and preparing them with joy and anticipation for confirmation are ways to show our youth what it means to live out our sacraments. Every Sunday, little eyes are watching each adult and following the lead of those they look up to. All of us have a sacred responsibility to live out our faith as an example to our youth.

Though Catholic school is ideal for raising youth in the traditions of our faith, devotions, feast days, and the sacraments, this isn't always possible. Ultimately, it is within our domestic church that true faith formation takes place. But we also rely on having a very strong and effective faith formation program at our parish. Parishes need to make sure these programs are supported and give life to the youth, and they must be a priority in all parishes! If we lack the passion and budget to provide a strong foundation for our children, how can we expect them to remain Catholic? We have a wonderful opportunity to bring Catholic teachings to life for our children.

Our Church is the foundation of living our vocation as parents and raising our children in the faith. We need to cultivate a deeper awareness of our Church's critical role in supporting the vocation of parents. In many simple or profound ways, we must encourage parents who desperately need to see the hand of Christ through the support of their Catholic community. Not only can we experience the deep joy of raising children to follow Christ, but we are answering Christ's call to "proclaim the good news to the whole creation" (Mark 16:15)—even toddlers and teenagers.

Caleb (thirty-seven years old) and Sheila (thirty-eight years old) McKinley were married in 2006 and have three children: Lucy (seven), James (five), and John (two). Sheila is a cradle Catholic and Caleb joined the Church in 2005. They attend St. Thomas More Parish in Oceanside, California.

Glitter, Glue, and the Gospel Message

HOW OUR PARISHES SUPPORT PARENTING CATHOLICS

by Billy and Kristin Byrnes

One of our favorite spiritual writers, Anne Lamott, describes the unquenchable desire and thirst we have in our lives as a "God-sized hole." Lamott says that we sometimes try to fill this hole with things that slip right through: gossip, alcohol, shopping, social media, to name a few. However, when we fill this hole with God, we are literally full of the graces of God; our cup overflows. To go a bit further, when we live our vocation, which is how and where God calls us, the hole is also filled. This includes both the challenges and the joys: the groggy 2:00 a.m. feedings, toddler meltdowns over the fact that a banana was peeled the wrong way, and the constant struggle to arrange childcare. Then there are moments of grace: snuggles on the couch while reading the adventures of *Thomas the Train*, 2:10 a.m. giggles from a well-fed baby, or the smile on William's face when he joins hands with his friend as they run down the aisle at church to attend children's liturgy. In this grace there is confirmation that we are truly living our vocation as parents.

Recently, we were at the park with our sons when multiple service vans pulled into the parking lot and out spilled dozens of older kids. They quickly overran the playground structure where our timid son, William, was gingerly crossing a rope bridge. Eyes wide, he backed slowly into Mom's legs and stuck himself there like that glitter from school projects. When I knelt down to talk to him, I found myself fumbling for the right words. "Are you nervous because the kids are so big?" I asked him. "And there are so many of them?" Or, I thought to myself, was it because most of them had Down's Syndrome? We did not want him to be afraid of these kids, but also, how do you explain Down's Syndrome to a toddler? I reverted to our favorite book of late, *Jitterbug Jam*, which tells the story of how a boy and a monster become friends. I asked him if the kids seemed a little different than perhaps other kids he's seen at the playground? "Yes," he confirmed. "Are they though, because at the end of the story the boy and monster, even though they have been told they could not be, become…what, honey?" "Friends," William said confidently. We may not all look the same, but we inherently are because we are created in the image and likeness of God. This is perhaps what I wanted to say, but instead of reaching for a Bible story, I found a children's book he loves at the forefront of my mind. Are Bible stories inaccessible to my toddler? Definitely not, but is he as familiar with them as he is with *Jitterbug Jam*, which we read over and over multiple times a week? Definitely not. How do we live our vocation as Catholic parents? How do we fill these "God-sized" holes? We would like to share about three values that have worked for us: family, community, and prayer.

The sparks that gave life to our little family of four can be attributed to the Jesuit and Franciscan Schools of Theology in

Berkeley, California, where we met while pursuing advanced degrees in theology. We knew once we were married that we wanted to start a family, but we wanted to make one dream a reality first. Our similar love of liberation theology had led us to graduate studies, and the passion was only strengthened while studying at our respective schools. After prayer and discernment, we were accepted into the Volunteer Missionary Movement as lay volunteers. We left our jobs at two well-respected Catholic high schools, sold most of our worldly belongings, moved what was left into a tiny public storage unit, said goodbye to family and friends, and left to live with and accompany the people of Nicaragua for two years. While the leaving was hard and the transition even harder, we were constantly affirmed of our decision in prayer; we were living our vocation, our call as a young, Catholic, married couple.

We left the United States in September of 2011, a newly formed family of two, and returned in the summer of 2013, with a third member of our family on the way. William likes to say he was born in Nicaragua, which is not entirely true. *Hecho en Nicaragua* is more accurate. He was born of our nightly prayers and pleadings with God to become parents, the deep longing we felt to grow our family, and the way we believed this was yet another vocation to which God was calling us.

Amidst the challenges of raising a child, and there are many, we felt confident in our vocation as parents. We struggle through the seemingly manic emotions that run rampant in a toddler, one moment flailing on the ground because he wanted the blue plate, not the red one, and the next moment laughing and wanting to curl into our laps to eat off that prized blue plate. There are the other moments that we just relish, like getting him ready for bed at night and asking him, "Where did you see God today?" Watching him parade around the house with a Salvadoran cross that we keep on our bookshelf, "playing church," and singing a simple Taizé chant for prayer before dinners during Lent. So we decided to grow our family again. As had happened with William, we were quickly staring at a tiny blue plus sign and were over the moon with excitement. This all came to a screeching halt after our first prenatal exam. Multiple doctor's visits later, over the course of a few weeks, we came to understand that we would never meet these babies (yes—there were two!). This took a toll on our prayer life. While I (Billy) continued to remain positive and confident that our good God was present in the darkness, I (Kristin) slid into despair and wondered if God had abandoned me.

The healing process really began once we started talking publicly about our miscarriage. On Good Friday, I (Kristin) was asked to speak at our parish, St. Charles, to offer my reflection on one of the last words of Jesus. My words were, "My God, my God, why have you abandoned me?" and though I only mentioned the miscarriage briefly, throngs of parents came up to me afterward, expressing their support. A few Sundays later, our pastor offered the Mass for these children we lost, and again people reached out in prayer and sympathy. Our story has a happy ending, or beginning as it is, and we welcomed our second son, Mateo, in February of 2017. His name means "God's gift," and with Mateo we have come to understand what an incredible miracle it is when we are able to cocreate with God.

In this vocation as parents we are never alone. This leads to the first way that we are supported: family. Both our families support our vocation in many ways: late night phone calls to my (Kristin's) dad or brother, who both happen to be pediatricians, weekly dinners with my (Billy's) mom, discerning preschools with my (Kristin's) mom, and watching William light up when he knows his aunt is coming over for dinner.

Another important way our family supports our vocation as parents is to give us time *away* from the boys. They recognize, probably from experience, that maintaining and nurturing our relationship as a married couple will surely make us stronger, more loving, patient, and generous parents. We often go back to the homily our Jesuit friend gave at our wedding, as he referenced a nineteenth-century painting on the sanctuary behind him where St. Francis is leaning into the body of the crucified Christ. Fr. Matt looked at us and said, "Throughout your marriage you must *lean* into one another." We have learned that when we do this we can draw strength during times of loss, as we did during our miscarriage. We can come up with better discipline strategies to offer our independent toddler, and we can better face the challenges presented by coworkers and students at the schools where we work. We must *lean* into one another as we live out our vocation as parents.

In addition to the support from our family, we are fortunate to have found an incredible community at St. Charles Parish. One desire we had when we became parents was to root ourselves in a vibrant parish so that our boys would be raised not only with the faith that we teach them at home, but also hear similar messages of love and acceptance at church. There are no formal ministries for young families at our parish in which we partake, but we are grateful for the community we have found. It is wonderful that William is learning to carve out time for God in his life and that the ritual of Mass is important. Recently, he has taken more interest in communion, and at dinner a few nights ago, he held up a piece of bread to his dad and said, "Body of Christ."

When Mateo was born there was a genuine sense of gratitude and joy, after knowing and understanding the loss we had experienced. The first Sunday we brought him to Mass, many families stopped us after to meet him and offer congratulations. A few offered to take William if we were ever in need of help. This is community. This is a grace. Again, not in formal ministries, but we have found abundant support for our vocation as parents at St. Charles.

Prayer is the final value that enacts and supports our vocation as parents. The parish community supports what we do at home with William and Mateo. Early on in William's life we developed a nightly routine, as many parents do. Part of this routine is our nightly prayer, which has taken on slightly different forms as he has grown up. One constant is that we say the Our Father and Hail Mary in Spanish. Knowing the words to these prayers, in Spanish or English, is hopefully the fertile ground for his own personal faith life and journey.

We believe that what we begin at home, supported by our families, can be nurtured by the parish community. So far we have found this to be true in most cases. Yet we know that our experience is not universal. Thanks to the leadership and support of our pastor, St. Charles has provided a loving and generous faith community that our boys will come to know and reach out to in times of need and joy.

Parenting Catholics need their parishes to lean on in a way that strengthens both their parenting and their Catholicism. There are three specific ways parishes can support parenting Catholics. They can provide some catechetical resources for parents to teach our faith at home. For example, we have a friend who put together and shared a wonderful Jesse Tree project for toddlers. Also, parishes can support small faith-sharing groups for parents. If one's own faith and prayer life is strong, it can be better transmitted to one's children. Last, social gatherings with free childcare would give parents an opportunity to get to know and build organic communities of their own within the parish. If we *lean in* to one another, and to Jesus, we can find the support and strength to be good parents, good Catholics, and good to

Glitter, Glue, and the Gospel Message

one another. In this way, parishes can help parenting Catholics live out our vocations and fill our "God-sized" holes.

Billy Byrnes, M.A. (thirty-six years old), and Kristin Byrnes, MDiv (thirty-eight years old), met while studying at the Graduate Theological Union. Married in 2009, they minister to high school students at two different Catholic schools in the Bay Area. They are parents to two inquisitive and adorable boys, William and Mateo, and are raising them amongst the loving community of St. Charles Parish.

Questions

1. Dr. Mary Ellen Konieczny reminds us that these are not representative, but instead are the experiences of highly active parenting Catholics. Yet, these essays still remind us of the ways parishes might better support parents. What challenges do these essays offer your own parish? What can you say you are doing well? Do you offer post-Cana, post-birth, or post-baptism support?

2. How can these essays encourage Catholic parents? What insights do these essays offer parents who attend Mass or other parish functions irregularly? Do parents feel comfortable and confident in being their children's first teachers in the faith? Do they see opportunities to be involved in parish activities *with* their children?

3. Of the five essays here, three mentioned emotional and spiritual pain because of issues surrounding infertility or miscarriages. Very few parishes offer this sort of pastoral support, and yet, these essays illustrate that this is both typical and very tragic. At best, parish culture neglects these needs; at worst, it exacerbates this with well-intentioned but uninformed comments. What active steps can parishes take in supporting these parents who suffer in secret or silence?

PART 2

Vocation through Identity and Practice

Catholic Lay Organizations in the United States

by Jeffrey M. Burns

For many years, I served as a youth minister at a multiethnic parish in East Oakland, California. Each year, my group included at least three or four extremely bright, inquisitive young men and women, the type of young people we used to push toward religious life. Today, most of them will pursue lay vocations. And every year, I worried about what would happen to them once they left the youth group and entered the larger Church. True, many might find sustenance in Newman Centers and campus ministries. But after that? Would they find a place in the Church? Would their talents be used to build the Church? Or would they join the many who drift away from the Church to the detriment of both the Church and themselves? This is a particularly pressing problem for young women (see Kendra McClelland's essay). What organizations will call to them?

A survey of Catholic lay organizations for youth and young adults in the United States is a bit discouraging. Though there are a few bright spots, and some exciting initiatives, by and large the terrain is a vast wasteland. Recent books by scholars Massimo Faggioli and Kevin Ahern see promising signs for youth movements and organizations in the rest of the world, but they lament that these groups have made little headway in the United States.[1] Lay movements such as Communion and Liberation, Focolare, the Community of Sant'Egidio, and others, though not primarily aimed at youth, have aspects that appeal to the young. Similarly, the charismatic movement has given rise to groups that stress traditional spirituality and eucharistic adoration, such as Life Teen and the Catholic Underground. Though popular in certain locales and among certain types of Catholics, these movements have limited appeal nationally.

In light of contemporary concerns, it is tempting to look back nostalgically at the preconciliar era (1918–62) with its apparently vibrant lay youth movements and organizations. The Church in the United States was just shifting from being a working class, immigrant Church to a Church that attempted to engage U.S. culture and society more fully. As more Catholics entered the middle class and left their ethnic urban neighborhoods for the suburbs, new lay associations flourished. Catholic defensiveness, stemming from the Church's longtime minority status, gave way to a new, confident public Catholicism.

In the 1920s, Jesuit Daniel Lord tapped into this trend by reviving and reinventing the youth Sodality of Our Lady, which "had become a moribund organization and little more than a collection of pious societies and prayer meetings."[2]

---

1. See Massimo Faggioli, *The Rising Laity: Ecclesial Movements since Vatican II* (Mahwah, NJ: Paulist Press, 2016); Kevin Ahern, "Youth Movements in a Global Church," in *Young Catholics Reshaping the Church*, ed. Solange Lefebvre, Maria Clara Bingerner, and Silvia Scatena, *Concilium* (2015/2): 28–40; and Kevin Ahern, *Structures of Grace: Catholic Organizations Serving the Global Common Good* (Maryknoll, NY: Orbis Books, 2015).

2. William D. Dinges, "'An Army of Youth': The Sodality Movement and the Practice of Apostolic Mission," *U.S. Catholic Historian* 19 (Summer 2001): 37.

Lord utilized the growing infrastructure of Catholic high schools and colleges to—as their anthem stated—create an "Army of youth, flying the standards of Truth," to develop a vanguard of Catholic youth to "restore all things in Christ." Lord wanted an articulate, courageous Catholic youth with a strong Catholic identity who could confront the issues of the day informed by Catholic teaching. He used drama, pageants, study clubs, and liturgies to rally Catholic youth, and he redesigned the sodality publication, *Queen's Work*, making it more relevant. In 1931, he initiated the Summer Schools of Catholic Action to make the Church's social teaching more accessible to youth. The sodalities flourished under Lord's direction, but by the late 1940s, they had begun to fade.

Other youth movements also flourished. The Catholic Student Mission Crusade, supporting domestic and foreign missions, claimed as many as five hundred thousand members during the 1930s.[3] The Catholic Youth Organization, founded in Chicago in 1931, rapidly adopted by most dioceses, engaged youth across the country in athletic competition.[4] The devotionally oriented Holy Name and Junior Holy Name Societies were present in most dioceses and parishes as well.

More significantly, a number of apostolic movements grew up in the post-World War II era, particularly groups inspired by Canon (later Cardinal) Joseph Cardijn's "See-Judge-Act" formula for Catholic Action. Young Christian Workers and Young Christian Students enjoyed limited success among high school and college students, but the Christian Family

---

3. See David J. Endres, *American Crusade: Catholic Youth in the Worldwide Mission Movement from World War I to Vatican II* (Eugene, OR: Wipf and Stock, 2010).

4. See Timothy B. Neary, *Crossing Parish Boundaries: Race, Sports, and Catholic Youth in Chicago, 1914–1954* (Chicago: University of Chicago Press, 2016).

Movement (CFM), founded in 1949, exploded in the 1950s and early 1960s. Cardijn's method of organizing small "cells" of ten to twelve members that operated a "like to like" ministry (that is, workers to workers, students to students) appealed to the emerging class of young, college-educated, Catholic professionals for whom the old ethnic parish no longer sufficed. What was their "like?" Most had young children, so family became their common link. Unlike most family movements, CFM did not simply turn inward, focusing on family relationships, but turned outward, attempting to transform the environment in which the family found itself to make it "easier for families to be good." The CFM brought couples together who "observed" their environment, "judged" whether what they observed was in accord with the "mind of Christ," and then "acted" to lessen the gap between what they observed and what they judged.

The CFM had appeal for at least four reasons. First, it was primarily lay directed (though CFM had chaplains), with participants enjoying wide discretion and authority. Second, women played a prominent role, organizing and leading meetings and sharing equality with their husbands. Third, the method was inductive rather than deductive, allowing for a great amount of creativity. Fourth, groups moved beyond study to real action. The movement flourished through the mid-1960s before declining precipitously.[5]

Young women found outlets in a number of apostolic movements beyond CFM. The Grail Movement trained young women as "apostles" through study, liturgical events, and service. In the early 1960s, other outlets included the missionary groups Papal Volunteers for Latin America (PAVLA) and Extension Lay Volunteers.

---

5. See Jeffrey M. Burns, *Disturbing the Peace: A History of the Christian Family Movement, 1949–1974* (Notre Dame, IN: University of Notre Dame Press, 1999).

Despite the variety of activities, historian David J. O'Brien claims the programs were "modest in size," and "limited in number and impact."[6] Clerical and episcopal control ensured the movements did not become too innovative.

The Second Vatican Council and the promulgation of the Decree on the Apostolate of the Laity (*Apostolicam Actuositatem*, 1965) inspired fresh hopes for the growth of Catholic lay organizations, but the promised growth never materialized. By 1972, Apostolic Delegate Archbishop Jean Jadot "told a student group that his biggest surprise since coming to the United States was the near total absence of lay organizations in this country."[7] The lack of organizations remains a concern to the present. What happened? The Council expanded lay opportunities, particularly within the Church, as more and more laypeople obtained positions formerly held by religious. Lay ecclesial ministry emerged. Furthermore, Catholic laity joined movements not distinctly Catholic, but to which the apostolic urge and Catholic social teaching propelled them, including the civil rights movement, the anti-Vietnam war protests, the farmworkers movement, and other struggles for human dignity. Since the 1960s, Catholic youth have engaged in many of the larger cultural struggles for justice: the rights of women, the LGBTQ community, immigrants, and refugees; protests against the death penalty, climate change, the School of the Americas, and the Dakota Pipeline; joining such movements as Black Lives Matters and others. One of the largest movements to attract Catholic youth is the right-to-life movement, though it is not limited to Catholics. Besides belonging to local groups, each year large numbers of Catholic youth gather with others on

6. David J. O'Brien, "Catholic Youth: The Presumed Become the Pursued," in *The Catholic Church in the Twentieth Century*, ed. John Deedy (Collegeville, MN: The Liturgical Press, 2000), 94.

7. O'Brien, "Catholic Youth," 95.

the anniversary of *Roe v. Wade* to protest against abortion in the United States with impressive marches in Washington, DC, and San Francisco. This variety of involvement demonstrates that Catholic youth have been engaged, though not necessarily through Catholic organizations.

The conservative impulse is central to some of the more successful associations for youth and young adults: the Steubenville Youth Conferences, Life Teen, the Catholic Underground, Evangelical Catholic, and others. These groups emphasize a traditional, eucharistic spirituality, fellowship, and encourage a closer encounter with Jesus. Life Teen asserts, "Eucharist-based ministry has the power to transform teens, transform parishes, and transform culture."[8] It hosts Life masses and Life nights, which focus on catechetics and contemporary social issues, and socials to promote community. Similarly, the Catholic Underground, inspired by the Franciscan Friars of the Renewal, hosts eucharistic adoration, followed by a Christian rock concert, praise, food, and fellowship. Though popular, the appeal of these groups is somewhat limited.

More mainstream are parish-based young adult programs that offer social gatherings, social justice outreach, opportunities for performing charitable acts, and opportunities for study. Generally one or two parishes in a diocese, such as St. Vincent De Paul in San Francisco or St. Brigid's in San Diego, serve as unofficial diocesan youth centers. Similarly, Young Catholic Professionals, formed in 2010, meets the same needs and serves a clientele similar to the early CFM.

Apostolic movements continue to attract idealistic youth, though no single national lay organization channels young adults' social commitment and passion. Outlets are found in the Catholic Worker Movement, which continues to

---

8. Life Teen website, accessed June 16, 2017, www.lifeteen.com.

draw dedicated young men and women (see Fumiaki Tosu's essay), and short-term volunteer groups, such as the Jesuit Volunteer Corps (see Gus Hardy's essay), remain appealing. Despite the multiplicity of organizations for Catholic youth and young adults, there is no national, popular movement or organization that captures the imagination, passion, and dedication of Catholic youth in the United States.

The essayists in this section reflect the diversity of approaches to youth involvement; they represent Evangelical Catholic, the Jesuit Volunteer Corps, Opus Dei, the Verbum Dei Missionary Fraternity, and the Catholic Worker Movement. Though the organizations reflect different approaches and different styles of Catholicism, the language used by each reflects a commonality. Certain words and desires repeat in the five essays: community, service, witness, authenticity; all reflect a desire to be challenged, a desire to transform themselves and the world, a desire to live a fully integrated life of prayer and action. All reflect the vast, untapped potential of idealistic youth primed to change the Church and the world. Will we be able to harness this energy?

Jeffrey M. Burns, PhD, is the Director of the Frances G. Harpst Center for Catholic Thought and Culture at the University of San Diego. He also directs the Academy of American Franciscan History at the Franciscan School of Theology in Oceanside, California. He is a deacon for the Dioceses of Oakland and San Diego, and has worked in youth ministry for more than thirty years.

Responding to Our Call

by Kendra McClelland

Nearly three years ago, I reached the culmination of the most pertinent discernment process of my life thus far: coming home to the Catholic Church. As a young adult woman aching for greater depth in her faith, the Eucharist drew my heart forth in haste to be intimately united with Jesus Christ. In the years leading up to my conversion, I fell in love with serving in women's Christian ministry, but as deep as my passion was, it was coupled with crippling frustration as I saw little to no professional vocation available for women in ministry before me. As the Lord led me on a clear path toward Catholicism, he breathed hope into my dreams as I began to envision a vocation of pastoral ministry within the Catholic Church. The possibilities for women serving in a pastoral ministry role in the Catholic Church far outnumbered the opportunities I had in my Protestant upbringing. Not only did this strengthen my conviction in the Lord's calling me home, but for the first time in my life, I believed I had found a place of belonging unlike ever before. The Catholic Church valued the unique gifts of my feminine soul and empowered me to not only serve as a volunteer leader in my parish community, but to pursue a master of divinity degree and embrace God's will for my professional vocation.

Through active involvement as a leader in the young adult community at my parish, I benefited from a developing awareness of my personal strengths and spiritual charisms, which served as additional confirmation in the vocational path God had led me toward. As I pursued opportunities for peer leadership and skills training, my path intersected with a Catholic lay organization: Evangelical Catholic. My parish hired Evangelical Catholic to transform our community culture to be evangelistic in nature, a rare phenomenon in the Catholic Church. Through my initial involvement in small groups, I experienced an environment of prayer, community, Scripture, and rich discussions. Before I knew it, I was facilitating small groups within the parish community and had begun facilitating the training groups for new facilitators as well. My professional background in leadership consulting perfectly intersected with empowering the lay faithful to become leaders within their parish communities. In training parishioners to facilitate small groups, mentor their peers, and extend beyond their comfort zones by inviting people from outside the parish community to join a small group, lay members of the Church stepped into a meaningful leadership role within the parish. Watching individuals discover their God-given talents and charisms, and helping them find the best niche within the parish community to share those gifts, brought exuberant joy to my heart.

It was not long before I found myself working with Evangelical Catholic, the organization that initiated this cultural transformation in my parish, coaching other parishes to implement this contagious spirit of evangelization within their own communities. The opportunity to serve as a coach for parishes through this transformational journey fulfills my professional vocational dreams. As a lay organization, Evangelical Catholic effectively partners with universities and parishes across the country to build a culture of a joyous and intentional evangelization. Its model of ministry follows the mission process of Jesus's ministry on earth, seeking to cultivate meaningful relationships, which grow disciples who are sent out to impact the world.

As a Catholic woman pursuing a professional career in ministry, Evangelical Catholic values and prioritizes dynamics of excellence that heightened my interest to be a part of this forward-thinking, evangelistic organization. One of the first topics they mentioned when discussing employment was that they believed in just wages for pastoral ministers. Far too often, pastoral ministers are hired for part-time positions that are underpaid and carry the additional expectation that they will put in extra hours during the evenings and weekends. With the intention of pursuing the vocation of marriage and a family, I felt reassured in the fact that my time and talents would be fairly compensated with the underlying understanding of my inherent worth as a pastoral minister of the Catholic Church. While I am not strongly motivated by monetary gain, I felt deeply valued as a person giving her life to the ministry of the Church when they shared this organizational value with me.

Evangelical Catholic was also particularly interested in strengthening female leadership within its organization, something that female pastoral ministers do not hear very often. Coming from a particular Protestant tradition that undervalued the role of women in the church, listening to this intention breathed a great deal of hope into my heart. Additionally, I felt that my femininity was regarded with the utmost respect and viewed as a source of wisdom and value to the organization rather than a setback. Finally, as a young adult, I have frequently encountered generational bias in both the workplace and the ministerial world. Even though I had served in a ministerial capacity for seven years, often when people saw how young I was, they began to question my abilities to serve in a professional ministerial role. In fact, this unfortunate reality contributed toward my pursuit of a master of divinity, providing the credentials for my passion as it enhanced my know-how. However, Evangelical Catholic expressed specific interest in young adults as a portal to the future of the Catholic Church with an eagerness for innovation and creativity in our ever-evolving technological world.

In each of these areas that the greater world found gaps and spoke lies to diminish my sense of purpose and worth, Evangelical Catholic saw potential, unique gifts, and a zealous heart. Before I began working with the organization, one of the consultants took time out of his schedule to serve as a professional mentor to me. On a monthly basis, we practiced conflict resolution with real-life examples in our respective ministerial communities. He challenged me to think creatively, and he listened to the ways I envisioned potential solutions or new approaches to longstanding gaps in ministry. I valued his time and insight as it helped me grow and evolve as a minister, and he expressed how much he appreciated mine as well. Our monthly collaboration spoke volumes to me because, regardless of whether any opportunities grew from the conversations, the dialogue was rich and intentional. At the time, I failed to realize he was coaching me to stretch intellectually and spiritually as a pastoral minister, and he did not realize that he was bringing my professional dreams to life.

In response to the Second Vatican Council's push for the Body of Christ to understand the role of the laity in a more profound way, this Body has begun to walk in entirely new ways. These steps illuminate the future with great hope for a joy-filled revelatory impact on earth to bring the lost and forgotten home to the arms of their loving Father. This is where my passion dwells. I believe the future of evangelization and ministry in the Catholic Church rests on two factors: (1) An empowering invitation from the clergy to the laity to play an active role in the growth and formation of the Body of Christ and (2) an ever-growing curiosity from the lay faithful to become evangelizers themselves.

Serving as a parish consultant for Evangelical Catholic, I am infinitely blessed by the enriching experiences shared with pastors, deacons, parish staff, and parish leadership alike. By helping these communities implement a culture of evangelization, the rigid walls of the parish are coming down, and as Pope Francis encourages us, they have become like curtains. Parish communities are embracing the lost sheep unlike ever before because they have focused their eyes to see the lost and softened their hearts to show them mercy. However, in every parish, this transformation began with the pastor's decision to empower the parish community to lead one another. With the support and encouragement from the pastor, the lay faithful deepen their self-awareness through intentional formation, which results in a deepening aware-ness of others and equips them to guide and care for their personal apostolate. When seeds of discipleship are planted with intention and nurtured in relationship, the sustainabil-ity and growth of the community is maximized. This process requires trust between the pastor and those he chooses to lead the community toward a greater evangelization. Just as Jesus carefully chose his disciples and generously invested in their development, pastors must do the same. Without the freedom and trust between a pastor and his lay leaders, effective ministry cannot come to fruition. However, when a pastor believes and invests in the gifts of the lay faithful, the opportunity for evangelization is endless because the Body of Christ expands her reach when she empowers each limb to fulfill its potential.

Every invitation awaits a response. Once pastors seek to empower the lay faithful toward a greater role in discipleship, it is up to the laity to fulfill their baptismal call to proclaim the good news of Jesus Christ in their vocation. When the people of God respond with curiosity and passion to strengthen their relationship with Christ in order to guide others to do the same, an environment of encounter is established, and this is where transformation takes place. Thus, I am filled with anticipation for the ways the Holy Spirit will lead organizations like Evangelical Catholic to play a significant role in helping parishes and universities across the country foment discipleship within the Body of Christ. It is my sincerest prayer that the Church opens more doors for those who have a vision and a heart to respond to the Great Commission. As a young woman with a professional vocation to serve as a lay pastoral minister, I am thankful to call the Catholic Church my home, and my deepest hope is that she continues to recognize the inherent value and prospective difference that both young adult Catholics and lay organizations will make in the future discipleship of the Church.

Kendra McClelland is a twenty-six-year-old Catholic woman with a master of divinity from the Franciscan School of Theology in Oceanside, California. As a convert to the Catholic Church, she feels called toward a professional vocation as a lay pastoral minister. She is dedicated to helping contemporary young men and women know their true worth and value in Christ.

Belonging, Missioning, and Being Present

A Short Digression on Life as a Jesuit Volunteer

by Gus Hardy

> When my tour of duty ends at the House of Charity, I will return home to New York. I have yet to find the differences between myself and the many people who pass through the House of Charity. But thanks to my time here, I will forever remember the similarities.
>
> —Matthew Lavan, Spokane '98–'99, 1975–2003
> (on banner in the Spokane JV House)

Mary called me the other day. After six months, one of her community mates finally made the decision to leave, and now it's down to just the two of them in Bethel. While it's been half a year since we met for the first and only time, I can tell you that she lives in Alaska and works at a public defender's office. She lives on a diet of beans and salmon, and used to box at Notre Dame. She's had a hard year, and she's called me to talk about it. Sure, we may have only met for five days at that camp in Portland, but she knows she can trust me with anything, even with my being stationed all the way out in Missoula, Montana. We end the conversation, and I use our house's twenty-year-old sandwich press to make grilled cheeses for Monica and Cat. They both came into the house, shoulders slumped and eyes weary with the stress of caring for battered women and the city's mentally ill, and promptly crashed in the basement, seeking a brief space of peace. The three of us sit, eat, talk, and joke. It'll be community night soon, and we'll need to get ready if we want the strength to be open and honest with each other about all matters of God and life that may come up tonight. All of us are Jesuit Volunteers—stressed, crazy, heart-on-fire, sad, joyful Jesuit volunteers—and none of us fully knows why the heck we came out here.

About a hundred and fifty of us in the Pacific Northwest alone began the year fresh out of college and ready (or so we all thought) to commit ourselves to a year of service. JVs (as we're better known) are scattered all over—at shelters in Boise and Anchorage, L'Arche homes in Tacoma and Spokane, even a church in Seattle that's built into the side of an old skyscraper and serves the city's poor. As the year's gone on, and we've tried to serve people in our own ways, some have broken down, been hospitalized, or—for their own reasons—chosen to leave. It's not an easy life by any means, and meanwhile, all our friends back home are reeling in starting salaries, furnishing their first "proper" apartments, and maybe even getting a little bit of travel in. In a situation like this, *everyone* questions why he or she chose to serve. In my case, however, it's reflecting on the choice to live like this that I find I have grown the closest to Christ.

In this age of information, mine is a generation that bears an immense weight of responsibility. Thousands of clips, sound bites, and articles about the gritty realities of the world beyond our privileged American dreams have shown us the truth. We have been bombarded by so much information, so fast, and at such an early age that none of us is blind. No one can claim to not be responsible or not know that injustice is wreaked in the world at every second. And so this generation seeks a kind of atonement—with some courageous enough to allow a bigger vision to reshape their lives. They seek careers, paths, vocations untainted by connections to polluters and oppressive regimes and financial systems. They seek to work hard and well, to effect change, to do good. Some do it for the sake of humanity, some for the sake of following Jesus.

To be a Jesuit Volunteer, to spend one's first independent year in a simple community while living a life of service, is to make that desire part of our being for the rest of our lives. In sharing prayer, food, meals, song, struggles, and all else that comes in communal life, we give our lives to those immediately around us, and they do the same. When our time ends and we're called away from our places of service, the people in our communities will remain with us forever. We'll carry our community mates wherever we go, and memories of them will linger with us as we make choices in life.

This "carrying" is just as much true in the case of those we serve as those we live with. People with disabilities, impoverished school children, the mentally impaired, or those who seek the shelter that we help provide—each of these people teaches us an essential lesson, that they are worth serving for the fact that they are human beings, with no other reason necessary. Economic calculations, values, how many resources they're worth—all of these regressions and analyses that reign supreme in our world—fly out the window in the life of a Jesuit Volunteer. Whatever hardships, joys, moments of despair, or other situations that these individuals face, we partake in.

In describing this effect, I wish I could use a word other than *haunting*, but that's actually the best way I can put it. These experiences of service will haunt all of us for the rest of our lives in the way that only truly life-changing work can. The cry of the poor will haunt us when we look for work and have to decide whether or not a career in politics or art or education or the hard sciences is ultimately going to help or hurt the least of our brothers and sisters. Dorothy Day said that for all her life, God haunted her. For all our lives, we will be haunted by the people of God whom we served.

These JV communities, these people we encounter through service, these values that JVs commit themselves to—these impart lessons to me every day in every corner of my life. And that, I believe, is the main reason that I and other JVs choose this life, this way of being in community with others. We may have different incentives—a desire to explore ourselves, a chance to see a side of our nation that we wouldn't otherwise have experienced, maybe even an opportunity to escape the world as we've always known it—but we all seek *formation*. In the chaotic world I spoke of earlier, we want to be tested, forged, and tempered, and this life offers us a chance to do that in an authentic, powerful way. The intellectual, spiritual, and physical challenges that we face cannot be found in any place other than community life. Community gives us life because we choose to center our entire lives around it, more than at any other simple nine-to-five job; community is not something you "clock out" of. It may only be for a year, but it is a year that takes boys and girls and turns them into men and women for others, for the rest of their lives.

As the year ends, I'm going to head into the world beyond my house with the twenty-year-old furniture and the crucifixes surrounded by prayer flags and poetry, knowing that I'm ready for any challenge that the world can offer. After a year of being thrown into a situation of utter poverty with little more than a desire to serve and a few others to live with, I have thrown my life to God and trusted that all will be well. In this, I and the other JVs have become the people that God needs for the kingdom to come to this world, formed by community and tempered by service.

And how can Jesuit Volunteers be supported by the Church as a whole? Well, actually, I'm thankful for how well supported we are already. Priests and parishes open their doors for us, local schools invite us to speak and help out, and a lucky house may find an anonymous gift on its porch from time to time from a generous parishioner. People have a sense of the sacrifices that JVs make, and they want to help out. However, there is one thing that I believe the Church can do, and do well.

Give us a chance to tell our stories, as the people whom we serve have told us theirs. Let us have forums and meetings with clergy and lay leaders when we return to our homes at the end of this service. Perhaps provide opportunities to testify to what we've seen in official ecclesial settings. Listen to us, as we've listened and been present to the world's most desperate. Take the time to understand the powerful personal transformation that comes from an experience such as this. But don't stop there—preach from the pulpit! Tell our stories to your congregations. Speak about the deep injustices in our nation and how all can serve and be transformed by it—and for the better! And as God's people are changed, the world will be as well—formed by reality, just as JVs have been.

As I write these words, it's Monday of Holy Week, 2017, and I'm getting ready to travel to Boise with my friend Shaun. His girlfriend is being received into the Church at the Easter Vigil, and together, we'll make the trek through Idaho to reach her. It will be a beautiful occasion, one that I could never have borne witness to had I not chosen to say yes to God, and follow the path to community life set before me. It could only have come about with endless hours of tempering fights and calming down weeping adults at a homeless shelter, of making pasta dinners for five at a time, and organizing prayer services. This yes, if said authentically, always leads to the facing and overcoming of challenges in life, and this time in community and service makes us all the more willing to say it with full hearts.

Gus Hardy is twenty-three years old. He grew up in Berkeley, California, and was educated by the Jesuits just down the bay at Santa Clara University. Received into the Catholic Church at the 2012 Easter Vigil, he currently serves as a Jesuit Volunteer in Montana, where he works at a homeless shelter by day and reads medieval history by night. Next year, he will attend Boston College for graduate studies in theology.

Opus Dei in the Periphery

A VOCATION STORY OF A YOUNG WOMAN IN THE SOUTH BRONX

by Stephanie Frias

Opus Dei is part of the Catholic Church, and its mission is to spread the Christian message that every person is called to holiness. It was in the third grade at the Rosedale Achievement Center in the South Bronx that I was introduced to the spirit of Opus Dei. My mother wanted me to attend a program in which I could grow in character, nurture a spirit of service, and have fun activities to do after school. Throughout the years, I came to love Rosedale. I did most of the activities from the third grade all the way up to high school, including tutoring, voice lessons, cooking, arts and crafts, and character development lessons. These character development classes would help us see that Catholic teaching hit close to home. For example, in covering generosity, we discussed the importance of helping our parents with chores. Last, I did the job training program in high school in which I learned important skills for professional work and held different internships covering law, real estate, and horticulture.

Throughout my college years, I gained a better understanding of Opus Dei. In the summer of 2008, before entering my sophomore year in college, I was interning at a prestigious makeup company blocks away from St. Patrick's Cathedral in New York City. I started going to daily Mass and confessing regularly. I remember having "good" confessions, telling the priest, "Father, I yelled at my mother." He responded, "Well, is your mother deaf?" Finding him down-to-earth, I told one of my friends this story, and she asked me, "What is the name of the priest?" I had no idea because he was not always there as he was just a visiting priest. After a couple of weeks, I discovered that he was an Opus Dei priest.

Because I had this encounter and I was single in my life, I thought, "I'm called to be a numerary! This is it. I can be like the saints I love." A numerary remains single and is fully available for the apostolic undertakings and the formation of the other members of Opus Dei. I was happy being single. At the time, I feared marriage like no other and, frankly, I thought marriage was too ordinary; God, I was sure, wanted me to do something more. Then, I fell in love with a French man who made me wonder what God was planning; I have been restless ever since. Other adventures with people affiliated with Opus Dei opened my eyes to the importance of vocations beyond single life. I spent three weeks with a colicky baby only to realize that parenting is serious! I remember thinking, "Wow, I get it; this is an actual vocation. Why would anyone want this? Babysitting is the perfect birth control." But God calls many to all sorts of vocations!

However, I still did not know if being married was my vocation. I would sometimes stop at my parish church, St. Joan of Arc in the Bronx, to speak to the priest about life and vocation. I remember I told him once, "Father, maybe I can be a nun! I just need to find an order where I don't have to cut my hair." He laughed, "Well, go find it." I actually did. However, while on retreat with what I like to call NYC rock star nuns, God made it clear to me that I was not called to be a nun. I started to get more involved with my parish, teaching third grade catechism classes. It was perfect timing, too, as I was working in operations at a beauty company and thinking of a career change during that time. I spent time talking to my parish priest about my vocation and decided to go on my second Opus Dei retreat, which further illuminated my vocation. One of the more critical moments was when I went to the confessional to talk to the priest. "You sound a little restless," he concluded. "I am, Father," I admitted, "That's the perfect word to describe me." He continued, "You should pray for peace and read the last verses of chapter 11 from Matthew." I read it: "Come to me, all you that are weary and are carrying heavy burdens, and I will give you rest. Take my yoke upon you, and learn from me; for I am gentle and humble in heart, and you will find rest for your souls. For my yoke is easy, and my burden is light" (Matt 11:28–30). That Christmas of 2014, while I was teaching in Korea, I wrote the letter to the vicar and I became a member of Opus Dei as a supernumerary, that is, someone who can get married and live in their own home.

On an average day now, I am trying to be an apostle, which entails a few things. I try to attend Mass each day. In the morning on the subway, I usually pray the rosary. I take at least thirty minutes in the morning and in the afternoon to simply give God my full focus. I visit the tabernacle every day and, thankfully, where I work there's a chapel upstairs. I also make an effort to read the Bible each day for at least five minutes. It sounds like a lot, but I've realized that God has given me so much more and doing this gives me little reminders throughout the day that God is with me. Additionally, my biweekly spiritual direction helps center the most important aspects of my life.

I currently work at IESE, Instituto de Estudios Superiores de la Empresa, which is part of the University of Navarra in Spain. As a program coordinator, I make sure the professors and the participants have all they need so the program runs smoothly. I also pray that my coworkers and I can get through the daily work struggles with a smile. Because of prayer, I came to realize that I am doing this for a bigger purpose than just myself, too, this company helps form leaders in today's business world and creates a global experience for the students.

Beyond work, I am living what I consider to be a normal life. I live with my family. I do brunch with friends. I go to the bars. Some friends have inquired, "How do you find time to go out, work, and fit God in, too?" I always respond, "I set my priorities and God is it. Then everything else just falls into place."

Now that you see all the various ways I have been tugged by God to do so many different kinds of work, I want to acknowledge that it wasn't just me and God, there were so many laity, clergy, and professed religious who helped me along the way. Some of the most important ways I was supported included going on retreats and to theology conferences, confessing weekly, attending monthly spiritual talks, and being given responsibilities in the parish. These were important for many reasons. First, the retreats and theology conferences provided me with the time and space to pray and reflect on what is God's purpose for me in life. I needed those times to think about how to find enchantment in the ordinary. I also needed to understand that every calling, every vocation is beautiful. I didn't have to be a nun or have a celibate vocation to be a saint. Second, the weekly confessions and monthly spiritual talks helped me understand that

VOCATION THROUGH IDENTITY AND PRACTICE

I am not alone in my search for a better life. There is hope! Third, providing volunteer work for me at the parish gave meaning to my faith and knowledge as to how to best teach each age group. I learned how to be courageous, to go teach, and to be a disciple. As Matthew 28:19 states clearly, God has commissioned us to go out and spread our faith: "Go therefore and make disciples of all nations, baptizing them in the name of the Father and of the Son and of the Holy Spirit." The Church, in short, has taught me how to be a saint in the middle of this world. The Church needs to strengthen Catholics by offering these programs to the faithful, so that we may all grow in holiness and find the courage to bring this good news to the world.

I think simply *living* is a witness and a way to serve the Church. This lets people know that you can be ordinary—have a good and fun life—and have God at the driver's seat, too. I believe I am called to serve the Church by living out this ordinary vocation. I'm not saying it's easy, but I'd like to say I'm still a work in progress—I'm living Opus Dei.

Stephanie Frias is twenty-seven years old and currently resides in her hometown of the South Bronx. She works as a program coordinator at IESE, a business school of the University of Navarra in Spain. She believes that ordinary life can be extraordinary. Stephanie loves cultivating new friendships and has an affinity for all things in life: family, food, wine, and Latin dancing.

160

Essence, Not Uses

by Kiona Medina

I was restless. Like most young adults, I had a restlessness familiar to all those who are searching. I was restless due to a deep desire for authenticity and a life I did not know how to live. Growing up in Colombia with a Catholic family and attending Mass regularly as a young adult, I felt that I knew faith and love...yet something was missing and it bothered me. Then, a gift opened. In my third year of college I met the Verbum Dei Missionary Community in San Francisco through their campus ministry. The missionaries preached about a very human and real God, a God who was Someone, a faith that was intertwined with daily life, and they themselves embodied a very authentic and free spirit. That's when fear entered. Did I have to become a sister to live so joyfully and authentically my relationship to God? Was there any other way?

The charism of Verbum Dei is prayer with the Word in a way that relates and speaks to our concrete realities. I was fascinated and deeply moved to learn to pray this way and experience the Word of God alive in my life. In one of their silent retreats, I prayed with Paul's conversion and felt in my prayer God asking me, "What are you looking for?" As I struggled to answer that question then and in the summer that followed, I realized that God did not want me to *serve* him, God wanted me to be in *relationship* with him. The explosion of freedom in my heart led me to realize that God desired my happiness. I felt the pull to continue digging deeper; I had found a treasure! I decided to join what the community called the "gap year" after I finished college, and I took the time to truly stay in the interior desert and discern. Entering the desert was not easy. I ended a two-year relationship, I canceled my acceptance into grad school, I moved out of where I lived comfortably for four years, and made many other smaller choices. I didn't fully understand. My brother was already in religious life, and though he supported me, the rest of my family and friends didn't understand. Nothing made sense except feeling a burning bush in my heart. Though my mind didn't get it, I had to get closer.

Prior to entering this year, the community invited me and a group of other young adults to visit the very first missionaries in Spain. Another gift opened. I met one of the first missionaries, who walked with me for hours, dialoguing about boyfriends, prayer, discernment, family, fears, and everything in between. At the end of our conversation, she said to me, "You have been walking around a swimming pool, wondering what it is like to swim." Deeply challenged and moved by that conversation, I returned to the United States and slowly stepped into the metaphorical pool. For the next six months I lived with two other young women who would become like my sisters and two other missionaries. We shared meals, morning and evening prayer, and I helped out with retreats and other activities in the community. I kept my job and learned to integrate a life of prayer in all that I did. During this time, I fell ill and felt emotionally exhausted at times as I looked for something that was deep within me all along. I kept asking myself, "What is the best way to serve him? What is the best use of my life? What am I afraid of?" I talked to spiritual directors, my family, friends; I

interviewed missionaries and dissected every vocation story
out there. All those searches helped a little, but the greatest
times of revelation occurred in brief moments of solitude:
a simple drive in the car on my own, in the chapel when
everybody had already left, sitting at the beach watching the
simple ebb and flow of life. The greatest challenge for me
was to accept that I was "just right" as I was, that my vocation was and continues to be very simple: to belong to him.
My vocational discernment unfolded when I realized that I
belonged to God just by being his daughter; I did not need to
do or serve or preach anything, but simply be the authentic
testimony of that belonging. After six months, and with an
incredible sense of freedom and peace in my heart, I moved
out of the religious community without knowing what was
next. There was so much to figure out: I had lost my job and
needed a place to live. The uncertainty that followed led me
to doubt and question how my path had unfolded. I continued to stay connected with the community and joined their
retreats and prayer groups, slowly gaining the understanding
and certainty that I needed to continue to be authentic in my
prayer. Nothing gave me more clarity than being honest with
God and having an honest heart-to-heart dialogue with him.
My discernment taught me to live from my essence, not my
uses, and I slowly integrated that by focusing on the ways
I chose to live from then on and how I embodied a life of
prayer as a layperson. It is indeed an ongoing process intertwined with the challenges of a work schedule, social life,
and personal commitments. Yet, in the midst of all that is the
constant presence of a God, who joined me in my vulnerability and showed me how deeply he is committed to my life.

About a year after this experience, I wrote to the first
missionary who had invited me to enter the pool and said
joyfully that I was floating in God's mercy and freedom. She
was elated to read about my discernment and encouraged

me to continue to trust him as he truly knows our deepest desires. A few months later, I entered the graduate school program I had postponed, and I continue to be involved with the Verbum Dei Community.

Throughout my discernment and my ongoing journey after, I am blessed to stay connected to a community of sisters, consecrated lay, married couples, and other lay members like myself. We all need each other. Whether one is discerning religious life or not, it is very important to know that one belongs in the Body of Christ, and to hear and respond to everyone's unique story. There are many communities, like Verbum Dei and the Franciscans, that offer opportunities for lay members in the Church to nurture their faith and spirituality. In the retreats that Verbum Dei offers, all of us get together to pray, do dynamics, and receive formation relevant to all the different aspects of our lives.

The Church could help young adults find the spiritual depth that community life offers by more readily connecting them with local opportunities. Another important part of my discernment was my involvement with a young adult group in my local parish. They have become my closest friends and an important part of my spiritual growth. Young adults need opportunities to grow in faith and to learn about topics relevant to their lives. The more intentional parishes and religious communities are about creating these spaces, the more young adults will feel a sense of belonging where they can explore their vocational calling.

I currently work as an expressive arts therapist and help the community integrate arts into our retreats. Indeed, all of us have something to offer and accept from others. I am full of gratitude as I reflect on my journey and discernment. I'm grateful to the many who helped and continue to inspire my spiritual walk. I treasure as the foundation of my faith a relationship with God that was, and is, freedom and peace.

I hope that all young adults are afforded an opportunity to have spaces and communities where they can belong, grow in faith, and live from their essence the freedom and peace that God dreams for their lives.

Kiona Medina is a twenty-eight-year-old, Colombian-born lay member of the Verbum Dei Missionary Fraternity. She is an expressive arts marriage and family therapist intern who currently lives in the San Francisco Bay Area. Her passions include integrating the arts and creative movement with spirituality through retreats, workshops, and in her work as a therapist.

Still, We Live

EXPERIMENTS IN RESURRECTION
AT THE CATHOLIC WORKER

by Fumiaki Tosu

What I want is to find wholeness in our broken world—a way to live amidst people and a planet torn apart by climate catastrophe, war, nuclear madness, and grinding poverty. In the Catholic Worker Movement, I have found a way to face the dying of our world, yet live. The question facing young adult Catholics in twenty-first-century America is the question of hope: How do we hold the devastating realities that confront us and still live with hope? Or, from the perspective of faith and the Church: Can the Christian community nurture the resistance and creativity necessary for humanity to survive this moment in our history?

Let us examine the facts: We know that without swift action today, the atmosphere will be so saturated with carbon within two or three years that it will be impossible to keep global warming to below two degrees Celsius, the temperature beyond which climate change can no longer be considered even remotely "manageable." During every year of this century, the United States has been engaged in at least one major war, killing hundreds of thousands of civilians and displacing millions more; rather than decommission our nuclear arsenal, President Obama authorized a $1 trillion nuclear weapons upgrade, moving us away from our commitments under the Nuclear Non-Proliferation Treaty. The wealth gap continues to grow in the United States, with the wealthiest 1 percent now owning more than 30 percent of the wealth in this country, and leaving the bottom 80 percent with merely 15 percent of our nation's money and resources.

These are the facts; this is the reality within which we live.

What is astounding is that most of us know this, yet continue to act as if it were not true. We work our day jobs, send our children to school, and take out mortgages, as if a house will provide us with security in thirty years when the climate will not permit us to grow enough food to feed us all.

What we need is an alternative vision of what our lives could be. Some think the Church is too enmeshed in the failed political, social, and economic structures of yesterday to offer a life-giving alternative for tomorrow. I believe the Gospels—as *the* story of life's triumph over the powers of death—offer precisely the narrative we need to navigate our present crisis. The Catholic Worker Movement is one attempt at living out this narrative.

One of my early encounters with the Catholic Worker Movement was in Los Angeles, serving soup at the "Hippie Kitchen" on Skid Row in the summer of 2011. I was on a three-month "tour" of various Catholic Worker communities in California, discerning whether the radical embrace of the Gospels as lived out in the Catholic Worker Movement was for me. A turning point in my discernment came one day when we held a vigil for peace in front of the Federal Building. That morning, after serving oatmeal on a street corner to day laborers, we hopped into our vans and headed downtown with our signs and placards: "U.S. Out of Iraq" and "No Blood for Oil." For the next hour, we marched silently around the Federal Building, praying for peace. As I slowly paced the perimeter of the building with my rosary in hand, I pondered the women and men who zoomed past us in cars or worked in the surrounding office buildings—good, ordinary people, presumably working hard to support their families, and who, in all likelihood, were not at that moment thinking about the wars in Iraq and Afghanistan. If pressed, most would have known that we were at war, and many might even have been against the wars. Yet, given the demands of career and family, most, I was sure, were not thinking about our wars on a daily basis (with the exception, of course, of those who had loved ones in the armed forces). This is not a judgment or condemnation—I know from personal experience how all-encompassing a career can be—but a statement of reality. It was in that context of general indifference to the wars in Iraq and Afghanistan that I was struck by how good it was that here, at the Catholic Worker, were people who made it their jobs not to forget that on that day, people were being killed in our name.

This struck me as momentously important. If people were being killed on my behalf, I wanted to at least acknowledge that it was happening. For me, this went beyond politics or one's position on the merits of the war: If my government was bombing human beings *for me*, the least I could do was remember that it was happening, whether I supported the war or opposed it. To live as if I could ignore the reality of war altogether seemed somehow dishonest and a diminishing of my humanity.

The Church is the community that remembers: This is my body, broken for you; this is my blood, poured out for you. *Do this in memory of me.* At the Catholic Worker, we try to remember Jesus, not only in the bread and wine, but in people whose bodies and spirits are broken on our streets, whose blood is spilt in our wars.

When Jackie came to live with us at Casa de Clara Catholic Worker in San Jose, her body had been broken and her blood spilt repeatedly by her abusive boyfriend. She has four daughters, the oldest of whom, at age twelve, had been repeatedly raped by the same abuser. We took her in, but what could we offer to someone in so much pain? We provided a safe home with family-style dinners and a community of friends, support finding work, and help with school. It was not nearly enough. During the fourteen months that Jackie's family lived with us, their lives were constantly in chaos. Her youngest threw tantrums nightly, and Jackie, exhausted from life, could do little; her oldest, now thirteen and not knowing how to process her pain, went into repeated bouts of depression and withdrawal followed by rage directed— for lack of another target—at her mother.

How powerless we feel in such situations! We listen and offer feeble words of support. We are like Veronica, wiping Jesus's brow on his way to the cross, or like the soldier who gave him a sponge soaked with vinegar moments before his death: we offer tokens of support, but are powerless to alter the main course of events. We give what is ours to give, then await God's action.

God does, indeed, act—of this we are witnesses. Just when all hope seems lost, after twenty, thirty, or fifty failures, God opens a way. One day, against all odds, Jackie and her family found a place to live, and it has been two years now that they have lived on their own. Her youngest has discovered basketball, and is thriving in school. I just returned from her ninth birthday party, an occasion filled with friends, laughter, and her beaming face shoved into her birthday cake. I am still working with the oldest daughter, trying to find a way to nudge, prod, cajole, and bribe her back into attending high school. I do not know if I will succeed; I do know that I want to keep showing up, so that when God does act, I am there to see it and proclaim it.

Resurrection is always unexpected, and it is always God's doing. It is the life that breaks into our world precisely when death seems certain. Our hope, then, comes from the only place hope has ever come from: Signs of resurrection—life right here in our broken world. The particular challenge for our generation is that today these signs are so often obscured. On the one hand, we are fed false hope through "solutions" that can only disappoint—for example, a technological fix to global warming, or an electoral fix to income inequality. On the other hand, we are distracted from the contemporary manifestations of the cross (and therefore of the resurrection) by career, entertainment, and a pervasive hyper-individualism.

What we need is a Church—a Church rooted in the Gospels and planted firmly in the margins of society—that witnesses to both the cross and the resurrection in our world. Only a Church that looks squarely at the realities of poverty, war, and climate catastrophe and sees within them the death of Jesus will be in a position to witness to his resurrection. Let us name the death that surrounds us—we will not flinch. Let us also proclaim life, Christ's victory over death. We need bold preaching, and bolder living. We need a Church that acts as if the Gospels were true, and Christians willing to stake their lives on it.

The resurrection is already happening. It arises in thousands of small pockets around the world, when communities choose life and creativity over death. We see it when municipalities assert local control over their energy production, when indigenous tribes join nonviolently to oppose an oil pipeline, when peacemakers link arms in a gesture of solidarity around mosques in the United States, or when citizens organize to monitor and report immigration raids in their neighborhoods. We see it, too, at the Catholic Worker. Each night, I eat dinner around a large dining room table with women and children struggling to make their way out of homelessness. Our five-year-old presider, Sophie, offers grace (it lasts about five seconds): "ThankYou-GodforthisFoodandEverybodyWhoGivesUsGoodThings. WeLoveEverybodyinthisFamilyandWeLoveGodAmen!" During the meal, we talk, we tease, we check-in, and then we all share in doing the dishes.

This is resurrection, life arising out of the ashes of violence and poverty. It is not always easy to see, and there are days when the intensity and amount of suffering threatens to crowd out hope. It is on such days that we must remember "the full message of the prophets....that the Christ should suffer and so enter into his glory" (Luke 24:25–26, The Jerusalem Bible).

"Christ should suffer and so enter into his glory." In other words, the cross always precedes resurrection. Our task is to go to that place where Christ suffers and to remain there. To dwell within suffering is always difficult, but it is the only place we can witness the resurrection. The beauty of the Catholic Worker Movement is the beauty of the Church: The Body of Christ, risen from within the wounds of this world.

Fumiaki Tosu, thirty-nine, lives and works at Casa de Clara Catholic Worker in San Jose, California, which provides transitional housing for women and children, hot shower services for neighbors living on the streets, as well as a food distribution program. Fumiaki has also spent time at the Los Angeles and Redwood City houses of hospitality.

Questions

1. These lay associations may be even more critical for young adults in an increasingly mobile society; for example, it may ease their transition to a new parish home after a long-distance move if they are able to meet up with a new Sant'Egidio group. What are some of the lay associations that you have been involved with? Which might connect the young adults in your parish with Christ, one another, and the wider world in a religiously significant way?

2. Dr. Jeffrey Burns demonstrates that contemporary American Catholicism is not characterized by the thriving lay associations that past Catholics enjoyed. He concludes his précis noting some common themes amid their diversity: "Certain words and desires repeat in the five essays: community, service, witness, authenticity; all reflect a desire to be challenged, a desire to transform themselves and the world, a desire to live a fully integrated life of prayer and action." Do your parish groups that minister to young adults tap into each of these? Which one(s) tend to fall by the wayside?

3. Burns continues with a challenge to fellow Catholics: "All [of these essays] reflect the vast, untapped potential of idealistic youth primed to change the Church and

world. Will we be able to harness this energy?" Or will young people leave the Church for outlets that more readily channel their energy? What practical steps is your parish community taking to help Catholic young adults propel their vision of Christian hope, justice, and love into the world? For example, do you partner with wider community organizations? Do you invite young adults active in the community to propose parish outreach projects?

Young Adults in a Home of Harmony

by Tricia C. Bruce

American Catholics are a sizable and diverse lot. As the largest single religious denomination in the United States, nearly 82 million Americans identify as Catholic. Almost half of Americans have some personal connection to Catholicism, whether through current affiliation, former affiliation, or the affiliation of a spouse or parent. Catholicism holds a prominent place in the United States landscape.[1]

It is not altogether surprising, then, that such a large swath of the American populous would also exhibit divergence along the lines of ideology, politics, liturgical preference, and other cultural and social issues. Not all American Catholics are alike. The very notion of catholicity evokes the idea of unity amid diversity. Pope Francis has likened the Church to a "'home of harmony,' where *unity and diversity* know how to merge in order to become a great source of

---

    1. Statistics on Catholics throughout essay come from Pew Research Center, "America's Changing Religious Landscape," May 12, 2015, http://www.pewforum.org/2015/05/12/americas-changing-religious-landscape/; and Pew Research Center, "U.S. Catholics Open to Non-traditional Families," September 2, 2015, http://www.pewforum.org/2015/09/02/u-s-catholics-open-to-non-traditional-families/.

wealth." Pope Francis tells us that together, diverse Catholics form "a symphony….Each one preserves its own unmistakable timbre and the sounds characteristic of each blend together around a common theme. Then there is the one who directs it, the conductor, and as the symphony is performed all play together in 'harmony,' but the timbre of each individual instrument is never eliminated; indeed, the uniqueness of each is greatly enhanced!"[2] Diversity can lend itself to breathtaking performances.

Nevertheless, sociologists observe regularly the bumps and missteps that accompany Americans' encounters with diverse others. Today's young adult Catholics inherit a milieu scarred by a legacy of polarization in the Church. They participate in and are beginning to lead a Church whose racial diversity is unrivaled. A Church wherein interpretations of Vatican II vary by progressive or traditionalist lenses. It is a Church, in other words, undergoing a period of reckoning and identity negotiation. Young adults will set the tenor of catholicity for a generation to come. The forthcoming pages showcase the work of four young adults doing exactly this.

Some twenty years ago, religious studies scholars Mary Jo Weaver and R. Scott Appleby edited a two-volume set depicting two progressive and traditional poles of U.S. Catholicism. *Being Right* and *What's Left* assert that, perhaps, "the authority question is the hinge on which the difference swings." Liberal Catholics challenge conventional modes of operation; conservatives reclaim those conventional modes. A conservative interpretation might see Vatican II as having gone far enough or too far; a liberal one might see Vatican II as having not gone far enough. Mary Jo Weaver expands,

---

2. Pope Francis, General Audience, St. Peter's Square, October 9, 2013, no. 3, accessed June 21, 2017, https://w2.vatican.va/content/francesco/en/audiences/2013/documents/papa-francesco_20131009_udienza-generale.html.

If conservative describes Catholics who are often oriented to the past and who accept traditional religious authority, then liberal can describe those Catholics who are oriented to the future and whose energies are attached to an array of ideas that challenge conventional definitions of religious authority even as they embrace Vatican II's definition of the Church as the "people of God."

Viewed in this way, a polarized Church reflects not only oppositional *sides*, but also *direction* of movement.[3]

More recently, Mary Ellen Konieczny, Charles C. Camosy, and I coedited a volume titled *Polarization in the US Catholic Church*. Its contributions span the gamut of Catholic thought, each author challenging not only the temptation to divide the Church through parish, media, and relationship choices, but also challenging the very premise that a so-called culture war accurately describes the Church. Clearly, the specter of polarization still haunts some Catholics, such as contributor Michael McGillicuddy, who describes the "scars" and resentment of culture wars sewn into his own faith formation. An entire section of the volume is titled "Naming the Wounds." Polarization has had a lived, visceral impact on many Catholics as they live out their day-to-day faith lives.[4]

On the other hand, the editors and contributors of

---

3. Mary Jo Weaver and R. Scott Appleby, eds., *Being Right: Conservative Catholics in America* (Bloomington, IN: Indiana University Press, 1995); Weaver, *What's Left? Liberal American Catholics* (Bloomington, IN: Indiana University Press, 1999); quotations from Weaver, 1999, xiii–xiv.

4. Mary Ellen Konieczny, Charles C. Camosy, and Tricia C. Bruce, *Polarization in the US Catholic Church: Naming the Wounds, Beginning to Heal* (Collegeville, MN: Liturgical Press, 2016); James Davison Hunter, *Culture Wars: The Struggle to Control the Family, Art, Education, Law, and Politics in America* (New York: Basic Books, 1992).

Polarization in the US Catholic Church acknowledge that the vast majority of American Catholics are moderate in their views, neither absorbed nor pulled directionally by a so-called "left/right" divide in the Church. "Cultural conflicts" might be a better term, writes Mary Ellen Konieczny. "Despite differences of class, race, and gender, we as Americans are held together by our many similarities—including, especially, our faith commitments, beliefs, and common sense of belonging—as well as the interpersonal ties we have with Catholic family members, friends, and people in our faith communities." This more nuanced and moderated vision of the U.S. Church is what might offer the most promise for healing and unity henceforth.[5]

So, which is it? Does polarization in the U.S. Catholic Church (indeed, in the United States overall) exist, shaping young adult Catholics' formation therein? Or are myriad perspectives simply different, more moderate than extreme, and better described as instruments in a conjoined symphony like Pope Francis so optimistically describes?

Looking to available empirical data on these questions, one measure to consider is that of political affiliation. Among Catholics, 37 percent identify as or "lean" Republican; 44 percent identify as or "lean" Democrat. Two in ten do not lean either way. In terms of political ideology, 37 percent of Catholics describe themselves as "conservative." Fewer—22 percent—describe themselves as "liberal." Many (36 percent, to be precise) do not identify with either ideological pole but are self-described political "moderates." The Catholic vote went to Democratic presidential candidate Barack Obama in 2008 and 2012, then split between Republican Donald Trump and Democrat Hillary Clinton in 2016. The spectrum of Catholic political persuasion is wide.

---

5. Konieczny, Camosy, and Bruce, *Polarization in the US Catholic Church*, xiv.

Asked more specifically about the role of government services, Catholics are fairly evenly split. About half (48 percent) want smaller government and fewer services; the other half (47 percent) want bigger government and more services. About half (46 percent) of Catholics say that government aid to the poor "does more harm than good"; the rest (48 percent) say it "does more good than harm." Abortion attitudes, too, divide Catholics: 48 percent say abortion should be legal in all/most cases; 47 percent say it should be illegal in all/most cases. These are among the most polarizing social issues that divide American Catholics. This polarization is real.[6]

Another measure that sociologists look to in assessing whether and how communities are divided is that of social distance, or the degree of separation coterminous with social dimensions such as race, class, or education. To what extent do Catholics meet, intermingle, and build relationships across social lines? More broadly, scholars note that U.S. cities and neighborhoods remain residentially segregated (increasingly so, even), particularly when it comes to race and class. The "big sort" is what journalist Bill Bishop calls this kind of in-group partitioning. Wealthy live by the wealthy; poor live by the poor. Whites often live by whites, people of color by people of color. To the extent that territorial parishes serve a neighborhood's residents, this partitioning spawns segregated Catholic parishes as well. Just 15 percent of Catholic parishes are "multiracial," containing more than 20 percent of a second racial group therein. Congregations are typically even less diverse racially than the neighborhoods they occupy.[7]

---

6. Konieczny, Camosy, and Bruce, *Polarization in the US Catholic Church*, xiv.

7. Bill Bishop, *The Big Sort: Why the Clustering of Like-Minded America Is Tearing Us Apart* (New York: Houghton Mifflin Harcourt, 2009); Korie L. Edwards, Brad Christerson, and Michael O. Emerson, "Race, Religious Organizations, and

Catholic parishes embed polarization in other ways, too. Territorial parishes generate parish cultures that emphasize some facets of Catholic identity and deemphasize others. Both Jerome Baggett and Mary Ellen Konieczny describe this dynamic in parishes they study ethnographically. "Personal" parishes explicitly emphasize specialization rather than generic service to all in their midst. Most personal parishes serve Catholics on the basis of shared race or ethnicity (e.g., personal parishes for Vietnamese Catholics or Black Catholics). But a growing number of personal parishes create homes for Catholics who prefer the traditional Latin Mass (TLM), or who have a social justice orientation. Attendees at TLM parishes skew younger, as well: growth comes not from elderly Catholics who recall the pre–Vatican II liturgy, but from young adult Catholics yearning for traditional forms of worship and authority. Parishes cohere like-minded Catholics together, apart from other Catholics. Dioceses must necessarily bridge what both territorial and personal parishes divide.[8]

For young adult Catholics pursuing the vocation of marriage, another place where social distance matters substantially is in the "marriage market," or the perception (whether explicit or implicit) of who constitutes a suitable marriage partner. Sociologists note that "assortative marriage," or

Integration," *Annual Review of Sociology* 39 (2013): 211–28; Peter Marcuse and Ronald van Kempen, "States, Cities, and the Partitioning of Urban Space," in *Of States and Cities: The Partitioning of Urban Space*, ed. Peter Marcuse and Ronald van Kempen (New York: Oxford University Press, 2002), 3–10; Michael O. Emerson and Rodney M. Woo, *People of the Dream: Multiracial Congregations in the United States* (Princeton, NJ: Princeton University Press, 2006).

8. Jerome P. Baggett, *Sense of the Faithful: How American Catholics Live Their Faith* (New York: Oxford University Press, 2009); Mary Ellen Konieczny, *The Spirit's Tether: Family, Work, and Religion among American Catholics* (New York: Oxford University Press, 2013); Tricia C. Bruce, "Polarized Preferences, Polarized Pews," in Konieczny, Camosy, and Bruce, *Polarization in the US Catholic Church*, 33–45; Tricia C. Bruce, *Parish and Place: Making Room for Diversity in the American Catholic Church* (New York: Oxford University Press, 2017).

marrying someone with demographic similarities to one's self, has strong effects on social inequality and prospects for mobility. Catholics are fairly split in educational attainment, for example: 46 percent have a high school education or less. As Americans sort, befriend, and marry following educational lines, this exacerbates social distance.

Social contact theory suggests that it takes interpersonal relationships to bridge difference and undercut social separation. Do Catholic Americans have this opportunity to build relationships if their neighborhoods and networks fail to embed diverse people and views? Conservatives report valuing communities among others who share their religion (57 percent versus 17 percent of liberals). Liberals are far more likely than conservatives to value communities with racial and ethnic diversity (76 versus 20 percent).[9]

Ironically, American Catholicism's increasing racial diversity may mean that these two dimensions will slowly fuse together. Catholics, after all, are much more likely to be first or second generation. Nearly one in three (28 percent) are foreign born, and another 15 percent are second generation. Fewer than three in five Catholics (58 percent) are white—a number that continues to shrink, fueled both by religious switching and immigration. Paired with aforementioned neighborhood preferences, this means that conservative Catholics who seek out Catholic neighbors will necessarily find themselves in the very racially diverse neighborhoods sought by liberals. Structures mix with agency to make for new and different neighbors.

All this suggests that polarization is indeed real, and evidenced through empirical data. But there is also a case to

---

9. G. W. Allport, *The Nature of Prejudice* (Cambridge, MA: Perseus Books, 1954); Pew Research Center, "Political Polarization in the American Public," June 12, 2014, http://www.people-press.org/2014/06/12/political-polarization-in-the-amer ican-public/.

be made that, perhaps especially for young adult Catholics, polarization is as much perception as it is reality. Sociologist Christian Smith writes that younger Catholics are less polarized because they are simply less invested and less informed about their faith, and more reluctant to judge anyone else. Hosffman Ospino suggests that Hispanic Catholics are largely unconcerned with polarizing issues, instead invested in issues of life, faith, and dignity. Given that half of American Catholics ages eighteen to twenty-nine are Hispanic—triple that of Catholic seniors—this portends a decreasingly polarized future Catholic America.[10]

This brings us back to the opening frame of this essay: American Catholics are a sizable and diverse lot. On the one hand, you can call this variety "polarization"—a cacophony of perspectives. On the other, you can call it a symphony—a retention effort, a sign of vibrancy. Pope Francis says,

> It is a beautiful image which tells us that the Church is like a great orchestra in which there is great variety. We are not all the same and we do not all have to be the same. We are all different, varied, each of us with his [or her] own special qualities. And this is the beauty of the Church: everyone brings his [or her] own gift, which God has given him [or her], for the sake of enriching others.[11]

A diverse U.S. Catholic Church makes room for young adults to explore who they are within a Church that has a place for them.

---

10. Hosffman Ospino, "The Unheeded Middle," in Konieczny, Camosy, and Bruce, *Polarization in the US Catholic Church*, 130–44; Christian Smith, "Reflection by Christian Smith," in Konieczny, Camosy, and Bruce, *Polarization in the US Catholic Church*, 16–21.

11. Pope Francis, General Audience, St. Peter's Square, October 9, 2013.

Tricia C. Bruce, PhD, is an Associate Professor of Sociology at Maryville College and the University of Texas at San Antonio. Her books include Faithful Revolution *(Oxford University Press, 2011),* Polarization in the US Catholic Church *(Liturgical Press, 2016), and* Parish and Place *(Oxford University Press, 2017). She coleads The American Parish Project and has conducted applied research for the United States Conference of Catholic Bishops.*

The Splendor of Tradition in Twenty-First-Century Catholic Evangelism

by Mark Kalpakgian

My first experience in Europe was as a twenty-year-old student during the Jubilee Year 2000. The traditions, customs, festivals, and glorious art and architecture kindled a reverence and wonder for the great Catholic tradition that has stayed with me ever since. Later, I was privileged to return to Europe for an extended period of time, spending nearly six years managing a university study-abroad program.

As we seek to evangelize the culture for Christ anew, it is vital to reintroduce the splendor and significance of this tradition in the contemporary context. Having worked closely with young adults over the past decade, I experienced firsthand the importance of celebrating the great spiritual, intellectual, artistic, and cultural traditions of Catholicism. Let's explore a few real-life examples within the Church's traditions of monasticism, architecture, apostles, saints, pilgrimage, and Catholic culture more generally.

THE KARTAUSE: THE MONASTIC TRADITION

The student program was located in Austria in a renovated, fourteenth-century Carthusian monastery ("Kartause"), a former residence of members of the Hapsburg dynasty. The Kartause's imposing Gothic roof spire rose up to heaven as a symbol of the intimate connection between heaven and earth, the temporal and the eternal. As a place of profound spiritual oasis, liturgical traditions such as the recitation of the Divine Office, the rosary, and eucharistic adoration imbued the daily rhythm of life.

Often just being immersed in this holy ambiance with its great monastic traditions—prayer, silence, contemplation, chant, and work and study—brought students closer to spiritual renewal and a deepening of vocation. Students regularly recounted how this happened through the various liturgical prayers in the chapel, in the permeating peacefulness of the grounds, and in the sacred music that reverberated in the church. The historical religious festivals and customs of the surrounding region such as the annual Corpus Christi procession and St. Martin's Day festival enriched their experience. Reflecting back, many student conversions resulted from an encounter with the traditional monastic, cultural, and liturgical elements that the Church has embraced over the centuries.

NOTRE DAME CATHEDRAL:
THE TRADITION OF SACRED ARCHITECTURE

It was July 2016, and I was in charge of leading public high school students on a summer trip to France and Spain.

The first stop was Paris. After touring the city and visiting the Louvre, the Latin Quarter, and the Arc de Triomphe, it was finally time to explore Notre Dame. Upon entering this famous medieval cathedral, constructed between the twelfth and fourteenth centuries and renovated in the eighteenth century, the students were in awe of the towering Gothic architecture, the magnificence of the stained glass, and the profound sense of the sublime in every nook and cranny.

As they stumbled outside the church one by one, I noticed many of the students in tears, even the nonreligious ones. As I sat quietly observing, I overheard them describe the church's impact: "I'm not sure what I felt, but I sensed the divine"; "I was moved by something transcendent in the cathedral"; "I felt called outside of myself"; "I have to reexamine my religious convictions…." The interpenetration of sacred art and architecture in Notre Dame produced an experience of *metanoia*, a conversion or change in one's way of life or thinking. Based on the cathedral's impact on secular students, I realized the value for the universal Church to continue the longstanding Catholic tradition of sacred art and beautiful architecture in its churches—even in modern times.

St. John Lateran: The Apostolic Tradition

In a rather unimpressive region of Rome lies the great papal archbasilica known as St. John Lateran. It is the oldest church in the West, and as the cathedral of Rome, it has precedence among the four major papal Roman basilicas. Walking down the main nave, one can't help but notice the massive statues of the apostles, ominously holding the instruments of their martyrdom. At the front of the church is the graceful *baldacchino*—a ceremonial canopy—over the high altar. At the top is a reliquary containing the heads of Sts. Peter and Paul. Beneath the *baldacchino* is the high altar, which can only be used by the pope. It contains a relic said to be part of St. Peter's communion table. To the left is the altar of the Holy Sacrament that, according to tradition, contains a cedar table used by Christ at the Last Supper.

As we celebrated Mass, one could feel the solemn and heroic presence of Peter, Paul, and the rest of the apostles. No longer was the papacy and the early Church an abstraction from ancient history; instead it became a personal encounter, a living reality that evokes assent from the heart. The Church of today should feast on the witness of the apostles, the keys of Peter, and the courage and zeal of Paul. These pillars of Catholicism are just that—cornerstones that support and nourish the Church up and down the ages.

Assisi: The Tradition of the Saints

The time spent in Assisi, Italy, the hometown of St. Francis of Assisi, was one of the highlights of the students' European experience. They had the opportunity to spend time in prayer and quiet, experiencing the most spiritually rich parts of the medieval city. They would visit the Portiuncula chapel located in the Basilica of St. Mary of the Angels, where the Franciscan movement started and where St. Francis received the first woman, St. Clare of Assisi, into his religious order. They would spend time at the church of St. Damiano, where Francis heard his call from the Lord: "Francis, Francis, go and repair My house which, as you can see, is falling into ruins."

Even after several visits to Assisi, I was repeatedly challenged to align my life more fully with the gospel. Listening to our guide, a Franciscan sister, explain that St. Francis stripped naked and gave up his wealth and privilege in front of his father and the local bishop, I questioned whether I was too attached to material things. Hearing that St. Francis rejoiced in all of creation, including the lepers of his day, was my joy lacking? Was my love and care for those on the fringes of society sufficient? By an encounter with the life and legacy of St. Francis of Assisi, we were inspired to reexamine the gospel and rebuild the Church.

MARIAZELL: THE TRADITION OF PILGRIMAGE

Pilgrimage is another great ancient tradition of Christendom. The word *pilgrim*, derived from the Latin *peregrinum*, conveys the idea of a journey to a holy place or shrine with a purpose to give thanks, to make sacrifices along the way, and to order one's life to the gospel. Ultimately, it is about honoring God. As such, we would lead a sixteen-mile pilgrimage on foot through the foothills of the Austrian Alps to the shrine of Our Lady of Mariazell, the most visited Marian shrine in Central Europe. Students hike in silence, pray together, and build solidarity as they make their way through the centuries-old trails in pristine forests and over rushing mountain streams. Tired, exhausted, and blistered at the end, we celebrated Mass in front of the miraculous image of Our Lady. Often, students would share that the pilgrimage was one of the highlights of their semester and a place of real encounter with the Lord and with the other students—the Body of Christ.

THE TRADITION OF VIBRANT CATHOLIC CULTURE

Just as the tradition of pilgrimage includes both physical and spiritual elements, Catholicism and its great humanizing traditions include the whole person—both body and soul. I witnessed students mature through an encounter with the rich and capacious traditions of Catholic culture:

at classical musical concerts located in churches, in monastic beer halls with friends, in philosophical discussions over cigars and bonfires, in festive Advent markets, and in solemn Good Friday processions.

While certain customs are best left in the pages of history, today we are often disconnected from tradition. Many of us have only tasted half the pie, leaving us nourished solely on modern ideas and practices, whether it is praying only in twentieth-century churches, listening only to contemporary music, reading modern theologians, or never having taken a pilgrimage on foot.

Today, more than ever, there is a *cri de coeur* to preserve the precious gems found in the illustrious mosaic of Catholicism throughout the ages. As Thomas Merton writes in *No Man Is an Island*, "Tradition, which is always old, is at the same time ever new because it is always reviving—born again in each new generation, to be lived and applied in a new and particular way." Time and time again, I have witnessed how young adults are inspired and moved by experiencing the beauty and tradition of the Church along the continuum of history. The adventure of faith includes not only our contemporary drama but also our ancient roots, customs, and doctrines. The Church—from the bishops to the faithful in the pews—should integrate these time-tested traditions into our modern lifestyle and milieu. A truly vibrant Church is relevant today, while also building on and connecting with our past.

A Decanted Tradition

The metaphor of wine is an apt one to describe the symbiotic relationship between tradition and progress, between the ancient and the modern, the old and the new. The very best wine comes from meticulously planted grapes that are grown over time, given constant attention, and prepared according to time-tested methods. The wine is aged and cellared. With time, care, and the right conditions, it deepens and develops complex nuances, aromas, and flavors. To get the best taste, however, one needs to decant the aged wine and pair it with the right foods.

Modernity yearns for a decanted, full-bodied tradition: the vibrant paradox of the old and new coming together to produce balance and completeness. Tradition, likewise, needs to breathe and encounter fresh air. Contemporary life needs the breadth and depth of age and time. In the quest for relevance, it is important to elevate our most beautiful Catholic traditions in liturgy, architecture, and culture. We need these time-tested truths and customs to mix with the current milieu to bring new life and verve to our Church's evangelical mission. As we go forth to evangelize and found a new civilization of love, we should build upon the pillars of Catholicism, the great traditions of our faith that ultimately lead us to Jesus Christ, who is ever ancient and ever new.

Mark Kalpakgian, thirty-seven, is an Armenian-rite Catholic who resides in North San Diego County with his wife, Niki, and four boys (with twins on the way)! He has held senior leadership positions in education and nonprofit management, both in Europe and in the United States. He is an avid outdoorsman who enjoys Southern California's beautiful beaches and zesty cuisine.

Corpus Christi

THE LIFE, HOPE, PEACE, JOY, AND LOVE OF THE SOUL

by Anonymous

I grew up in a very devout Catholic family. My family and I would gather every evening to pray the Rosary, read Scripture, and study the lives of the saints. We would attend Mass every Sunday and some weekdays. Once a month, my parents would take my sisters and I to perpetual eucharistic adoration. I was very young and enjoyed going because we would get to stay up late, eat *pan dulce* (sweet bread), and drink *chocolatito* (hot chocolate), and the people there were very kind. We sang songs and prayed as a community before the Blessed Sacrament. As a child, I remember seeing the great devotion that my parents had for the Eucharist. My father would prostrate before the Blessed Sacrament and I would imitate him. He would tell me that Jesus was present in the Eucharist. And I remember telling him that I didn't see Jesus. I would ask him, "*Papi*, how is Jesus there?" He would explain to me that the priest called the Holy Spirit and he changed the bread and the wine into Jesus. Jesus is hidden, my father would say, in the host, so we won't be scared to consume him, then he goes into our hearts and gives us his love. I still didn't really understand, but I believed anything he would tell me since he was so good to me and to others.

I went on to attend a Catholic elementary school that also contributed to my religious formation. The nuns from the nearby convent would often attend our school Mass. I remember that I would observe their reverence and devotion toward the Eucharist. And they would tell my classmates and I that Jesus remained in the Blessed Sacrament because he wanted to be with us, and that it made him very happy when we went to visit him.

When I later attended a four-year university, one of my English professors encouraged my interest in Our Blessed Mother. She had a great devotion to Mary, and allowed me to write a research paper on Mary's apparitions. I read all of the messages of the most popular apparitions, but the messages from Medjugorje resonated the most. They were simple, pure, humble, meaningful, and they produced a great love, peace, hope, faith, and joy in my heart. These were consistent with the Virgin that I had encountered in the Bible, Christian tradition, and personal experiences. The messages invite her children to pray the Rosary every day, attend Holy Mass, read the Bible, confess, say penance, fast, conversion, experience God's pure love, and see Jesus in everyone. She reminds us of Satan's existence and how we should yearn for heaven. This was a defining moment in my life because as I tried to live her beautiful messages with all my heart, my spirituality increased. I began attending daily Mass and adoring the Blessed Sacrament; this made me want to learn more about God, so I earned a minor in theology and religious studies.

After I graduated, I started attending my home parish again, which had a new pastor. The Masses were longer than before, and he preached amazing homilies. For example, when the pastor read the passage from the Gospel of John describing Jesus as the bread of life, he would explain that the Eucharist was the living bread that came down from heaven, and that whoever ate Jesus's flesh and drank his blood had the promise of eternal life. When discussing God's presence, he would say that God is present in his Word, in the sacraments, in the Church, but that the highest kind of presence was in the Holy Eucharist because he is there in his whole physical (body, blood, soul, and divinity) form. He preached on the eucharistic miracles, where the host had been turning into *real human flesh* throughout history. Through his homilies I learned about St. Francis's, St. Anthony's, and St. Padre Pio's strong faith in the real presence of God in the Eucharist. I learned that some saints and mystics lived on the Eucharist for years, such as St. Rita, Luisa Piccarreta, and Theresa Neumann.

The pastor's homilies increased my love, faith, understanding, reverence, and appreciation for the Eucharist. I started to confess once a week and prepare my heart with prayer before Mass. I came to realize that by receiving holy communion every day, God was shaping my life and destiny through revealing a new identity of discipleship. I understood that the Eucharist was washing away my venial sins, protecting me from deadly mortal sins, and producing life within me. I was being transformed through his body and blood that was giving me strength, courage, grace, joy, peace, love, hope, faith, and was assisting me in doing his divine will.

I began to get involved in my parish through altar serving, arranging the flowers, and cleaning the sanctuary. The president of the Legion of Mary invited me to their meetings, and I then became a member and an extraordinary minister of holy communion. I began taking the pilgrim statue of Our Lady of Fatima to homes and teaching families how to pray the Rosary. I started taking the Eucharist to the sick in the hospitals and to the homebound. I also began serving the poor through the Legion of Mary, which would provide meals for the homeless; every member would bring a dish, and we would share a meal with the poor. These gatherings and visitations to the hospital cultivated a greater love for the poor and the sick within me, helping me to see Christ in them.

In spending longer hours before the Blessed Sacrament, I started to experience the presence of God on a whole new level. I began to truly see him with my eyes of faith, and discovered what a great privilege it was to be before our Lord. This Lord, who is our Creator, gave his life for us, and humbly makes himself present in his great desire to be among us so we can experience his boundless love, goodness, and mercy.

Over time, what made the practice of ministry so meaningful was the realization of God's presence in the community. I came to experience the reality of God's presence not only in the Eucharist, but also in everyone, especially in those who are suffering. This remains one of my primary motivations to serve the Church community.

Every day after Mass, I spent time praying the Rosary and reflecting in the chapel, asking God to let me live in his divine will. I reflected on my upbringing, beliefs (e.g., Bible, Church teachings, Mary, and the lives of the saints), religious experiences, and the anticipation of seeing the kingdom of God coming upon the earth. I further reflected on how my service to God was being confirmed through the compliments, encouragement, and feedback of others. I felt that God was calling me to provide a greater service in the Church, and I wanted to receive a better training for this, so I enrolled in a masters of divinity program. This vocational discernment was a response to God's call that unfolded throughout my whole life. It involved my family upbringing, education, the sacraments, the Church community, and my religious experiences.

However, I cannot go out and help the Church transform the world through God's love if my heart is not continuously pure, humble, and filled with God's love, peace, and joy. So I ask the Church to assist me in faithfully giving witness to the gospel by increasing my love, holiness, faith, and hope. I desire to grow in these aspects and for the Church to do the same. The Church functions as a whole because she is influenced and impacted by her members. My life involves an ongoing conversion in my spiritual journey toward God. The witness of the Church will assist me in my own conversion, and I know that my conversion will likewise assist others. Therefore, I am humbly requesting the following:

1. For the Church to provide more hours and days for the sacrament of reconciliation. During confession, I also desire that the priests give more serious and thoughtful pastoral counsel as to how to prevent and avoid sin.

2. I ask for the Church to offer more teachings and catechetical opportunities on the real presence of God in the Eucharist so that the Church may attain a greater love, faith, understanding, reverence, devotion, and appreciation for the Blessed Sacrament. And since Christ is wholly present even in the smallest particle of the host, I beg the Church to use patens when distributing holy communion, and not to give the host in the hand anymore, to avoid his body from falling on the floor. I ask for every Mass to serve the blood of Christ, in order for the faithful to more fully partake in the Lord's Supper.

3. I desire more hours for eucharistic adoration to give the worship due to God and to provide the Church with more opportunities for grace, blessing, mercy, hope, love, faith, light, and spiritual renewal.

4. I hope to see clergy, lay ministers, and laity creating more prayer groups that bring peace, love, and unity that purifies, strengthens, and protects Church communities from every evil.

5. I ask that the Church speak more about heaven, purgatory, and hell, and to explain the existence and attacks of the evil one so that we may take the salvation of souls more seriously.

6. I would like to hear more homilies on God's miracles in Sacred Scripture and in the lives of the saints, as well as the miracles that continue today in order to increase our faith and give thanks and praise to God for his glorious deeds.

7. Finally, I desire for the Church to offer more Masses in Latin, since they contain a great sense of holiness, beauty, and devotion. Latin Masses assist in increasing our faith and love toward the Eucharist. This moves us to do his divine will as we serve and love God and one another in a way that truly gives witness to the Gospel.

This contributor is a traditionalist Catholic and a Mexican young adult. The Holy Eucharist is the center of the author's life. The contributor enjoys contemplating and adoring the Lord in the Blessed Sacrament, spending time in nature, and being with family and friends. The author volunteers at the local parish and in the community. The writer's role models are Jesus, Mary, the saints, his or her father, and Pope Francis.

Responding to a Call from a "Both/And" God in an "Either/Or" Church

CALLED SIMULTANEOUSLY TO MARRIAGE AND PRIESTHOOD

by Eric M. van Maarth

Like many young Catholics, I came in from the outside. I was raised in my family's Lutheran tradition, and our faith life was very strong. Since I was a child, I have felt a strong attraction to ministry in the Church. I remember playing "church" on the front porch of our house. Pretending I was the pastor, I consecrated chocolate chip cookies and Dr. Pepper, which I distributed to my brother and the other neighborhood kids. I even baptized the family dog! By seventh grade I was determined to be a Lutheran minister.

Unfortunately, like so many young people today, I drifted away from the Church in college. During that time of exploration, I learned valuable lessons and insights from other spiritual and secular traditions. I also learned about my own strengths and weaknesses, reconsidered my values, and reflected on my relationship with the Divine. For as long as I was away from the Church, however, I felt the absence of a personal and loving God. Thanks to many conversations with my Catholic roommate, I realized that in rejecting certain tenants of my denomination of origin, I had mistakenly dismissed all of Christianity. I decided Christianity deserved a second look. During my senior year of college, I participated in the Rite of Christian Initiation for Adults and was confirmed at Easter. Along with my new Catholic identity, however, the old sense of calling to sacramental ministry returned. Reluctant to renounce marriage, I cautiously began a period of discernment that would last years and was, in the end, agonizing.

I was introduced to the Capuchin Franciscans, and over time became increasingly involved with them. After volunteering for a year with the Capuchin Volunteer Corps, I lived for another year in a friary as a candidate. The call that I felt to the priesthood and its accompanying sense of urgency led to my reluctant breakup with my girlfriend of two-and-a-half years. The sense of that loss stayed with me throughout my time with the Capuchins and long after. As I entered postulancy, I prayed the words of Psalm 51: "The sacrifice acceptable to God is a broken spirit; / a broken and contrite heart, O God, you will not despise" (v. 17).

My brief time with the Capuchins was extremely blessed. The formation I experienced with them led to a total reorientation of my life. I loved the Franciscan tradition and vision. I loved the friars and their work, and living in a house with brothers made the prospect of celibacy less daunting. At the end of my year of postulancy, however, I discerned that I could not go forward with the formation process. I had hoped that someday everything would be okay, that God would come wave a magic wand and make my life more bearable because I had followed God's call. One day, however, I realized God was not going to come in and save me from my heartbreak and angst. I was not ready to proceed with the formation process until I could get some resolution around the issue of celibacy. I realized that I felt called to do the work of a priest, to share the sacraments with others, but at the end of the day, I yearned to return to a wife and home.

Leaving the Capuchins was difficult. I had come to love them, and I felt my soul being torn between two calls: the priesthood and married life. I felt angry, abandoned, betrayed, tricked, even seduced by God (cf. Jer 20:7). I felt I had been called by God to end a relationship with someone I loved to pursue the priesthood only for it to end in pain and confusion. This led to a crisis of faith that lasted several years.

Over time, however, I gradually found peace. I credit this largely with meeting my wonderful wife. We were married nearly four years ago, and since then I have experienced more of God's grace than I could have hoped for. If the angst I felt during my brief time in religious life was a spirit of desolation, then the peace I feel today is certainly a spirit of consolation. Another source of peace and joy is in my enrollment in the Franciscan School of Theology. I hope to finally be able to respond to God's call to service in the Church.

But not as a priest.

Although I discerned that I was not called to celibacy, the strong pull to sacramental ministry remains. The desire to pray the eucharistic liturgy together with others who are hungry for God, to share God's gift of love and forgiveness in the sacrament of reconciliation, to comfort the sick and dying in the anointing of the sick, is still strong. Aside from baptism and holy matrimony, however, the celebration of most sacraments of the Church is restricted exclusively to celibate men.

I am not denying that celibacy has value. Men and women everywhere are legitimately called to celibacy in religious life. My question is whether it is essential to sacramental ministry. Although a celibate priesthood is conducive to the practical matters of running a diocese or parish, it doesn't have anything to do with the essence or theology of the priesthood. If it did, the Church could not recognize its previous and current married priests as valid. Furthermore, from the Lutheran perspective in which I was raised, mandatory priestly celibacy makes no sense. Indeed, to most people outside—and many inside—the Catholic Church, priestly celibacy is seen as a holdover from the medieval ages for the purpose of maintaining power and money within the hierarchy. Also, it oftentimes leads to unhappy priests, many of whom leave the priesthood in order to answer their other calling.

In contrast, I have known many Christian clergy who are married. These Lutheran ministers, Episcopal priests, and Byzantine Catholic priests are wonderful pastors who can relate to the daily trials of their parishioners, perhaps more so than their celibate colleagues. Their families are joyfully embraced as part of the Christian community where they serve. I have also known wonderful men who left the priesthood to marry and would love to continue to serve as priests. It is true that it can be difficult for pastors and their families to maintain a balance. The choice to serve as a married minister, however, is one that rightfully includes the minister and his family together with a church administrator on a case-by-case basis rather than by the church administrator alone.

The gospel of Jesus Christ is radical, and the kingdom of God includes everyone from all walks of life. All Christians are called to pray, to participate in liturgy, to use the gifts God gives them, and to live lives of service in communion with others. It is counterintuitive to me that sacramental ministry and oversight in the Church should be restricted to celibate men. I feel that maintaining a celibate priesthood is unjust to many Catholics, including married men who are called and qualified by the Holy Spirit to sacramental ministry. It is unjust to priests and bishops who have been laicized and are restricted from exercising their eternal priesthood. It is unjust to the whole people of God, who increasingly lack access to the sacraments Christ gave them, or who are reluctant to speak with their pastors because they can't relate to the challenges in their daily lives as married Catholics. Finally, it is unjust to many priests who, although having freely chosen celibacy, may suffer loneliness and feel unfulfilled their entire lives. I believe the way to address these issues is to make celibacy for priests optional. Precedents for a married priesthood are found in Scripture, Church history, current Lutheran and Episcopal ministers converting to Roman Catholicism, non-Roman rites within the Catholic Church, and *every single other Christian community in the world.*

This raises a question I ask myself literally every day: Why remain Catholic, then? Thanks to the impetus of the Second Vatican Council and the ecumenical dialogue that has followed, there are very few differences between Catholics and Lutherans in terms of theology, sacraments, and liturgy. Many Lutherans admit that the Lutheran Reformation would not have happened in today's Catholic Church. The differences that remain are mostly about anthropology and church authority. Furthermore, I am not native to the Roman Church. I am in some respects a stranger in a strange land, a naturalized citizen. Why not return to my previous tradition? It would certainly resolve a number of personal and vocational issues in my life, and yet I choose to remain.

Truthfully, I am often not sure. There are many small reasons. The Catholic Church offers continuity with a long past (which includes married priests, bishops, and even popes). It offers a connection to over one billion Christians today from around the world who gather to pray and celebrate the Eucharist. The children and young people I see in the pews on Sunday indicate that the Spirit is still with the Catholic Church and promises to remain into the future. Besides, I see remaining in the Church in respectful dialogue as a form of loyal obedience; I *could* leave, but I don't. Finally, I stay because of my hope for Christian unity, which must include the Catholic Church if it is to be achieved at all. For our part, however, we must respond to the Holy Spirit if we are to survive and thrive in this world.

Pope Francis gives me great hope that the Catholic Church is truly listening to the Holy Spirit. I believe the Holy Father is inspired as he urges us to go out into the world, to embrace the poverty of Christ, to give ourselves to each other and not count the cost, to proclaim the love of God to all people, and to listen to and embrace the Other. These naturally lead to growth and change in the individual, and it is no different for the Church as a whole.

As priests continue to dwindle, laypeople must pick up the mantle (if not the stole). That is why I have chosen to obtain a master of divinity degree. I have often been told that I have the gifts and talents needed to be a priest. Soon I will have the education as well. As a chaplain, I will be able to counsel and console, to listen, to pray, and even bring communion to the sick. I find it tragic and absurd that I will have to tell patients that I cannot offer them the sacraments of reconciliation or anointing of the sick because I have a wife.

My need from the Church, and that of the people of God, is for ordination to the Roman Catholic priesthood to be opened to married men. By changing this discipline, the pastors of the Church would be honoring God, who has called married men to sacramental ministry in the past and is clearly still doing so today. They would open the door for thousands of new priests and the return of thousands more in the United States alone, allowing the underserved people of God to be fed, nourished, and healed by the sacraments. Finally, the primary obstacle would be lifted from the lives of countless men who feel a deep longing to respond to God's call, including my own. I would finally be able to respond to the call I have heard in the depths of my being since I was a child.

Eric M. van Maarth was born and raised in Colorado. He is currently a student in the master of divinity (MDiv) program at the Franciscan School of Theology. He lives with his wife in Oceanside, California.

The Francis Effect

HOPE AND LIBERATION IN RURAL APPALACHIA

by Brian and Kathleen DeRouen

When Jorge Bergoglio took the name Francis and, wearing simple robes, introduced himself as pope, we—along with much of the world—took notice. Simplicity and humility were not among the things that we had come to expect amid the pomp and ritual of the Vatican, and yet here they were. Pope Francis's simplicity of dress and choice of words in those first moments stirred something inside of us. Although we did not immediately know how to articulate the feeling he gave us, it was clear that Pope Francis was doing things differently and the Church, the world, and the two of us were feeling the first stirrings of the Francis Effect.

Each pope makes an impact on the Church; however, for this impact to be felt immediately in rural West Virginia is unusual. While our personal social media pages bring us stories from *America* magazine and the *National Catholic Reporter*, our friends and neighbors in Monroe County have never heard of these publications. Around here Fox News needs to cover an issue for people to talk about it, and, well, Fox has been covering him. From the car Pope Francis chooses to drive to the women, refugees, Muslims, and prisoners whose feet he has chosen to wash on Holy Thursday, he has the attention of the world. From *Laudato Si'* to his comments on capitalism, border walls, and atheists, Pope Francis is blazing a distinct path.

Pope John Paul II introduced the papacy to the world in a new way, visiting 129 countries outside of Italy. He served as an ambassador for the Church and chose to be a visible leader to Catholics and non-Catholics alike. Benedict XVI turned the focus of the papacy inward. He led the Church as an intellectual giant and defender of the traditions of the Church in an increasingly secular world. He revitalized the customs and traditions of the papacy and encouraged the world's Catholics to remember what sets us apart. Pope Francis has emphasized his role as pastor and, in a literal way, has been a pope amongst the people, specifically the poor and oppressed. As Catholics, this is precisely what we need from our Church. We need leadership, which spans the political spectrum, demonstrating that there is not one way to live the faith. As young progressive Catholics, we have benefited from what John Paul II and Benedict XVI provided, but we have *yearned* for what Pope Francis is offering. We desire to be inspired, challenged, and encouraged to talk; we want to seek out perspectives different from our own. We also need to know, as people of faith inspired by the Sermon on the Mount and social justice, that the hierarchy is with us.

As we reflected on the Francis Effect, we realized that finding contrasts within the Church helped us each to define our faith long before Pope Francis was elected. The spiritual paths that led us to our shared faith life were disparate ones, with one of us a cradle Catholic and the other finding the Church during college after being raised as an Evangelical Protestant. While faith was the cornerstone of each of our family lives, it was our studies and travels in El Salvador and Nicaragua that helped us to discover and live our faith as we do today. It was the suffering Church of Central America, standing in contrast with the comfortable parishes we had known, which helped us to begin the process of understanding our vocation.

Time in El Salvador and Nicaragua introduced us to liberation theology and the lives, work, and martyrdom of Jean Donovan, Rutilio Grande, and Ben Linder. The dirt roads of Latin America, the very ones they had walked, were so different than the ones on which we grew up. The Stations of the Cross in the University of Central America chapel were brutal sketches of tortured campesinos rather than ornate carvings of a Caucasian Christ. Learning of Ben Linder, an American engineer working to bring small-scale hydroelectricity to rural Nicaragua, was both unsettling and inspiring. He was beloved by the children of his adopted nation not because of the vaccination campaign he was working on, but because of his juggling and unicycling clown performances. He was murdered by the Contras and subsequently condemned by the United States government for putting himself in harm's way and entering a war zone in which, they claimed, he had no business being. We knew that Christ had called us to take up our cross and follow him, and yet, up until this point we had understood serving the Church as working at parish festival fish fries. While Linder's death made headlines, it was his life and joy that caught our attention and demonstrated for us what vocation looked like. We wanted the opportunity to take risks and find a different path as guided by the Spirit.

The idea of a persecuted Church full of vibrancy and struggle, walking amongst the poor, is something that we recognized clearly in the Gospels but found entirely foreign to our upper-middle-class Church experiences. From birth we had been raised as followers of Christ, and while our faith was central to our identities, our faith lives did not take the form of vocation until we witnessed the experiences of Catholics living outside of our first world bubble.

Fifteen plus years after the scales fell from our eyes during our visits to Central America, and having found one another, we are once again in the mountains. Not those of the Chalatenango Department of El Salvador, but rather southern West Virginia. The similarities between the two are not what one would expect when comparing first and third world nations. There are families living on our street without electricity or running water. The prescription opioid epidemic is leaving children without parents in numbers comparable to a war zone and crippling poverty has taken hold of most every holler. Our neighbors are the unrecognized Christ from Matthew 25. Three young fathers from our neighborhood have recently received prison sentences of thirty years or more, a young mother overdosed, and one more was killed in a drunk driving accident. The iconic photos that aroused a nation's compassion and helped spawn the war on poverty were taken in these mountains and a majority of the struggles chronicled remain.

Our home is a West Virginia county that covers almost five hundred square miles, does not have a single stoplight, and has fewer than fourteen thousand residents. Much like the Bethlehem of Christ's birth, nothing but unflattering stereotypes and backward thinking is expected from a place like this. West Virginia is ranked at or close to the bottom among the fifty states in regards to education, health, employment, income, and quality of life. Extractive industries have exploited the mountains, poisoning the rivers and children. The people are tired. This state—and Appalachia as a whole as much as anywhere—is desperately in need of hope, inspiration, and a positive direction forward.

Fortunately, hope is not an all-or-nothing commodity. The tiniest little bit from any source can bring light to the darkest of situations, and each one of us as people of faith can bring it forth. This neighborhood could not be more distant from the theology 101 classrooms and bustling campus ministry offices in which we thought we would spend our careers, but it is where we have found ourselves. We run the Alderson Hospitality House, a nonprofit bed-and-breakfast, serving friends and family of women incarcerated at the federal prison in our tiny mountain town. We do not go to work every day because our home and our work are one. Our children do not welcome us home from work at the end of each day because they are active participants in it with us and our faith is lived in the preparing of meals and making of beds. The families that come to our door are in crisis, and in their faces and in those of our neighbors we see Christ.

It is a rare and blessed thing these days to find work that inspires and sustains, and that is exactly what we have stumbled upon. Our dining room table is a place of tears and uproarious laughter, of longing, sorrow, and courage. Our guests are at a broken place in their lives and thus are wide open, raw, and real. We rarely speak explicitly of religion, but the faith that imbues the Hospitality House is one of liberation, and it is shared over the breaking of French bread and slurping of spaghetti on Friday nights. We are a community of parents and children, believers and skeptics; each of us is rich in ways and poor in others. We are a community both within and apart from mainstream American society and are the faces behind the statistics of the criminal justice system and prison industrial complex.

Finding and living our vocation does not mean that all is perfect; toilets still clog and electric bills remain difficult to pay. Last week our older boy got in trouble for flipping another student off at school, and sometimes we are the broken ones as we lose our composure with a challenging guest. We recognize, however, that the weight we feel is not our own. Our family is whole as we pray about and hope for future reunions with our guests, but sadness is a palpable component of our ministry. Likewise, frustrations with inconsiderate guests, a broken system, an oblivious public, failed public policy, and absent/silent churches—including our own—continually mount. For these reasons and many others, we need the Francis Effect. We need to read about the pope visiting juvenile detention centers and sharing meals with people struggling through homelessness. We would love to see the hierarchy in our nation follow his example and set one of their own by taking the time to literally feed the hungry, clothe the naked, and visit the prisoner. The Church our Holy Father envisioned, one that is poor and with the poor, is one in which—like our neighborhood—we find ourselves at home and there is no place we would rather be.

Brian and Kathleen DeRouen run the Alderson Hospitality House with their feral sons, Micah Henri and Vitale Francis. They met during graduate school at the University of Dayton, where they studied pastoral ministry and theology. When they are not doing laundry and preparing meals at the house, Brian can be found running ultramarathons and Kathleen is known as "Mary Magda-Slam" of the Greenbrier River Rollers roller derby league. They are passionate about their pet pig, Larry, vegetarianism, faith, the environment, feminism, nonviolence, and the town of Alderson, West Virginia, where Brian runs the local food pantry and Kathleen is a founding member of the Alderson Community Food Hub.

Questions

1. Dr. Tricia Bruce writes in her précis that while there is some evidence of polarization in the U.S. Church, there is considerable overlap among Catholics as well. And, as she notes, Pope Francis is comfortable with this ideological diversity, likening it to a symphony with various timbres coming together in a lovely harmony. To what extent do you experience American Catholicism as a symphony or a cacophony?

2. How do you feel about Catholics who identify as conservative/traditional or progressive/liberal? Do you feel like either of these labels suits you? Before reading these essays, what were some of the positions that you believed these ideological orientations would have elevated?

3. These essays discussed very different things, yet they did not say anything that contradicted one another. What are core principles from the traditionalist essays? What are the most central issues for the authors who identify as progressive? What might be the common ground they share?

Hispanic Young Catholics

by Hosffman Ospino

About 60 percent of all Catholics younger than eighteen and nearly half (46 percent) of all Catholic millennials (ages eighteen to thirty-four) in the United States are Hispanic.[1] The numbers speak loudly and clearly. We no longer need to imagine a future when Hispanics become a numeric majority among U.S. Catholics. That future is already here. In many corners of the United States and in thousands of faith communities, to speak of Catholicism is to speak of how Hispanic Catholics live and celebrate being in relationship with Jesus Christ.

Two simple yes-or-no questions for the reader: Are you and your parish/organization genuinely engaging young Hispanic Catholics? Have you taken the appropriate time to understand the experiences of this important population? These answers should determine a path of action, with the

---

1. Cf. Hosffman Ospino and Patricia Weitzel-O'Neill, *Catholic Schools in an Increasingly Hispanic Church: A Summary Report of Findings from the National Survey of Catholic Schools Serving Hispanic Families* (Huntington, IN: Our Sunday Visitor Press, 2016), 5; Michael Lipka, "A Closer Look at Catholic America," Pew Research Center, September 14, 2015, http://www.pewresearch.org/fact-tank/2015/09/14/a-closer-look-at-catholic-america/.

following observations serving as a roadmap. How well we engage young Hispanic Catholics *now* will significantly define the vibrancy of U.S. Catholicism for the rest of this century.

HISPANIC AND (STILL) CATHOLIC

Although Hispanics have been present in the U.S. territory for more than five hundred years, during the last half-century, the Hispanic presence has experienced accelerated growth, literally doubling every ten years. Migration waves from Latin America and the Spanish-speaking Caribbean have played a major role. About 20 million Hispanic immigrants live in the country today; about two-thirds self-identify as Catholic. Nevertheless, it is the children and grandchildren of these immigrants who are driving much of the demographic change in the Catholic Church. Two-thirds of Hispanics are U.S. born. Catholic self-identification is not as strong in this group as in the case of the immigrant generation, yet most young Hispanics still see themselves as Catholic.

Hispanics are in general a very young population. The average age is twenty-nine. About 58 percent of Hispanics are younger than thirty-three. We know that nine out of ten Hispanics younger than eighteen (93 percent) and about half of Hispanic millennials were born in the United States. The majority of these young women and men have embraced many core aspects of the predominant culture in which they live. They speak English as their everyday language, their lives are shaped by the regular use of technology and social media, and they find themselves constantly negotiating the influence of multiple cultural trends like their peers. They are American young people in the full sense of the phrase.

At the same time, most young Latinos/as remain culturally Hispanic. This means that they continue to be nurtured

211

by values and practices from the various Hispanic/Latino cultures that coexist in neighborhoods, towns, and cities throughout the United States of America. The Hispanic cultural and religious influence is channeled in various ways, most importantly through the family. The majority of young Hispanics presently live in households with at least one immigrant parent or relative. Pastoral experience indicates that immigrants tend to be more intentional in the process of fostering a sense of religious identity among the younger generations, usually drawing upon what they learned in their countries of origin.

Young Latinos/as are deeply influenced by a strong Catholic imagination that pervades much of Hispanic cultures. Young Hispanics are more likely than other young Catholics to participate in Marian devotions and other practices of popular Catholicism. One cannot minimize the importance of the *quinceañera* ritual—with its mixture of religious and secular elements—among young Hispanics and their families. The use of iconic representations of Jesus and Mary is common within this group.[2] Young adult Hispanic Catholic couples often baptize their children and bring them for first communion and confirmation, even though most are not sacramentally married nor actively involved in parish life.

Fluid Identities, Challenging Paradigms

Pastoral leaders and educators working with young Hispanic Catholics need to remain aware of the various factors that make the experience of this group particularly complex. Not only must they journey along the normal process

---

2. See Tomás, V. Sanabria, "Personal Religious Beliefs and Experiences," in *Pathways of Hope and Faith among Hispanic Teens*, ed. Ken Johnson-Mondragón (Stockton, CA: Instituto Fe y Vida, 2007), 44–68.

of becoming adults and negotiating the challenges of growing up in the U.S. sociocultural context, but they must also sort out who they are as Hispanics in the United States.

In the early 2000s, Instituto Fe y Vida, Inc., acknowledging that there is not one all-encompassing category that fully captures the experience of young Hispanics, proposed four pastoral categories to name the fluid reality of Latino/a adolescents: identity seekers, mainstream movers, immigrant workers, and gang members and high-risk teens.[3] These categories remain helpful and easily correlate to the experience of Hispanic young adults. From a religious perspective and considering their growing numbers, I would add a fifth category: Hispanic "nones" (that is, nonreligiously affiliated), with particular attention to former Catholics. There is much to learn from this group to assess present pastoral initiatives and envision new ones.

Young Hispanic Catholics are most likely bilingual and bicultural. These young women and men are both Hispanic and American. They are Catholic like their immigrant relatives and religious like other young Christians in the country figuring out how to incorporate their faith into their lives amidst pluralism. When contending with these binaries, adults and pastoral leaders are often tempted to expect that young Hispanics have to choose one or the other. Such expectation reflects an either/or mentality that often prevails at home, at church, and in the larger society.

In various ministerial contexts, immigrant adults typically want U.S. born, young Hispanics to remain culturally and religiously like them. In turn, Catholics of different backgrounds often expect that these young women and men embrace models of ministry that have worked well primarily with Euro-American young Catholics as if such models were

---

3. See Ken Johnson-Mondragón, "Socioreligious Demographics of Hispanic Teenagers," in *Pathways of Hope and Faith among Hispanic Teens*, 38.

culturally neutral and always adaptable. Another common expectation is that young Hispanics become fully "Americanized," hinting at the idea that to do this they must abandon the language and cultural roots of their relatives. All such expectations are rather unrealistic and impractical. Pushing them too much can have negative consequences. Let us not forget that youth ministry initiatives normally reflect the vision of reality that we hold as well as our understanding of young people.

Catholic parishes and dioceses nationwide continue to discern best approaches to meet the spiritual and pastoral needs of Hispanic youth. Communities that bank on the idea that young Hispanics should learn and practice their faith more like their immigrant relatives tend to invest in initiatives that are mostly in Spanish and replicate models that were developed somewhere else yet may not have the same effectiveness within the U.S. socioreligious context. Communities that over-rely on assimilationist perspectives get caught up in a vicious cycle of ignoring or dismissing the potential of what young Hispanics bring in terms of faith and culture, while imposing idealized models that may not necessarily respond to the needs of communities that are culturally diverse, multilingual, and not always middle or upper class.

The main consequence of this prevalent either/or mentality is the marginalization of this important group of Catholics, upon whom much of the future of U.S. Catholicism depends. Marginalization in turn leads to isolation, and ultimately to defection. It is painful, yet not surprising, that, in recent decades, about 14 million Hispanics (one in four) stopped self-identifying as Catholic, most of them young and born in the United States. They drifted away.[4] These are not

---

4. Cary Funk and Jessica Hamar Martinez, "The Shifting Religious Identity of Latinos in the United States," Pew Research Center, May 7, 2014, http://www.pewforum.org/2014/05/07/the-shifting-religious-identity-of-latinos-in-the-united-states/.

necessarily disaffected young Catholics or people inclined to reject religion altogether. In fact, one can confidently assert that, given their rootedness in the vibrant Hispanic cultures from which they draw inspiration, religion still plays an important role in their lives.

In the not-so-distant past, Catholic schools and colleges played a major role in supporting Catholic youth. These spaces proved to be very effective in preparing millions of young Catholics to succeed in society and to grow in their faith. Tens of thousands of young women and men from Catholic educational institutions went on to exercising important leadership roles in the Church (e.g., priests, vowed religious, lay ecclesial ministers) and the larger society. Nonetheless, now that Hispanics are the majority of young Catholics, very few benefit from such institutions. As of 2017, only 4 percent of school-age Catholic children are enrolled in Catholic schools (about 317,000 of 8 million) and barely 10 percent of students enrolled in Catholic colleges (approximately 90,000) are Hispanic.[5]

A worrisome combination of prejudice, unrealistic expectations, and lack of investment in intentional pastoral accompaniment is imperiling how young Hispanic Catholics discern their vocations as Christian disciples here and now as well as their commitment to faith communities that often fall short from understanding and affirming their potential.

SEIZE THE MOMENT

My hope is that this brief analysis serves as a wake-up call and a motivation for Catholic pastoral leaders and organizations

5. Ospino and Weitzel-O'Neill, *Catholic Schools in an Increasingly Hispanic Church*; see also Hosffman Ospino, ed., *Our Catholic Children: Ministry with Hispanic Youth and Young Adults* (Huntington, IN: Our Sunday Visitor, *forthcoming*).

to redouble our outreach efforts toward this population. We must seize the moment! Seizing the moment demands making major commitments. I want to suggest three.[6] First, we must ensure that young Hispanics see the Church as a home where they belong. Parishes and schools in particular need to make a preferential option for pastoral initiatives that sincerely welcome and engage these young Catholics. Second, we must create spaces where young Hispanics encounter Jesus Christ in truly transforming ways and nurture their Christian vocation. This is a time for faith formation initiatives that are creative and take culture, language, and social location seriously. Third, we must accompany young Hispanic Catholics in the contexts and realities in which their lives unfold. Millions of them live in the peripheries of Church and society. Ministry to young Hispanic Catholics in the United States must be defined by its prophetic character.

Young Hispanics are a blessing to the Catholic Church in the United States. It is time to embrace this blessing.

Hosffman Ospino, PhD, is an Associate Professor of Hispanic Ministry and Religious Education at Boston College. His research explores how the relationship between faith and culture shapes Christian ministerial and educational practices. He served as the principal investigator for the National Study of Catholic Parishes with Hispanic Ministry *(2014) and the* National Survey of Catholic Schools Serving Hispanic Families *(2016). He has authored and edited nine books.*

---

6. See National Catholic Network de Pastoral Juvenil Hispana–La RED, *Conclusions: First National Encounter for Hispanic Youth and Young Adult Ministry* (Washington, DC: USCCB, 2008). These priorities appeared repeatedly throughout this document. The meeting took place in 2006.

Ordinary Rhythm

by Gerardo Rojas Mayorga

I am the oldest of three children, and I spent most of my childhood in a beautiful town two hours from Mexico City. Growing up in Valle de Bravo, I felt like I was living in paradise. This was not just because of the majestic forests, mountains, and waterfalls that surrounded this valley; mostly it was because I grew up in a family that was joyful. Community is a strong value in Mexican culture. I am grateful that a loving family was my first experience of this value. This joy and love I experienced growing up manifested in the way my father loved and respected my mother, in the way my parents took care of my siblings and me, and by the way God was made present in our daily lives.

Prayer was part of our ordinary rhythm of life. As soon as we woke up, we were encouraged to thank God and ask for his assistance in the day ahead. Every meal was eaten as a family and a typical blessing preceded each of them. Time spent in the car always began with prayer, and for long trips my mother would always lead us in praying the Rosary. Whenever we passed by a church, we did the sign of the cross. At night my parents would pray with us before going to bed and make the sign of the cross over our bodies. This experience was not exclusive to my immediate family.

217

I could expect the same rituals and prayers from my friend's family and my cousins' families. My faith in God was lived and shared in community. Although I probably did not notice it at the time, this rhythm of prayer taught me to be grateful for each moment of the day and to have faith in God's care. In fact, faith in God was essential for us, especially in times of uncertainty. Both of my parents grew up, graduated from college, and worked in Mexico City. However, when I was four years old, my parents made the brave decision to leave Mexico City. I call this decision brave because by going away from the city, they were also going away from the family support and job security that they enjoyed there. However, the one thing that has always accompanied them is their faith in God's providence. I remember many times hearing my father tell me about his favorite Scripture passage: "So do not worry about tomorrow, for tomorrow will bring worries of its own. Today's trouble is enough for today" (Matt 6:34). Faith in God has shaped most of my parents' decisions. That is why we lived in Valle de Bravo for eight years; a town with no supermarkets, malls, or many paved roads. Mexico City's infrastructure made more sense in terms of stability. However, Valle's natural beauty made God's grace and providence real. This faith in God is also why we now live in San Diego, California. When I was thirteen years old, my parents decided that the best future for our family awaited us across the border; then they trusted God to provide the rest. San Diego has been our home ever since; however, it quickly became clear to me that the rhythm of prayer that covered life and culture growing up in Mexico would face challenges in the United States.

The first thing I appreciated about San Diego is how clean, orderly, and safe everything felt. I remember using the post office for the first time and marveling at the reality that my letter would be delivered in a timely and safe manner to its destination. My experience with mail growing up in Valle de Bravo was very different. There, if mail arrived, it was always through divine providence! Like the mail, I encountered many things in American culture that actually *worked*. It also became very clear that study, hard work, and success were very important values. Without realizing it, the dependence on God that was part of my everyday life in Mexico, was slowly making room for newfound knowledge. I was beginning to learn that all that was needed to fulfill a dream or goal was to simply work hard. This did not mean that God and faith had to go out the window. In fact, one of the first things I learned as an eighth grader was that my life had to be compartmentalized. This was the biggest cultural challenge I faced. I was used to having friends and classmates that were more like me in language, faith practice, family structure, and so forth. In San Diego, it was not difficult to make friends, but they had to be kept in compartments; math class friends, soccer team friends, youth group friends, and whatever other activities I was involved with. Instead of being part of a community, I was joining groups based on a specific interest. I soon realized that my relationship with God was beginning to become boxed in. God was not someone I shared with others or brought up in public. He was there still, but only there for me privately so that he would not make others uncomfortable.

Nevertheless, because of the incredible amount of uncertainty that governs a newly immigrated family, there was never a shortage of prayer at home. The joy that we experienced as a family in Mexico also remained with us. This helped me to realize that my parents' love and care for each other and us; coupling this with their unwavering faith in God's providence was all we needed to experience joy. Prayer continued to grace our meals and bring us together at night. It also became an essential part of my discernment for higher education. I remember being certain that God would place me wherever he needed me to be, so my prayer was always for me to understand and accomplish what he had planned. As you can imagine, this reliance on God did not stem from me alone; it was modeled after the example of my parents. Time after time God revealed his goodness to them and through them, so there was no doubt in my mind that his loving care would grace my life as long as I was open to it. *Gracias a Dios* the University of Notre Dame accepted my application and offered enough financial aid to make my attendance possible. I decided to attend the university because it was the best way to guarantee success. What I did not realize at the time was that my relationship with God needed strengthening, and I was blessed to be going to a place that would provide that.

For the first time since leaving Valle de Bravo I was once again immersed in a Catholic culture, feeling that same experience of community that integrated my life back there. The dorm that I moved into had a chapel, as did every other dorm on campus. Mass and prayer opportunities were available at many times and in many places. Best of all, I was able to make many friends who shared my faith and values. Unlike any other place I had visited in the United States, Notre Dame helped me experience a great sense of belonging. There I felt that my unique God-given gifts had a place, that my cultural background and love of God had a purpose and were of value. Most of all, I felt that my life did not need to be lived in compartments anymore; I could belong to a community and be my full self. I learned that if I allowed faith and culture back into the rhythm of what I did throughout the day, it would only enhance the fruits of my efforts. I experienced these positive reinforcements in many ways, from the prayerful atmosphere found throughout the beauty of the campus to the support and friendship of roommates, classmates, and professors. I came to understand that my Catholic faith, my Mexican nationality, and my own experience of God were gifts that would enrich the lives of those around me. Through God's will and the mentorship of many people, I now enjoy a profession as a lay ecclesial minister. However, what I am most grateful for is the understanding of God's love. Not an academic understanding, but the personal knowledge of having experienced his love through family, friends, and the beauty of creation. As a father and a husband, I realize that my most important task is to echo the love I have experienced so that it may reach those that need an encounter with the beauty and goodness of God. I owe my own understanding of this love to those that accompanied me and continue to do so.

My past and current experiences cause me to take special notice of the pastoral needs of families with young children and single adults. Parish communities need to find creative ways to support families so that they can be true witnesses of God's love and beauty. For many of our young people, the love of God is not obvious because it is not experienced at home. This is understandable as many parents either feel unprepared to bring this to their children or they see it as just one more thing to do after a long day. Parishes could support ill-equipped and overworked parents by sponsoring a retreat or day of prayer and reflection.

Given the strong emphasis on the individual in today's society, young people who are transitioning into adulthood need communities that will help them understand their God-given gifts and talents. On a college campus, this can be done through small faith-sharing communities, Bible study groups, and social service projects. Similar activities should also be made available to young adults who are not part of a college campus.

Neither of these projects will happen on their own; they

need deliberate effort. My time facilitating the recent Synod on the Family in the Diocese of San Diego taught me that Church leaders better accompany families and single young adults when they listen, learn, and respond in a thoughtful, intentional way. Every region and parish has its own challenges to face; clergy and lay collaboration offers the most promising and responsible way to understand and address these problems.

Gerardo Rojas Mayorga, MA, was born in Mexico City and raised in Valle de Bravo, Estado De Mexico. Gerardo's family immigrated to San Diego, California, when he was thirteen years old. Gerardo graduated from the University of Notre Dame with a BA and an MA in theology. He is serving as the Director of the Office for Youth Ministry in the Diocese of San Diego. He is thirty-five years old, has been married for ten years, and is the father of three children.

Mi Familia

Belonging as a Young Adult Mexican American Catholic

by María Olivia Galván

On the occasion of the upcoming Synod on Young People, the Faith and Vocational Discernment called upon by His Holiness Pope Francis, I take this opportunity to draw upon my experience as a young adult Latina Catholic living in the United States. I will reflect upon the familial, societal, and cultural gifts that have formed me, and I will offer insights so that our Church may respond to the needs of our young people in light of the challenges we face today.

I am a millennial, first-generation, American-born, Latina Catholic with a master's degree in pastoral theology. Both of my parents are from Mexico. My grandparents and father are from Guadalajara, Jalisco, and my mother is from Tijuana, Baja California. My father immigrated to the United States early in his childhood, and my mother arrived in the early 1980s. My younger brother and I were born and raised in Southern California, and would often visit our extended family in Tijuana.

The importance of family for Mexicans and Mexican Americans cannot be understated, and this centrality of family has shaped much of who I am today. I am fortunate to have been brought up in a household that honors my Latino roots, language, culture, history, and traditions. Simultaneously, I learned about the American culture, its language, and history in both my home and in school. Growing up in a bilingual and bicultural environment allowed me to communicate effectively in both languages and integrate myself into academic, social, and professional settings. Family, faith tradition, and culture continue to serve as the firm foundation on which I understand my very being. These gifts have inevitably shaped and formed my identity and, subsequently, my sense of belonging in society and to a faith community.

Coming from a large Latino extended family, our culture and faith traditions were always celebrated with joy. I first learned my Catholic faith—its prayers, devotions, doctrines, and Mass—in Spanish. It was not until I was in high school that I began to attend Mass in English and learn the prayers in English as well. In my family, church attendance and active involvement was inculcated at a very young age. Through the examples of my parents and grandparents, I was taught to love God, our Church, and people, in both word and actions. My moral beliefs, faith, and interpersonal formation began at home; my self continues to be deeply rooted in my family. My family's immense love demonstrated that I belonged and that I was a gift to be shared with others. They taught me to love, to be understanding, to honor my family and faith, to be proud of my cultural heritage, to hold fast to truth, and to share this joy with others.

My parents' marriage has always been an inspiration to me as well. I have seen the beauty of their love, respect for one another, and most importantly, the way they live their relationship in Christ. Their witness of faith has given me a model to follow. I believe that within the vocation of marriage lies the future of the Church. Given my parents' exemplary marriage, I hope that one day I, too, will live out my vocation with the amount of love and dedication with which they have lived theirs.

In great part, the essence of my cultural roots lies in being attuned to my surroundings, particularly in identifying opportunities for intentional engagement and presence. My parents taught me intentionality when they would take my brother and me to Casa de los Pobres in Tijuana to share the things we enjoyed the most with those less fortunate. I experienced firsthand the joy and gratitude of so many children. In their eyes, there was a sense of awe and disbelief upon receiving the gifts they were given, because they expected nothing. This changed me and to this day these experiences shape my thoughts and actions as I seek to be an answered prayer to others.

My parents also taught us the importance of presence through the way we ate dinner. Dinnertime was sacred space. Our guest of honor was Jesus, and our discussion was always led in gratitude for the gift of family and the blessings that were before us. My parents and grandparents would share fascinating stories of how they experienced God's presence in their lives and in the people they encountered. They would describe moments when their faith was tested; even in the midst of facing difficult situations, they would praise God and his divine providence. Dinner was not just a typical meal, it was an experience, providing a chance to reflect upon the ways we serve God and one another. Without a doubt, this has served as vocational guidance and formation throughout my discernment.

I often find myself looking back at those experiences that have greatly impacted my life, and I ask myself these questions: Am I doing enough? Am I utilizing my gifts to their fullest potential? Throughout my academic and professional career, I was fortunate to have the support of professors and mentors who helped me identify the gifts I have and where I may best put them to use. As a single laywoman serving in diocesan ministry, I see my professional call to service fulfilled in this role.

Another source of support and accompaniment was my parish community, especially one of my catechists. As a youth, I recall feeling the great love she exemplified when sharing the Word of God with me and the rest of the students. Years later, she invited me to come assist her in class. She mentored and guided me, and it was her vivid example of being a gift of God to others that drew me to become a catechist when I was seventeen. All these gifts—these people and encounters—have helped form the person I am today. I write this aware that I come from a long legacy of lived experiences and wisdom given to me by others; these will forever stay with me.

The challenges we face today are everywhere; the imposition of societal, political, even cultural norms are successfully swaying our young people's fundamental beliefs and distancing them from the Church. Without the proper guidance, sense of belonging, and understanding of who we are, the question of what we are called to do is too quickly brushed aside. In order to counteract these pulling forces, our Catholic Church can respond pastorally in these ways:

1. Supporting families and accompanying them in their journey of faith. As I mentioned earlier, my family was my foundation, but my parish community was instrumental in reinforcing these values. This must be perfected in all parishes. Create a support system, a ministry of outreach and hospitality that welcomes, engages, and supports families and children. If the presence of the Church is there and readily available, families will feel like they matter and belong. I have heard on numerous occasions that families feel discouraged or disengaged because they are not acknowledged,

welcomed, or supported. If we want to reach our young people, we must begin with the heads of the households.

2. Being a bold Church. Young people often complain that the reason they do not come to church is because it is boring. So now that we have heard it, how can we respond? We need to provide a place where young Catholics are welcomed and feel they belong. One way in which many young people begin to ponder the ways they might respond to God's call is through experiences that make faith come alive. Parishes should offer opportunities for social justice, allowing young adults to encounter Jesus in and through the gift of service, just as I did when I was growing up. Give them responsibilities that will enliven the Church and make their presence known to the community. This will hold them accountable while it encourages them to take their faith seriously.

3. Engaging our Latino young people and being responsive to their needs. As a Latina, I see the great need of outreach that exists for the culturally diverse presence we have not only within the Diocese of San Diego, but nationwide. The future leaders of our Church are in our midst. As a bilingual, bicultural, young adult diocesan director, I am the realization of the future Church that was spoken of in years past. Our Church needs to identify, mentor, guide, and empower our Latino young people. They make up the majority of Catholics under thirty today and their presence within American Catholicism is steadily growing. The efforts we begin today in favor of their formation will bear abundant fruit in the years ahead.

My hope is that the voices, reflections, and experiences shared in this collection will weave a tapestry of common themes that will empower our Church to actively seek opportunities to engage and inspire young adults. Young people are our hope for the future; however, their discernment and call to vocation cannot be nurtured if it is not lived and experienced within family life and supported within a faith community. The signs of the times call for us to be bold, to imagine and create new ways of addressing the needs of our young and emerging church. We are all called to share the love of Christ in transformative ways, ways that will lead our young people to an enthusiastic response to God's call.

María Olivia Galván, is a thirty-four-year-old, first-generation, American-born Latina. Native to Chula Vista, California, María obtained her master's degree in pastoral theology with an emphasis on pastoral leadership from Loyola Marymount University in Los Angeles. She currently serves as the Director for the Office for Evangelization & Catechetical Ministry in the Diocese of San Diego.

Questions

1. Dr. Hosffman Ospino asked two questions of the reader at the outset: "Are you and your parish/organization genuinely engaging young Hispanic Catholics? Have you taken the appropriate time to understand the experiences of this important population?" Regardless of whether you answered yes or no, what are some ways that you can better welcome and minister Hispanic Catholics in your region?

2. Ospino also mentioned that the number of religiously unaffiliated is growing among Latinos/as. What are some of the reasons this may be happening? What clues do the essays offer in catching Latino/a Catholics, especially young adults, on the margins?

3. In stark contrast to the more individualist mores of American culture, both essays underscored the importance of family and community. How can the wider American Church better incorporate this deep sense of solidarity into its fabric? What other lessons can non-Latino/a Catholics learn from these voices and fellow Latino/a Catholics?

Black Catholic Young Adults

A BROADER CONTEXT

by Tia Noelle Pratt

I spent the beginning of my childhood as a member of a predominantly African American parish. In such a parish, the idea of being both black and Catholic was not the least bit unusual—especially in a family with a Catholic tradition going back hundreds of years. It was not until I was a young adult that I learned that conventional wisdom holds that being both black and Catholic occurs so infrequently that some consider it a disparate identity.[1] As an undergraduate student, I began researching African American Catholic identity in order to better understand why such conventional wisdom prevailed in a society that claims large numbers of both Roman Catholics and African Americans. As I continued my research in graduate school and in my career, I continually encountered a false perception that Roman Catholicism is too staid, cerebral, and ritualistic to appeal to African Americans.[2]

---

1. Jenice Armstrong, "Blacks and Catholicism: It's not an Oxymoron," *The Philadelphia Daily News*, September 28, 2015, http://www.philly.com/philly/news/pope/20150928_Blacks_and_Catholicism__It_s_not_an_oxymoron.html.

2. Rev. Edward K. Braxton, "Black Catholics in America: A Challenge to the

While there are over 74 million Roman Catholics in the United States and nearly 42 million African Americans, there are only 3 million African American Catholics.[3] The dissemblance in these numbers have little to do with the rituals that are hallmarks of Roman Catholic practice. Rather, the reality of why these numbers do not add up becomes clear only when the consequences of systemic racism are included in the conversation. As sociologist Joe R. Feagin says, "From the 1600s to the 2000s, this country's major institutions have been racially hierarchical, white supremacist, and inegalitarian...each part of U.S. society—the economy, politics, education, religion, the family—reflects the fundamental reality of systemic racism."[4] A plethora of scholarship on the Catholic Church in the United States articulates this point in demonstrating that black Catholics in the United States have spent centuries on the fringes of American Catholicism, leaving them marginalized not only in society but also in their Church.[5] Slavery, exclusion from the priesthood

Church's Catholicity," in *One Lord, One Faith, One Baptism: The Hopes and Experiences of the Black Community in the Archdiocese of New York*, vol. 2, *Appendices* (New York: Archdiocese of New York, Office of Pastoral Research, 1988), 63–82; and C. Eric Lincoln, *Race, Religion, and the Continuing American Dilemma* (New York: Hill and Wang, 1999).

3. Center for Applied Research in the Apostolate, "Frequently Requested Church Statistics," accessed May 22, 2017, http://cara.georgetown.edu/frequently-requested -church-statistics/; U.S. Census, "Quick Facts: United States," accessed May 22, 2017, https://www.census.gov/quickfacts/table/PST045216/00; and United States Conference of Catholic Bishops (USCCB), "African-American Demographics," updated February 2017, http://www.usccb.org/issues-and-action/cultural-diversity/ african-american/demographics/.

4. Joe R. Feagin, "Toward an Integrated Theory of Systemic Racism," in *The Changing Terrain of Race and Ethnicity*, ed. Maria Krysan and Amanda E. Lewis (New York: Russell Sage Foundation, 2004), 203–223, at 204 and 206.

5. Cyprian Davis, *The History of Black Catholics in the United States* (New York: Crossroad Publishers, 1990); John T. McGreevy, *Parish Boundaries: The Catholic Encounter with Race in the Twentieth-Century Urban North* (Chicago: The University of Chicago Press, 1996); Thomas Murphy, *Jesuit Slaveholding in Maryland, 1717–1838* (New York: Routledge, 2001); and Stephen J. Ochs,

and religious life, and segregated sanctuaries and communion lines are just a few ways black Catholics have been ostracized. While this scholarship depicts the severity of this marginalization, it does not do enough to illuminate the repercussions of more than four hundred years of alienation and oppression.

My research shows that African American Catholics have combined the traditions of Roman Catholicism and the African American religious tradition into a unique identity as a way to reject the myth that being both black and Catholic is a disparate identity.[6] This combination is most clearly articulated at Mass, where my research has identified three styles of liturgy—*traditional, spirited,* and *gospel*—that incorporate homilies, music, and church aesthetics to create a distinct "cultural expression that leaves parishioners satisfied in their worship experience."[7] In his contribution to this volume, Ansel Augustine conveys the essence of a gospel Mass when he describes his own parish: "Mass lasts about two hours and our music and homilies are filled with messages that offer hope and encouragement in the face of the injustices of violence, murder, racism, and poverty in our communities."[8] These expressive and robust liturgies demonstrate just one way that black Catholics form a rich identity from two distinct traditions.

In researching and writing about black Catholic identity, I have spent my entire adult life in an effort to illuminate the ways systemic racism informs African Americans'

Desegregating the Altar: The Josephites and the Struggle for Black Priests, 1871–1960 (Baton Rouge, LA: Louisiana University Press, 1990).

6. Tia Noelle Pratt, "Black Catholics' Identity Work," in *American Parishes: Remaking Local Catholicism,* ed. Gary Adler, Tricia C. Bruce, and Brian Starks (New York: Fordham University Press, *forthcoming*).

7. Pratt, "Black Catholics' Identity Work," 4.

8. Ansel Augustine, "Black Catholicism: A Gift to Be Shared," found in this volume.

present and future in the Roman Catholic Church. Millennial generation black Catholics embody the intersection of two key constituencies in the Church: racial minorities and young adults. These two groups are pivotal for the Church's growth—and perhaps its very survival—over the coming decades. Racial minorities are becoming an increasingly larger share of the Roman Catholic population in the United States.[9] In fact, among the post–Vatican II and millennial generations of Catholics—who comprise more than 50 percent of the total U.S. Catholic population—Catholics "are almost equal proportions non-Hispanic white and Hispanic or other race or ethnicity (such as African American, Asian American, Native American)."[10]

Meanwhile, the millennial generation overall is more socially and politically engaged and more social justice oriented than any generation in a half-century. Yet, our current generation of young adults is disaffected and disillusioned with institutions to a new and deeply concerning degree.[11] Black Catholic young adults are certainly not immune to this phenomenon. Institutions—especially the Roman Catholic Church—ignore this at their peril. Rather than ignoring young adults and assuming their disaffection will dissipate

9. Pew Research Center, "'Nones' on the Rise," October 9, 2012, http://www.pewforum.org/2012/10/09/nones-on-the-rise-demographics/.

10. Charles E. Zech, Mary L. Gautier, Mark M. Gray, Jonathon L. Wiggins, and Thomas P. Gaunt, *Catholic Parishes of the 21st Century* (New York: Oxford University Press, 2017), 14–15.

11. Mark M. Gray, "Young People Are Leaving the Faith. Here's Why," *OSV Newsweekly*, August 27, 2016, https://www.osv.com/OSVNewsweekly/PapalVisit/Articles/Article/TabId/2727/ArtMID/20933/ArticleID/20512/Young-people-are-leaving-the-faith-Heres-why.aspx; David Masci, "Q&A: Why Millennials Are Less Religious than Older Americans," Pew Research Center, January 8, 2016, http://www.pewresearch.org/fact-tank/2016/01/08/qa-why-millennials-are-less-religious-than-older-americans/; and Tia Noelle Pratt, "Catholic Young Adults' Attitudes towards the Church's Pro-Life Teachings: A Bellwether for the Church's Political Strategy?" *Interdisciplinary Journal of Research on Religion* 10, no. 3 (2014): 1–21.

as they get older, the Roman Catholic Church needs to actively engage young adults by specifically reaching out to them on the issues that are of concern to the millennial generation. Issues such as climate change, immigration, and gun violence specifically attract and engage young adults and are also issues with which the Roman Catholic Church has a long history of engagement and action.[12] In short, these issues form a place where the concerns of black Catholic young adults and their Church intersect.

In keeping with his teaching of Encounter, Pope Francis has chosen "Young People, Faith and Vocational Discernment" as the theme for the fifteenth General Assembly of the Ordinary Synod of Bishops in October 2018. This theme could not be timelier given Catholic young adults increasing disaffection with the Church. For African American Catholic young adults, this is a challenge of particular concern because they must also contend with the Church's legacy of systemic racism, which for many years manifested itself in

---

12. USCCB, "Confronting A Culture of Violence: A Catholic Framework for Action," 1994, accessed May 29, 2017, http://www.usccb.org/issues-and-action/ human-life-and-dignity/violence/confronting-a-culture-of-violence-a-catholic -framework-for-action.cfm; USCCB, "Welcoming the Stranger among Us: United in Diversity," November 15, 2000, http://www.usccb.org/issues-and-action/cultural -diversity/pastoral-care-of-migrants-refugees-and-travelers/resources/welcoming -the-stranger-among-us-unity-in-diversity.cfm; USCCB, "Global Climate Change: A Plea for Dialogue, Prudence and the Common Good," June 15, 2001, http:// www.usccb.org/issues-and-action/human-life-and-dignity/environment/global -climate-change-a-plea-for-dialogue-prudence-and-the-common-good.cfm; USCCB, "Testimony Submitted for the Record on Behalf of the United States Conference of Catholic Bishops," February 12, 2013, http://www.usccb.org/issues-and-action/ human-life-and-dignity/criminal-justice-restorative-justice/upload/USCCB-Senate -Testimony-Proposals-to-Reduce-Gun-Violence-2013.pdf; USCCB, "Demographics," updated February 2017, http://www.usccb.org/issues-and-action/cultural-diversity/ african-american/demographics/; and USCCB and Catholic Bishops of Mexico, "Strangers No Longer: Together on the Journey of Hope," January 22, 2003, http:// www.usccb.org/issues-and-action/human-life-and-dignity/immigration/strangers -no-longer-together-on-the-journey-of-hope.cfm.

a dearth of opportunities for ordained and religious life for African American Catholics. Consequently, black Catholic young adults belong to an institution where they see few episcopal, clerical, and consecrated leaders who look like them. For black Catholics and those who work in black Catholic ministry, the disaffection of Catholic young adults is only one part of the issue at hand. It is essential to also contend with the systemic racism that still plagues the Church. As Ansel Augustine writes, "At times, we feel like 'motherless children' fighting for the Church we love to love us back."[13] Shingai Chigwedere, another contributor to this volume, reiterates this point saying, "As a Black Catholic, it can be hard to feel that sense of belonging when I don't encounter many parishioners who look like me."[14] To truly live Pope Francis's message of Encounter, the synod—along with diocesan and parish leaders—must encounter black Catholic young adults not only as young people, but also as African Americans, and as women and men who are an essential part of the Church. For far too long, black Catholics in the United States have not seen their own image reflected in their religious leaders in a substantive way. Out of the 3 million African American Catholics in the United States, there are only 250 priests, 437 deacons, 400 religious sisters, and 50 religious brothers who are African American.[15] These staggering numbers—a consequence of hundreds of years of marginalization—illuminate the need for the Church to authentically encounter African American Catholics by acknowledging the Church's mistreatment of African Americans and intentionally reflect on what this disenfranchisement has done to a community who, as Augustine writes in his essay in this volume, wants "the Church [they] love to love [them] back."

---

13. Augustine, "Black Catholicism," found in this volume.
14. Shingai Chigwedere, "Finding Myself in the Church," found in this volume.
15. USCCB, "African-American Demographics."

An encounter of this magnitude will neither be quick nor easy. Yet, it has enormous potential and must be done. It is only through an effort this great that the Church can begin to alleviate the disaffection seen in the millennial generation and do the necessary work to increase religious vocations among African Americans. Encountering one another, and Jesus, at this level can lead to a Church that is inclusive in worship styles, ministry, and vocations. This level of encounter, inclusion, and diversity is essential for the Church to be not only Catholic, but also catholic.

Tia Noelle Pratt, PhD, is a sociologist of religion specializing in the Roman Catholic Church in the United States. Specifically, her research includes experiences of African American Catholics, systemic racism in the U.S. Catholic Church, and millennial generation Catholics. She is a visiting instructor in the sociology department at St. Joseph's University in Philadelphia. Tia Noelle has recently begun work on a book about systemic racism in the U.S. Catholic Church and its impact on identity work among African American Catholics.

Finding Myself in the Church

by Shingai Chigwedere

I love my faith! I cannot imagine being anything other than Catholic. My mom is one of my spiritual role models. She was raised Methodist and converted to Catholicism in 1997. She raised my siblings and I in the Catholic faith and ensured we received our sacraments. As a non-Catholic, she made a promise to raise the children Catholic to the best of her ability. She did an amazing job! My mom embodies the generous spirit of the black Catholic Church I have experienced. I was born in Zimbabwe, a country that is 99 percent black. The Mass is a very spiritual and lively celebration. The community is welcoming. The hymns are accompanied by drums and rattles, creating these beautiful, melodious sounds. Anyone can feel free to stand up in their pew, clap, and sway back and forth to the music. The youth frequently sing and dance in front of the altar. At the presentations of the gifts, the giftbearers perform a simple dance up the aisle. The Mass celebration engages all your senses. In addition, there is a strong sense of community, with black elders all around with whom you can connect. You see a lot of black families, and as a single black Catholic, that is really nice to see. My description may sound familiar because I have also experienced many of these characteristics in some black Catholic churches in the United States. However, this has not been the standard experience for me in the suburban parishes to which I have belonged. Overall, I have had a pretty good Catholic experience, but I find most Catholic churches in the United States to be far less expressive.

Belonging to a community is an important thread in my life and for black Catholics more generally. There are experiences I cherish and opportunities I have taken because of the fellowship and belonging I found. As I moved around the country, I always ended up living in the suburbs. Frequently, I was one of a handful of black members in my parish. When I started working after graduating from college, I found myself making every effort to attend daily Mass each evening. I was yearning for a sense of belonging and community. I joined a Bible study, attended faith formation events and retreats, and helped with youth and young adult ministry. Through this, I started falling more in love with Jesus and with the eucharistic celebration. At faith formation events and other fellowship opportunities at church, I found myself always being the only black, or one of two, and the youngest, usually by ten to fifteen years. It was a bit isolating even in the midst of belonging to a parish. I did not have readily available tools to help me navigate my faith and my career aspirations as a twenty-something, Catholic, black, African woman.

I understand the word *catholic* means universal, which I equate with *diverse*. I wondered where my black Catholic brothers and sisters were. I have heard from some that there isn't a connection for them with Jesus and this Church where nobody looks like them. I think about all the black priests I encounter; they are mostly African. In my twenty-three years living in the United States, I met my first non-African black priest this year. It can be hard to expect vocations to the priesthood when you can't envision the possibilities because you don't see them as examples in your daily life. It can be hard to feel that sense of belonging when, as a black Catholic, I don't encounter many parishioners who look like me. It was always encouraging for me to see a black eucharistic minister, lector, or choir member. This was a big deal because it provided examples, showing me ways that I could become more involved at my parish. This is all about inclusion, which is what Jesus preached.

One of my pastoral disappointments has been with the most recent racial strife in the United States, specifically in the city of Chicago, which is dealing with unprecedented violence. While we pray for an end to violence and for healing in our communities, I struggle with the fact that we don't have real conversations about it in our suburban parishes. I think dialogue can help us see each other as people, as God's children, and remove the fear of the unknown that causes the hate that leads to violence. It hurts to see my black brothers and sisters suffering injustice or becoming victims of violence and yet see my parish community on the sidelines. It can be awkward to start a conversation about the Black Lives Matter movement when you are the only Black person in the room. It can be perceived that I am speaking for all black people when all I want is to just have an open discussion, with all opinions welcome. I know that our Catholic faith calls us to solidarity with the poor, which means taking action to help change sociopolitical and economic structures and policies. Even though the violence does not directly affect us in the suburbs, the dialogue is necessary because it helps us to work toward a solution. Otherwise, we become bystanders watching our neighbors die from something we can, and must, help prevent. That to me is the antithesis of the gospel message.

As a black Catholic, I enjoy seeing depictions of Jesus
with darker skin. That actually helps me to relate to him
more. This year, through Ignatian imaginative prayer, I have
envisioned and encountered Jesus as not only a black man,
but an Arab man, and a Jewish man. It is wonderful that St.
Augustine, one of my favorite saints, was from Northern
Africa, from the same continent I am from! We have an opportunity to recognize the diversity of the Catholic community
with simple things like celebrating black saints. Wouldn't
that be a nice tie-in during Black History Month? Our children and young adults would see that there are great holy
men and women who look like them and were canonized.
Talk about a powerful way to spotlight role models while
showcasing the inclusive aspect of our Church.

In college, I cannot recall actively trying to discern my
vocation. I was more focused on discerning my professional
career. In 2009, I felt the need to approach my faith in a more
integrated manner. My Catholic faith became a regular part
of my life, and today, I cannot separate the two. For the past
five years, I have felt God calling me to a deeper participation in the Catholic Church. When I moved to the Chicago
suburbs in 2013, the pastoral associate at my new parish
was very welcoming and helped me integrate into the community. It was through a conversation with her about the
pastoral associate's role that I heard about something called
"pastoral studies." I had been feeling called for two years to
go back to school but had no idea what I was supposed to
study. I am halfway through a master of arts in pastoral studies at Loyola University in Chicago. If it wasn't for our pastoral associate, I don't know if I would be in school right now.
For me, the words of Marie Wilson, "You can't be what you
can't see," ring true here. In my suburban experience in the
United States, I cannot say that I have met any black pastoral
associates or directors of religious education or directors of

liturgy. Interestingly, I had never, ever thought about working for the Church, let alone in a parish setting. I don't know whether my myopic view of vocations is directly connected to my not seeing lay black Catholic leaders, but that absence did not help.

God has not yet revealed what I am supposed to do with this degree. I have read some books and met some great parishioners and professors who have shared their own journeys. I am very aware that my future opportunity as a lay minister will require a significant pay cut from my current job in corporate America. I invested in this degree because God very clearly called me to this, and I think part of my struggle is that you can do so many different things with this degree. Unlike a seminarian who gets a theological education and is guaranteed a job, I am in a different state. It would be helpful to have some pastoral guidance from the Church for such a transition.

I am energized by the wonderful things going on in the Church today. Pope Francis has reengaged many Catholics and struck a chord with the world as a loving and *authentic* spiritual leader. My desire is for the Church to grow again with parishioners who are engaged and driven by a deep relationship with Jesus Christ. The first important element to my vocation is a call to help the Church become a welcoming community that *extends invitations* to young adults to bring them into the fold. As a black Catholic, an inclusive and supportive community is important. Older adults in the church community see potential in those in their twenties and thirties, and I think we need to intentionally invite black Catholic young adults to take on visible leadership roles. By having these visible leaders, other black Catholics may then start thinking differently about their vocational options. We need to do a better job of guiding black Catholic young adults to the available resources and connecting them with mentors. As a Church, we can talk more about lay religious communities or single life. We can offer faith formation events that provide guidance and resources or have panels for parishioners to describe their journey. After all, we tend to learn more profoundly through experiences, so hearing from others could help inform, encourage, and support these important vocations. I love my Catholic Church and have great hope in our future.

Shingai Chigwedere is a forty-one-year-old joyfully Catholic, black, African woman living in suburban Chicago. She was born in Zimbabwe, moved to Canada at age nine, then to the United States at fourteen. Her father was a nonpracticing Catholic and her mother was Methodist. Shingai went to Catholic elementary and high schools.

Black Catholicism

A GIFT TO BE SHARED

by Ansel Augustine

The black Catholic community has always been very close-knit. Remembering and honoring the sacrifices of our ancestors, reflecting on the obstacles our elders overcame just so that we could worship in dignity, and looking at the struggles our youth face today inspire us to worship and experience our Catholic faith in a unique way. Growing up in New Orleans at St. Peter Claver Church in Treme, I had a unique experience of Catholicism. My parish has a world-renowned gospel choir. Our church is decorated with images of Christ, Mary, Joseph, and saints whose features are black like those who worship in the pews. Mass lasts about two hours and our music and homilies are filled with messages that offer hope and encouragement in the face of the injustices of violence, murder, racism, and poverty in our communities. In fact, during my first day of work at the archdiocese, I was brought into our vault at the chancery by an archivist who showed me the baptismal record of my great-great-grandfather who was a slave from Haiti and was baptized at St. Augustine's Church here in New Orleans. I did not know how to react to this information and was overwhelmed when I continued to reflect on the struggle that is the black, but more specifically the black Catholic, experience in this country.

I have been blessed to be invited to speak all across the country, and often, I am the only black Catholic among the speakers. Sometimes when I am at these events, people ask, "What is up with all that 'black' stuff?" or "Why does something have to be labeled as 'black and Catholic' and not just 'Catholic?'" The reason things are labeled "black and Catholic" is no different than when our brothers and sisters of other cultural backgrounds magnify their particular expressions of Catholicism. Our experiences in America through slavery, Jim Crow, and present racial and economic struggles have shaped the way we express our faith. Our African traditions also influence the ways we express our Catholicism. Our song, preaching, environment, and focus on social justice are all part of the black Catholic experience. Cultural expression among black Catholics, specifically African American Catholics, includes our artwork, dress, history, music, and others. We have a unique history that is just as much a part of the Church as anyone else's.

Black Catholics have been around since the foundation of the Church. Many scholars have shown that black people played significant roles throughout the Bible, from the Old Testament tribes to Simon of Cyrene who helped Jesus carry his cross. Black Catholics were among the first Catholics to set foot in this country, in St. Augustine, Florida, in 1513 and Los Angeles, California, in 1765. Although we have been here since the beginning, in days past the Church has viewed us as "second-class citizens," telling us on occasion when we could receive communion and where we could sit in certain churches. Also, at times the Church has viewed our expression of faith as not "authentically Catholic," or has ignored our contributions to the faith. This is why many of my peers and their families have left the Church. It is the Church's silence on topics of racism, unjust laws, mass incarceration, violence, poverty, police brutality, and so forth that continue to turn young adults of color away from the Church. Many ask the leaders to be just as vocal about the numerous right to life issues as they are about abortion. Our communities are hurting and many black Catholic young adults believe that the Church does not care. This pastoral neglect is the reason why, through my ministry, I try to bridge the gap between the hurt of my community and the typical silence of the Church.

I have worked in ministry for over eighteen years, from youth ministry to serving on the boards for the National Young Adult Ministry Association and the National Federation for Catholic Youth Ministry. In all of my positions I have had to be an advocate for black Catholics and fight for a place for my people "at the table," both in and out of the Church. Hurricane Katrina was a challenging time for my faith. Sometimes I would bring our youth ministry kids to other Catholic parishes; we were treated like we did not belong because we were the only black people there. This was insulting and hurtful because we saw people not practicing what our faith teaches about the dignity of human beings. I have had similar experiences with Catholic Youth Organization. At times we feel like "motherless children" fighting for the Church we love to love us back. These barriers inspire me to dedicate my life to educating everyone on the gifts of my community, both on the individual level and in teaching courses at the Institute for Black Catholic Studies at Xavier University of Louisiana.

When I was younger, serving in ministry was the last thing on my mind. I wanted to be a DJ, and I even had a job at one of our local radio stations. It was my home parish, especially Fr. Michael Jacques, SSE, who helped me discover my vocation as a lay minister within the Church. Fr. Mike moved down south from Maine. He was an Edmundite priest who came to New Orleans in 1984 and served as our pastor at St. Peter Claver until he died in 2013. The main thing that made Fr. Mike such a successful and loved white pastor within the black community was that he came into the parish with an open mind and not a "savior" mentality. He learned about our culture and our contributions, and he himself was transformed. He challenged us to become advocates for change within our community. He taught and preached that it is our baptismal duty to fight the injustices that plague our community. It was because of his encouragement, along that of Sr. Eva Regina Martin, SSF, that I went to school, and it was their mentoring that shaped me into the lay minister I am today. They met me where I was and loved me into who I am today; their pastoral care has served as the basis of my own ministry, which is grounded not in judgement, but love. I offer the loving challenge to the powers that be to look around and discover who is not represented and offer ways for us to build bridges so that all are included in the Church. *Catholic*, after all, means "universal."

So what can the Church do? There are many things that are causing young adult black Catholics to feel disconnected with the Church. I pose the following questions to help guide the bishops to demonstrate that the needs of the black Catholic community are important to the whole Church:

> How can the Catholic Church live out the ideas mentioned in Bishop Braxton's pastoral letter on racism and the Black Lives Matter movement?
>
> How can the Catholic Church address the new form of slavery in mass incarceration that is affecting the black community?
>
> How can the Catholic Church train vocation directors to work effectively with the black Catholic

community to raise, nurture, and keep African American vocations in priestly, religious, and lay life?

How can the Catholic Church help the pro-life movement address the pro-life issues beyond abortion that affect the black community (e.g., racism, poverty, mass incarceration, gentrification)? Also, how can the Catholic Church educate the pro-life movement to not demonize the black community when it comes to abortion?

How can the Catholic Church enlighten its members on the gifts, challenges, and contributions of African American Catholics to the Catholic Church and teach them not to regard us as second-class members or view our worship styles as somehow less authentically Catholic?

The story of black Catholics needs to be included in this ongoing Catholic story. To illustrate the peripheral existence of black Catholics, did you know that November is Black Catholic History Month? Did you know that there were three popes of African descent: St. Victor, St. Melchiades, and St. Gelasius? Did you know that there are presently four African Americans whose causes are up for canonization: Venerable Pierre Toussaint (New York), Venerable Henriette Delille (New Orleans), Mother Mary Lange (Baltimore), and Fr. Augustus Tolton (Chicago)? Most Catholics do not and this is why positions like mine as well as organizations like the Knights and Ladies of Peter Claver and others exist. We help make sure that black Catholics—African American, Caribbean, African, and others—have a place where we can collectively voice our experiences and articulate the gifts we offer to the wider church. These programs that are labeled "black" are not meant to separate, but to provide an avenue to enrich and educate all Catholics on our rich history. Our history, our dedication to the faith, and our contributions to the Church remind all of us that black Catholics are not a problem to be dealt with, but a gift to be shared with the rest of the Body of Christ.

Ansel Augustine, DMin, is thirty-nine years old and has worked in ministry for almost twenty years. He has served in his hometown of New Orleans, Louisiana, and on a national level in various capacities. Ansel has served in the Archdiocesan CYO/Youth & Young Adult Ministry Office and as the Director of the Office of Black Catholic Ministries for the archdiocese. He was also one of the contributors to the African American Catholic Youth Bible.

Questions

1. Dr. Tia Pratt opened her précis noting that some scholars have asserted that black religiosity and Catholicism are incompatible. To what extent did you (or do you) agree? Where do you think this notion of incompatibility comes from? What are some of the inherent assumptions about both black religiosity and Catholicism that underlie this belief?

2. Both of the experiential writers discussed their frustrations with the silence and inaction of so many churches in the face of violence committed against black people and other issues in the black community (e.g., mass incarceration). What should be the proper response to this at the parish level? The diocesan level? The level of the USCCB? How should you as an individual respond?

3. As Pratt notes, American Catholics—both as individuals and corporately—have explicitly excluded black Catholics from aspects of Catholic life. Dr. Augustine notes that this continues in less explicit ways today, such as being made to feel unwelcome or a diminishing of uniquely black dimensions of Catholicism. How can Catholics begin to make amends for the sins of Catholics past as well as acknowledge that black Catholicism is a full and valuable part of the American Catholic experience?

Asian and Pacific Islander American Catholic Young Adults

PERSPECTIVES AND CHALLENGES

by Stephen M. Cherry and Tricia C. Bruce

Catholic young adults of Asian or Pacific Islander (API) descents are a valuable part of the American Catholic Church. Like their parents, they represent a vast diversity of country origins, ethnic backgrounds, native languages, and religious histories. Nearly three-quarters of all Asian and Pacific Islanders in the United States today are foreign born. The rate of API migration to the United States now outpaces that of all other racial groups, including Latinos, making them the fastest growing contingent of new Americans. Second-generation Asian Americans (those born in the United States to immigrant parents) make up the next largest share of Asian and Pacific Islanders. Findings from our 2014–15 national study of Asian and Pacific Islander Catholics in the United States, commissioned by the United

States Conference of Catholic Bishops, shed light on the experiences and challenges of API young adults today.

On average, API Americans have higher education levels and household incomes than any other racial group. They are also, in general, fairly religious. One out of every five Asian and Pacific Islanders in the United States is Catholic, for a total of nearly three million nationally. The population of young API Catholics in the United States is growing. Their presence, influence upon, and retention in Catholic parishes throughout the country are already shaping the future of American Catholicism.

Like Asian Americans in general, the migration and community history of API Catholics varies substantially. At the ethnic and national origins levels, they are as diverse. Filipinos, for example, settled in the swamps of Louisiana as early as 1587. Many Asian immigrants first came to the United States in significant numbers more than a century ago, largely as low-skilled male laborers concentrated on the West Coast of the United States. One of the oldest Chinese Catholic parishes, St. Bridget, started serving Chinese immigrant laborers and their children in Los Angeles's nearby Chinatown in the 1920s. Hawaii has also been one of the largest migrant destinations for nonnative APIs. Native Hawaiians, by comparison, do not exhibit the same kind of migration history experienced by other API populations.

Laws regulating immigration to the United States have heavily influenced the size and extent of API American populations over time. Racially restrictive immigration laws introduced in 1924 substantially curbed non-European immigration, excluding Asian immigrants entirely. Many Asians who migrated to the United States in subsequent years came as military spouses and children. Revision to immigration laws in 1965 ended a long period of anti-Asian restriction, thereby revitalizing the United States as a destination for

Asians and Pacific Islanders. Growth has been fairly steady ever since. Even among communities comprised of predominantly first-generation API migrants, many have a presence in their diocese that spans decades. Some parishes, for example, formed amidst Vietnamese Catholics' refugee flight from persecution and poverty in the early 1980s. Others, including some communities of Burmese Catholics, arrived to the United States more recently.

Country of origin can matter substantially for whether or not an API young adult identifies as "Asian" American or as a specific Asian ethnicity (e.g., "Vietnamese American"). Some prefer to identify as just "American." Who is doing the asking may elicit different responses. For example, if the person asking is a white American, young API Catholics may identify as "Asian American." If an Asian American is asking the question, they might respond with, for example, "Chinese American." Sociologists of race and ethnicity acknowledge that racial identities are constructed through a combination of internal and external opinions. This means that an API young adult may be identified by others in ways that may or may not match his or her self-proclaimed identity. For example, a young person of Indian descent born in the United States may be seen by others as foreign despite her birthplace and self-perception as a native American.

Whether foreign born or native born, API Catholics bring a rich understanding of faith and religious practice into their day-to-day lives as Americans. For some young API Catholics, their ethnic and Catholic identities are nearly synonymous. American young adults born in the Philippines, for example, may see their Filipino identity and Catholic identity as inseparable given that Catholicism is so culturally pervasive in the Philippines. The overwhelming majority of Filipinos are Catholic. Other API young adults, by contrast, may navigate a near incompatibility between their ethnic and

Catholic identities. Outside of parish interactions, API youth may be faced with imposed labels that do not allow for them to be seen as Christian, let alone Catholic. By identifying as Catholic, API youth might find acceptance among American-born Christian peers but, at another level, experience skepticism toward their culturally specific faith practices. Some Asian American Catholics talk of being "othered" religiously among family, peer groups, or neighbors just as they are "othered" racially as people of color.

The Second Vatican Council (1962–65) brought a greater openness to incorporating Asian and other local cultures into parish life. For many API Catholics, this translates into the option for Mass in preferred languages, meaningful ethnic imagery in church, and Asian-specific cultural traditions throughout the liturgical year. An increasing number of Catholic parishes offer Mass in Asian languages. Some predominately API parishes cater to different generations and blended families by celebrating multiple Masses at different times. some in Asian languages, others in English. API American Catholics are more likely than other Catholics to speak a non-English language at home. Many say that they prefer prayers, Mass, and other sacraments in Asian languages. This also helps to explain why API Catholics frequently drive past a geographically closer parish to belong to a parish that more closely meets their specialized ministry needs. API Catholics twenty-five years old and younger are less likely than their parents to speak an Asian language fluently, particularly if they were born in the United States. Those born in the United States often straddle two linguistic worlds, speaking an Asian language at home with family and English outside the home. This kind of linguistic bridging is common among second-generation immigrants in the United States.

Many API Catholics describe enduring tensions between the culture they or their parents left behind, and the normative culture introduced by becoming "American." Catholic parishes can act as key sites of cultural preservation, serving as spaces where distinctively Asian expressions of faith and life may be taught, preserved, and carried forth. Young adults frequently feel pressured by family, particularly parents, to embrace traditions, while simultaneously pressured by friends to fit in. This can lead to cultural incompatibility or even cultural clash. Some API young adults embrace dominant American cultural patterns learned through peer and community socialization, perhaps as a strategy to distance themselves from "foreign" stereotypes regardless of their own nativity. This desire to be seen as "American," however, may come at the cost of their parents' beloved cultural heritage.

The strength of API Catholicity among young adults will depend heavily upon the community they were raised in, the concentration of coethnic Catholics in their area, and the degree to which their parents are religiously active in their parish church. One of the greatest concerns API Catholic parents raise is that of children maintaining the Catholic faith across generations. Many first-generation Asian and Pacific Island community members state that they are concerned that their children, the second generation, do not participate as heavily in Catholic traditions, speak their language, understand their heritage, or know what their parents went through to get to the United States. Faith and cultural retention can operate hand-in-hand, but never seamlessly.

In many respects, API young adults are less religious. They attend Mass less often than their parents after leaving home. They read the Bible less often. They are also less likely to venerate national and regional saints or practice novenas. API Catholic young adults have arguably become more American by becoming less religious. Nevertheless, this trajectory can be offset by the religious involvement of family and peers. Parish youth ministry offerings also influence young API

Catholics' levels of religiosity. Parishes with sizable numbers of API young adults are more likely to foster religious activity, especially where the church actively develops such programming. Parishes with strong API ministries connect API Catholics with peers who can help support each other's Catholic practices and provide spaces to address shared issues of identity. Catholic ministries on college campuses likewise play an important role in activating and maintaining the faith lives of API young adults.

All of these variables, paired with significant transitions that all emerging adults undergo, intersect and work together to shape the personal and collective identities of API American Catholic young adults today. The contemporary American Church is uniquely positioned to provide resources to foster leadership roles as API young adults mature further to adulthood and can help mitigate potential clashes across generational lines.

Stephen M. Cherry, PhD, is an Associate Professor of Sociology at the University of Houston Clear Lake. He is the author of Faith, Family and Filipino American Community Life *(Rutgers University Press, 2014) and coauthor/editor of* Global Religious Movements across Borders: Sacred Service *(Ashgate, 2014). In 2006, he received the Society for the Scientific Study of Religion Distinguished Article Award.*

Tricia C. Bruce, PhD, is an Associate Professor of Sociology at Maryville College and the University of Texas at San Antonio. Her books include Faithful Revolution *(Oxford University Press, 2011),* Polarization in the US Catholic Church *(Liturgical Press, 2016), and* Parish and Place *(Oxford University Press, 2017). She coleads The American Parish Project and has conducted applied research for the United States Conference of Catholic Bishops.*

Rosaries and Liturgical Accoutrements

DOORWAYS ON MY SACRED, ORDINARY PATH

by John Michael Reyes

I have been to the Philippines three times. From 2013, I vividly remember my mom's hometown church, with a shrine to St. Joseph just to the left of the sanctuary. My mom walks through the cavernous church with the local bishop to the familiar shine. She sifts through dried flowers, finding a plaque. Like those visiting the Vietnam Wall, she caresses her fingers over the plaque, which reads, "Donated by Dalmacio Briones, Sr. and family," and tears flood her eyes. She and I were visiting the Philippines after the death of her mother, Veurita "Vita" Briones. Having buried my grandmother in the States earlier in the year, my mom desired to go through my grandmother's estate, and I wanted to explore my family's history and culture. Thus, we both visited the Philippines ultimately to find something. Surprisingly, it was in that church that I, too, found what I was looking for: I saw the connection between my culture and identity, and realized that my faith is central to both.

From the beginning of my life, my domestic church loved me into the faith. In Filipino culture, one cannot underestimate the role that mothers have in the family. Growing up, my mom and I did something that most kids and parents did not. I remember preparing for school by not only eating breakfast and watching cartoons, but also by praying the Rosary. Together we sat on her bedroom floor in front of various Blessed Mother statues, the Santo Niño statues with copes that she and a local tailor had sewn, dozens of prayer cards taped to the walls, and old palm branches of Palm Sundays past. It felt like tough love at times because not a day would go by that we would not observe the devotion. Sometimes if we did not pray at home, I would longingly watch my classmates in the schoolyard while the Rosary cassette "did its thing," only joining them after the final Sign of the Cross.

The intertwined celebration of Filipino cultural identity and Catholic spirituality is so important; praying the Rosary is one of many ways we continue the beloved traditions and rituals from the homeland. The Rosary became a daily, living sacrifice to encounter God, and is particularly consoling to Filipinos in the event of a death. Prayer begins on the day of death and continues for nine days, with another novena concluding the fortieth day after the death (when the soul is believed to enter heaven), and another novena ending on the first year anniversary of the death.

All this I experienced at the death of my maternal grandmother. The liturgist in me found the power of prayer and ritual to be soothing. Amid our emotions, the repetition of the prayers was calming. I think that is why Filipinos pray the Rosary; in the midst of grief, the Rosary allows us to enter a different state of mind, which eventually brings about a greater healing. The strong maternal respect in Filipino culture also elevates the importance of the Rosary, honoring the Blessed Mother who is also our mother. When my extended family members think of church, they think of the novenas for the dead prayed through the Rosary, complete with litanies, long prayers, and culminating with the comedic "Good evening" by the jokester uncles that bring us from sacred time to secular, "dinner" time. This dinnertime—actually any food time—is an integral part of Filipino life because we pride ourselves on gatherings with an abundant offering of food. Food is a communal time of generosity; even when finances were difficult, we would scrape everything together to ensure everyone had something.

My childhood parish and school were only five blocks away, and just as my family loved me into the faith, the parish church was where I caught and grew in my faith. I sang in the school's church choir and was an altar server (because who didn't want to get paid for helping with a funeral or a wedding, hanging out with friends in the sacristy while igniting incense charcoal?). This early liturgical participation was opening my eyes and heart to a deeper understanding of the Catholic Church's rites. I was beginning to see the ways we bring liturgy to life through prayerful and simple preparation, reflecting upon God's presence in the experience. A Canossian sister took time to answer my questions, and later asked for my input on things in the liturgical environment. She invited me to prepare the liturgies and even gave me her breviary, which I quickly misplaced because I did not know how to use it. One evening while my family and I were in the middle of Mass, the sister asked me into the reception hall. It was Holy Thursday, and little did I know she wanted me to help prepare the Altar of Repose. I prepared the tabernacle by opening its doors, lighting all the candles around it, and *tjuzing* banners and the incense brazier. She gave me tasks that few get the opportunity to do, and rarely in their youth. I felt honored to be so close to sacred objects that connected me to God, showing me that everyday things become holy for holy people. Plus, this was a chance for me to help; Filipinos like to help. This comes out of a social norm called *utang na loob*, meaning "debt of gratitude"; for us, giving back to the Church is a no-brainer. Historically, Filipinos have gone through much hardship and would turn to religion for help, guidance, and community. My parents supported my time in church because I could be an example to others in my giving back, particularly for other Filipino families wanting to raise a good son.

My journey has definitely been a bed of roses; hidden thorns have pricked. My Filipino family does not fully understand what I do on a day-to-day basis because I am not a priest, but I do ecclesial work. Yet there are glimpses of them understanding Catholic lay participation, realizing that Catholicism is not just following what Sister or Father says. My extended family jokes when I try to explain things of the Church, maybe because it is too much for them to handle. Considering the superstitions that have plagued Filipino culture, catechetical moments are often met with resistance rather than openness. When family members see me serving as an MC at a liturgy, or providing comfort for those grieving, they see my vocation made real. It is not easy, but I am glad that I help them see past the mystique of ministry or of the Church, and into its humanity.

I have three hopes from the Church going forward. First, young adults need the Church to take our stories seriously. We need to be specifically told that our stories matter and will have an impact because we are the new generation of leaders. Filipinos are storytellers, usually with song and always with food surrounding them. As I look back through my ministerial career, I see a pattern: People who were in authority invited me to try things that many people would never ask me to do simply because I was young. These people would say, "John Michael, you do it. Go ahead." And later they would help me unpack my experience through my stories. They invited my story into the story of the community, demonstrating that I am integral to the mission of the Church. Taking the words of Jesus, I suggest that we "go and do likewise" (Luke 10:37).

Second, lay ministers' salaries need to be equitable given the societies in which they minister; it's a matter of justice. As a lay minister, a profession in the Church is a different path than, say, working a six-figure job. Yet, in graduate school, I was not often reminded to take my own financial worth seriously; the emphasis was usually on serving others, which is appropriate for ministerial formation. Once employed, I was happy, but a lay minister's salary does not go far in the Bay Area! Sometimes the cost of living outweighs my desire to continue in ministry. The Church should have an honest conversation regarding its financial situation. What are our financial priorities? What does a "just wage" mean for lay ministers? Can we accept that working for the Church is not financially lucrative, but that the graces outweigh this? I think this is a deeper problem of not having a paradigm shift once laypeople entered ministry. Laypeople are not generally living in community and cannot afford the vulnerability that comes with voluntary poverty. The Church needs to support its ministers so that they can effectively support the people of God they are commissioned to minister to.

Finally, the Church needs to better support the API community by inviting and apprenticing API people into leadership roles. Unless the Church begins to see more API leadership, our Church will remain what is often thought of as Anglo led. If we see API people in leadership, it can expand our imagination, helping us to see Catholics of color not just as guests, but hosts, as well. Thus, API Catholics are part of the Church, both shaping it and shaped by it, not an exotic subset.

We cannot understand how to transform our world unless we tell our stories. May we continue to share the stories of our lives to embody the essence of God's love made real, of our shared and yet unique humanity. May we have the courage to share our stories so that others are invited to share theirs, giving life to the world.

John Michael Reyes, MDiv, a twenty-nine-year-old native of San Francisco, California, holds a master of divinity from the Jesuit School of Theology. Currently a campus minister at Santa Clara University, he has ministered as a liturgist, spiritual director, and hospital chaplain. In recent years, he served as liturgy coordinator for national gatherings, such as the Los Angeles Religious Education Congress.

Embracing the In-Between

by Jessica Gapasin Dennis

There are two questions I've been asked my entire life. Where are you from? And, what do you want to be when you grow up? My answers have changed and evolved over the years, and I've spent most of my young adulthood actively worrying if I'll ever answer these questions to my satisfaction. What I've learned is just how much my understanding of who I am (my identity) is intricately connected to how I understand my role in the world (my vocation).

Discerning my vocation has been an ongoing process of sifting through all the competing voices that clamor for my attention to tell me who I am. While there have been times that God's voice has been a thunderclap amidst the noise, I've found that more often than not, the Spirit speaks in a still, small voice. The catch is whether or not I'm paying attention. As a second generation Filipino American, I've always felt like a nomad, never quite at home, my identity fluid and constantly shifting as I straddle the line between two very different worlds—the Filipino culture I inherited from my parents and the American culture I was born into.

I am the daughter of immigrants, both highly educated

professionals who migrated from the Philippines in the 1970s. I grew up hearing stories of life in rural Philippines. My mom lived in a village so remote it didn't have regular access to books, and she would look forward every week to when the newspaper was delivered. My dad told stories of how he and his eleven siblings slept in a one-room *bahay kubo* (a hut on stilts) and how Tatay (his father) once won a sweepstakes and used the winnings to buy a bus he named after my Uncle Bong.

While I grew up in a mostly white, middle-class neighborhood, my family belonged to a tight-knit Filipino American community, where faith and culture were deeply intertwined, sometimes indistinguishable from each other. Every Filipino my parents' age was "auntie" or "uncle." We were taught to ask for a blessing from our elders (*mano po*) after Mass, and whenever there was any sort of gathering, the greatest hits of Filipino cuisine always made an appearance. When my parents became involved in the Charismatic Renewal in the early 1990s, Friday night prayer meetings went late into the night—not because they prayed for hours on end, but because the adults always lost track of time after the meeting, gathering around the table eating and telling stories in a mix of Tagalog and English, peppered with *Ilocano* and *Visayan*.

In this particular phase of my life, I understood my vocation as closely tied to the legacy that my parents began when they uprooted themselves and built a new life for them and future generations. Like many of my friends, I recognized the hard work and many sacrifices my parents made to change their situation for the better, and I felt a deep obligation to respond and show by my actions that their choices had not been in vain.

I decided early on to pursue my parents' dream (let's be honest, every Filipino parents' dream): to have a doctor in the family. It became my dream because it was their dream. I never questioned or resented my choice. In my eyes, this was the best way to respond to everything they had done and given me. I was a driven and competitive student—my dad had been valedictorian at his high school, and my mom was salutatorian at hers—and they encouraged me in my pursuit to be the best at everything. I was devastated when I realized two years into college that my desire to pursue this dream was not enough to override my absolute hatred of organic chemistry. To this day, I distinctly remember wanting to throw myself down the steps of the lecture hall; I hated it that much.

I was twenty-five when I moved across the country to Washington, DC, at a time when I wanted to see what was outside my northern California suburban bubble. It was the first time where many of the people I encountered had never met a Filipino before. Strangers would come up to me and ask where I was from or if I was Filipino. It didn't occur to me how weird this was—conversations that started with total strangers all because of my ethnicity—until my boyfriend (later husband) pointed it out. As a white man, the concept of anyone asking him about his ethnic background was completely foreign. For me, it happened so often that I didn't even think about it.

Over ten years later, the process of integrating my Filipinoness and Americanness no longer feels like I'm constantly switching hats for every occasion. I've learned how to be comfortable with—even embracing of—my in-betweenness, and have come to recognize my role as a bridge builder. I'm not completely a member of any one group or culture; rather, I am both/and—an inherently Catholic concept. As I've become increasingly fluent in the language of the in-between, I've felt called in many aspects of my life to stretch and get out of my comfort zone, to seek out situations where I am exposed to differing viewpoints and ways of life.

When I felt called to study theology, it was at an institution that was the theological opposite of the charismatic Catholic community in which I was formed. My husband is white and Protestant, and our conversation about faith, religion, race, and ethnicity is ongoing. I credit him for teaching by example that true dialogue is not two people taking turns reciting talking points. Authentic dialogue involves equal conversation partners, both open to having their minds changed. Our marriage has challenged my perception that becoming more of myself automatically implies that the other becomes less of themselves. If anything, it's the exact opposite—when each person is allowed to come to the table with their whole being, without apology or caveats, everyone involved is implicitly invited to do the same.

These days, especially in my Catholic circles, I am often the only brown person and the only person under forty. I grapple with the pressure of being the *de facto* ambassador of not just Filipino Americans, but minorities as a whole. It is difficult for me to understand the Catholicism handed down to me from my parents without also recognizing that it came as a result of colonial oppression of indigenous Filipinos when the Spaniards first came to the islands. And yet all of it—the good and the bad—are part of my story, and it is up to me to discern how I live it out and pass it along to my children.

Previously, whenever I imagined hearing God's call for my life, I thought it would be this grand epiphany, everything would click, and I would know that I'd finally arrived. Nowadays, I find myself coming back to this story of Elijah as he waits to hear from God:

> [The Lord] said, "Go out and stand on the mountain before the Lord, for the Lord is about to pass by." Now there was a great wind, so strong that

> it was splitting mountains and breaking rocks in pieces before the LORD, but the LORD was not in the wind; and after the wind an earthquake, but the LORD was not in the earthquake; and after the earthquake a fire, but the LORD was not in the fire; and after the fire a sound of sheer silence (1 Kgs 19:11–12).

As I approach the end of young adulthood, I realize now that I've come to know my vocation as a result of listening and paying attention to that still, small voice whenever I've come to life's crossroads. I'd grown so used to God working with me through grand gestures and lightning strikes that little did I know, there was a trail of breadcrumbs all along.

God was there when I answered the call to be a youth minister, a music minister, a high school religion teacher, a director of religious education, a stay-at-home mom. God is here now as I explore life working from home as a marketing assistant and web/graphic designer, as a novice in social justice and political activism. As disparate and unrelated all these pieces of my life may seem, the invisible thread through all of it has been my passion for sharing Christ's message that we are deeply loved—just as we are—in a way that is accessible and relevant to a diverse audience.

My hope is that the Church can be a place where people feel safe enough to be transparent about their journeys, where someone at any stage of life can learn and practice the skills of discernment and find common ground, not just with like-minded people, but with others from a diverse set of backgrounds and beliefs.

My hope is that our understanding of the Catholic Church as universal includes the recognition that we become a truer reflection of God when *all* cultures are included and represented, that being united in Christ isn't the same as rigid uniformity. My hope is that we embrace fully the Catholic idea of *unity in diversity*, that unity becomes reality through thoughtful dialogue. We must recognize that real unity can only be achieved when we, as a Church, are willing, unafraid, and intentional about having frank conversations about race and culture, when we can acknowledge that there are times when the Church got it wrong. I believe the Church can truly be a light to the nations when we integrate all the wisdom that our society has learned thus far—through history, science, psychology, sociology, anthropology, theology, all of it—and from it, present the message of the gospel in a compelling way to the world when it needs to hear it the most.

My hope, at the end of the day, is that as my daughters grow up in the Church, they know, at the very depths of their being, that they are seen and loved by a limitless God, that they are members of a Church that is equipping them to change the world, that an act of love, no matter how small or seemingly insignificant, is how we answer our call to bring Christ to the world.

Jessica Gapasin Dennis, MAPS, is thirty-six years old and lives in northern Virginia with her husband (aka the most patient man in the world) and their two crazy, amazing girls, ages two and five. She holds an MA in pastoral studies from the Washington Theological Union and left full-time ministry in 2013 for a stint in stay-at-home motherhood. She currently works from home and blogs regularly at leanintheworld.com.

Questions

1. A theme running throughout Drs. Stephen Cherry and Tricia Bruce's précis is the diversity within the API community. How well does your parish respond to the variety of API ethnicities present in the parish and local community?

2. Both of the experiential writers were Filipino and noted the importance of food in gatherings. What were some of the other important elements of being an API Catholic you have noticed, in either these essays or your own experiences? What are some of the important cultural markers within your own identity—religious, ethnic, or otherwise?

3. The important role of elders was noted in the précis as well as the essays. What are the strengths and shortcomings to having such intense family ties? How does having esteem for elders both constrain and enable one's ability to discern a vocation?

4. Both of the essayists demonstrated the central role of stories in their personal and social worlds. What role do stories have in your own life? Within Catholicism more broadly? How well are we hearing the stories of API Catholics and the other groups of young adults within this book?

Young LGBTQ Catholics

MAINSTREAMING DIFFERENCE

by Michele Dillon

Recent changes in the American religious and cultural landscape have particular salience for young LGBTQ Catholics. Since the 1990s, the proportion of Americans who express no religious affiliation has more than doubled—now comprising a full quarter of the population. Young people—eighteen to twenty-nine year olds—are far more likely than others to have no affiliation, so much so in fact that they are twice as likely to be unaffiliated (39 percent) as to be Catholic (15 percent), their generation's second largest religious identity group.[1] Another major change has been the accelerated cultural acceptance of same-sex relationships, and most notably, in June 2015, the U.S. Supreme Court's legalization of same-sex marriage. Although we cannot say that change in either of these domains caused the other, they remain highly interrelated. Three-quarters (73 percent) of young people support gay marriage; and religiously

---

1. Robert Jones, Daniel Cox, Betsy Cooper, and Rachel Lienesch, "Exodus: Why Americans Are Leaving Religion—and Why They're Unlikely to Come Back," PRRI, September 22, 2016, https://www.prri.org/wp-content/uploads/2016/09/PRRI-RNS -Unaffiliated-Report.pdf.

unaffiliated Americans (85 percent) are among the most supportive, even as a large majority of Catholics (68 percent) and white mainline Protestants (62 percent) do so, too.[2] Young LGBTQ Americans are thus living in a very different environment than that experienced by even their somewhat older peers, born as few as fifteen years earlier.

An Emergent, Gay-Friendly Church

There are also signs of the emergence of a more gay-friendly Catholic Church.[3] Since the 1970s, when gay rights became a public issue, Church officials have given much attention to articulating Church doctrine on the immorality of homosexuality. The Church's opposition to gay sex is informed by its natural law understanding of the binary of natural sexual male/female difference and an ensuing sexual complementarity that is open to life. The Vatican's Congregation for the Doctrine of the Faith (CDF) used highly negative language in the 1970s and 1980s in outlining its opposition to homosexuality and same-sex relationships, categorizing gay sexuality as "objectively disordered," and "homosexual acts" as "intrinsically disordered" and "self-indulgent." In more recent years, advocacy against same-sex marriage has been a central piece of the U.S. bishops' public agenda, emerging around 2005, when the Massachusetts State Supreme Court became the first to allow same-sex marriage. The Church argues that gay marriage is harmful to society and the common good because it gives legal approval to "gravely

2. Daniel Cox and Robert P. Jones, "Majority of Americans Oppose Transgender Bathroom Restrictions," PRRI, March 10, 2017, 2, https://www.prri.org/research/lgbt-transgender-bathroom-discrimination-religious-liberty/.

3. My discussion in this essay draws on arguments and sources cited in Michele Dillon, *Post-Secular Catholicism* (New York: Oxford University Press, 2018), chap. 4.

immoral" private behavior, and as such, is equivalent to public "toleration of evil." By extension, Church officials also oppose the rearing of children by same-sex couples.

Against this backdrop of negativity, Pope Francis is symbolically disrupting Church discourse on gay sexuality. He does so in a number of ways. Early in his papacy he argued for the need to rebalance the Church's priorities and to move away from its obsession with sexual issues. He is the first senior church official to publicly use the word *gay* in talking about LGBTQ individuals—thus showing attunement to the preferred language of the LGBTQ community and of doctrinal and political moderates. He also projects a nonjudgmental attitude, infamously stating that "if someone is gay and he searches for the Lord and has good will, who am I to judge?"[4] In accord with his broader emphasis on "a church of encounter and accompaniment," one that values and walks with people in all their marginality and complexity, he subsequently elaborated:

> A person once asked me, in a provocative manner, if I approved of homosexuality. I replied with another question: "Tell me: when God looks at a gay person, does he endorse the existence of this person with love, or reject, and condemn this person?" We must always consider the person. Here we enter into the mystery of the human being. In life, God accompanies persons, and we must accompany them, starting with their situation.[5]

---

4. James Martin, "Pope on Gays: 'Who Am I to Judge?'" *America*, July 29, 2013, https://www.americamagazine.org/content/all-things-pope-gays-who-am-i-judge.

5. Antonio Spadero, "A Big Heart Open to God: An interview with Pope Francis," *America*, September 20, 2013, https://www.americamagazine.org/faith/2013/09/30/big-heart-open-god-interview-pope-francis.

This clearly is a very positive, person-centered theology.

Francis's decentering of gay issues from the Church's public agenda is also seen in his remarks on family life. In his historic speech to the joint houses of Congress during his trip to the United States in September 2015, Francis spoke of the contemporary challenges to the institution of marriage. He framed these largely in terms of the economic problems couples and families confront. Notably, he did not mention the increased legal and cultural acceptance of same-sex marriage as one such challenge. Additionally, even though Francis frequently affirms Church teaching that "marriage is between a man and a woman," in *Amoris Laetitia* (no. 52), he also formally acknowledges the stability same-sex unions can offer. Further, he has not contradicted the influential German Cardinal Reinhard Marx's publicly stated view that the Church should not oppose structures in society that respect gay rights, including civil unions. Additionally, echoing a view also expressed by Cardinal Marx, Francis has stated that the Church should seek forgiveness from gays for how it has treated them. These gay-friendly nods matter. They are critical moments in the institutionalization of the Church's—and society's—acceptance of gays. Today, for example, 66 percent of American Catholics and 85 percent of eighteen to twenty-nine-year-old Catholics say that homosexuality should be accepted in society; further, only one-third (35 percent) of Catholics say it is a sin to "engage in homosexual behavior."[6]

---

6. Michael Lipka, "Young U.S. Catholics Overwhelmingly Accepting of Homosexuality," Pew Research Center, October 16, 2014, http://www.pewresearch .org/fact-tank/2014/10/16/young-u-s-catholics-overwhelmingly-accepting-of -homosexuality/; Pew Research Center, "Where the Public Stands on Religious Liberty vs. Nondiscrimination," September 28, 2016, http://www.pewforum.org/ 2016/09/28/where-the-public-stands-on-religious-liberty-vs-nondiscrimination/; and Pew Research Center, "In Gay Marriage Debate, Both Supporters and Opponents See Legal Recognition as 'Inevitable,'" June 6, 2013, http://assets.pewresearch.org/

THE NORMALIZATION OF GAY ROLES

The normalization of the idea that one can be LGBTQ *and* Catholic has been a long process—and it is ongoing. Counterpoised against Church teaching that being gay is contradictory of Catholic identity, Catholic activist groups such as DignityUSA and New Ways Ministry, among others (e.g., Call to Action), have played a pivotal role in affirming the authenticity of LGBTQ Catholics' identities and everyday experiences.[7] An indicator of their success and of the broader mainstreaming of gay Catholic identity on college campuses and in a growing number of parishes over the past several years, many young gay Catholics today do not feel the same spiritual and social pull as their same-age peers a couple of decades ago did to participate in Dignity and other gay-specific Catholic liturgies. Yet, as evidenced, for example, by the popularity of New Ways Ministry pilgrimages to Rome and LGBTQ Catholics' commitment to participate in the World Meeting of Families in Philadelphia in 2015, they are proud to collectively celebrate their intersecting identities. This is so even as they also seek to mainstream themselves into full participation as gay Catholics in the Church's sacramental and communal life.

Given the significance of marriage and parenting in the life course of the individual, the increased normalization of these processes among LGBTQ couples is noteworthy. There is accumulating evidence of the active commitment of gays to parenting and family formation. Close to one-fifth (19 percent) of same-sex couple households include children under age eighteen; among those under age fifty, either living alone

wp-content/uploads/sites/5/legacy-pdf/06-06-13%20LGBT%20General%20Public%20Release.pdf.

7. See Michele Dillon, *Catholic Identity: Balancing Reason, Faith, and Power* (New York: Cambridge University Press, 1999), 85–95, 115–63.

or with a spouse or partner, almost half of LGBTQ women and one-fifth of men are raising a child.[8] The increased parenting activity of LGBTQ couples is matched by the acceptance Americans have toward LGBTQ parenting couples. Two-thirds of Americans (66 percent) approve of gay parents raising children.[9] Postponed marriage and lower fertility are increasingly normative among current cohorts of young Americans. For young LGBTQ Catholics, the social incentive to get married and/or to become a parent may be further dampened by the Catholic Church's hesitancy to affirm such decisions. However, should young LGBTQ Catholics decide to embark on these paths, they will surely welcome the role-modeling provided as a result of the increased normalization of these major life events among LGBTQ individuals.

Young LGBTQ Catholics considering church-related work may be given pause by restrictions on gay employees. High profile cases of gay teachers in Catholic schools being fired after publicly coming out and similar restrictions against publicly out gays who are parish employees and volunteers (e.g., in the Philadelphia archdiocese) maintain the stigmatization of gay Catholics. Gay men considering the priesthood may pause, especially in the face of recent Vatican guidelines on the training of priests. The document repeats earlier Church language that men who "practice homosexuality, present deep-seated homosexual tendencies or support the so-called 'gay culture'" should not be considered eligible for the priesthood. It also repeats language from *The Catechism of the Catholic Church*, noting that "Such

---

8. Gary J. Gates, "LGBT Parenting in the U.S.," The Williams Institute, February 2013, https://williamsinstitute.law.ucla.edu/wp-content/uploads/LGBT-Parenting.pdf.

9. Pew Research Center, "U.S. Catholics Open to Non-Traditional Families," September 2, 2015, http://www.pewforum.org/2015/09/02/u-s-catholics-open-to-non-traditional-families/.

persons...find themselves in a situation that gravely hinders them from relating correctly to men and women. One must in no way overlook the negative consequences that can derive from the ordination of persons with deep-seated homosexual tendencies." A Vatican official further explained that the guidelines are intended to guard against sex abuse by priests.[10] The many prejudices against gays contained in the guidelines—that they are more likely than heterosexual priests to not maintain celibacy, to engage in pedophilia, and to not relate well to women—seem like a reversal of the attitude projected by Francis. Nonetheless, despite the negative message conveyed, the guidelines are unlikely to reverse Catholics' growing acceptance of gay equality and their perception that such views accord with Church teaching.[11]

Michele Dillon, PhD, is Professor of Sociology at the University of New Hampshire. Much of her research and writing focuses on American Catholicism. She is particularly interested in issues of hierarchical authority and individual interpretive autonomy, and their negotiation with respect to Church teachings on sex, gender, and family. Her latest book is Post-Secular Catholicism *(Oxford University Press, 2018).*

---

10. The guidelines for priestly formation were issued by the Vatican's Congregation for the Clergy on December 8, 2016, http://www.clerus.va/content/dam/clerus/Ratio%20Fundamentalis/The%20Gift%20of%20the%20Priestly%20Vocation.pdf.

11. Daniel Cox and Robert P. Jones, "The Francis Effect? U.S. Catholic Attitudes on Pope Francis, the Catholic Church, and American Politics," PRRI, August 25, 2015, https://www.prri.org/research/survey-the-francis-effect-u-s-catholic-attitudes-on-pope-francis-the-catholic-church-and-american-politics/.

Is Now and Ever Shall Be

Integrating My Catholic and Sexual Identity

by Aaron Bianco

Catholicism has been a part of my life since the day I was born. Before I can remember, I was baptized and have always felt at home in the Catholic Church. My mother brought us to Sunday school, which evolved into CCD. Nights and weekends were spent volunteering at the church and being involved in social functions surrounding the church. While most people were happy with their level of involvement in the church, I felt a higher calling. I spent more time at church volunteering; I was involved in almost every aspect of parish life. I watched my peers play sports, go to school dances and movies, and have nights out, but I was happy to be at church. Long before I knew I was gay, or what gay was, I was Catholic. I loved the tradition and history that came along with being Catholic, and I was proud to be part of something so well defined and historical.

In my twenties, I discovered I wanted to be a priest.

276

Around the same time, I also realized I was gay. At the time, I wasn't able to comprehend how one could have such a connection with God and be gay. I faced confusion and a sense of self-loathing. My response was to further shove myself into the Church and try to ignore all the feelings that came naturally to me. I enrolled in seminary and did my best to keep my feelings and desires to myself. It was at seminary that I reached my breaking point. I could no longer hide my sexuality. After prayer and conversations with God, I knew I wasn't sinning, and being gay was exactly how God made me. However, I thought that becoming a priest would force me to jam myself further into the closet, a closet that I hated being in. The societal pressures and the sentiment of the Church forced me to leave the seminary and parish life for a long while.

While I spent time away from the Church, I often searched for a meaningful relationship with God outside of the Church. I never felt satisfied with any of the services I went to that were open to the LGBTQ community. People often told me that I should just leave Catholicism and find a religion I like, but being Catholic is not just my religion. Catholicism was my family, my friends, and my culture. Leaving would mean a loss of a huge part of who I was. How could I just walk away from something that defined almost everything about me?

While I sorted it out and dealt with my inner struggle, life moved on. I finished school with a master's degree in theology and promptly found work in the private sector. I still went to Mass on a regular basis and did my best to be a "good Catholic" (whatever that means). This went on for years. I met my husband, who is also Catholic. We settled down together and remained practicing Catholics. We both experienced similar upbringings in the Church and both confided in and consoled one another regarding our place in the Church. Fortunately, we belonged to a wonderful, inclusive parish in New York City and life seemed good. In New York we were able to live in a little bubble that gave us a space where we could easily be both gay and Catholic.

The trouble with living in this bubble was that the struggle of our LGBTQ brothers and sisters outside still existed; we could easily ignore this in our sheltered space in our community and parish. This bubble burst in 2008 when, for family and career reasons, we moved to California. I imagined California as being as open-minded as New York City, and maybe it was, but we moved to California at the same time that Proposition 8 was being placed on the ballot. Prop 8 was a proposition that would define marriage as exclusively between one woman and one man. It brought gay relationships to the front of everyone's mind. It was at this moment I realized just how homophobic the Church still was. I watched "good Christians" spew hate and venom toward the LGBTQ community. I watched as people ignored hundreds of verses in the Bible where Jesus tells us to love and understand each other in favor of a few vague references toward homosexuality. Ultimately, Prop 8 passed and the LGBTQ community suffered another loss; they were told that the majority of voters in California did not deem their love and commitment worthy of basic legal protections. This loss inspired me to get involved in the Catholic Church again, and I sought to establish an LGBTQ-friendly parish in San Diego.

By the grace of God, I found a place in my local Church. Francis was elected pope and things seemed to be moving in the right direction. I watched interview after interview and spent countless hours watching Francis say things and express a real love and understanding for the LGBTQ community. I couldn't believe that the leader of the Catholic Church was saying such welcoming and affirming things.

Unfortunately, the trickle-down effect can often take longer than we want. While the pope was making groundbreaking statements of LGBTQ inclusion, many Catholics turned a deaf ear to the pontiff and continued to look at the gay community as second-class citizens in the Church. While I was happy with my new job at a parish where the priest I worked for was welcoming and loving, I was careful to keep my private life to myself. I figured change would need to come slowly. I was never ashamed of being gay; I just knew that some things take time. Unfortunately, I was outed by a parishioner. This normally wouldn't have been a big deal, but this parishioner was a large donor to the parish and there were larger forces at play. In an effort to spare the parish any unnecessary heartache, my name was removed from the bulletin and I lost the title of pastoral associate. I thought I was in a place where I could be myself and do the job I loved, but I was let down, feeling heartbroken again. The pastor of the church remained supportive of me, and I kept my job for about a year after I was outed. I was able to run the church's RCIA program and start up an active, vibrant young adult group.

Eventually, the pastor of my church was moved, and we were assigned a new pastor. I knew my status was in limbo, and I was losing the man who had always acted justly and believed in me, regardless of my sexual orientation. I began my search for employment outside of the Church. I did this for a while, but did not find it fulfilling. As luck would have it, I was offered another position working for the Church. I was asked by the pastor, with full support of the bishop, to help establish an LGBTQ-friendly parish, create a task force, and work on making the diocese a welcoming place for everyone. I was excited at the opportunity and I went right to work.

Currently, I have the support of my bishop and the pastor of my parish. While each day presents new challenges, I feel like I am in a place where I can make some important changes. That's not to say I do not have setbacks or hear negative comments, but the good outweighs the bad, especially having the encouragement of good and holy people. Living in a world where everything around us happens in an instant, it can be hard to work toward long, slow change. Change in an organization as large as the Catholic Church can be glacially slow, and I'm okay with that. It can be hard to stay positive, but nothing worth fighting for is ever easy. Rome, after all, was not built in a day.

For lay straight people in the Church: I think it is important for you to meet us (LGBTQ Catholics) where we are. You have to understand that most of us don't feel like we are sinning. There seems to be a big focus on the LGBTQ community's place in the Church that doesn't exist for other groups who are living "outside" of Church teachings. For example, divorced and remarried Catholics or Catholics using contraceptives are welcomed in nearly every parish. Why shouldn't gays be welcomed in the same way? The "witch hunt" for LGBTQ Catholics still exists. Even when LGBTQ parishioners are supposedly welcomed in one particular church, the need to hide one's true identity as a gay person seems prevalent.

For my fellow Catholics who support the Church's teaching on homosexuality: My sexuality should not be a reason why we cannot still communicate and celebrate Mass together. The *Catechism of the Catholic Church* states, "They [homosexuals] must be accepted with respect, compassion, and sensitivity. Every sign of unjust discrimination in their regard should be avoided" (CCC 2358). We can disagree and still come together. Life is a series of compromises; in order to get along in this world, we must accept each other as fellow persons. Any legitimate Christian would have to acknowledge that we are taught to love. I think that people become so divided by issues that they ignore the common ground we share. Our focus should be the reason we are all at Mass: to be fed in Word and Sacrament and to be sent to live out the gospel message.

For the clergy of the Church: You undoubtedly have

gays and lesbians in your parishes, schools, and families. The LGBTQ community is asking for nothing more than to be treated with dignity and respect as children of God. At your ordination, you were called to serve all of God's people. That includes those who may be living outside of what you believe to be acceptable. Pope Francis continually calls the Church to accompany all people wherever they are on their journey. The best example of pastoral accompaniment will be witnessed at the parish level. Show us the love of which Christ is capable.

Aaron Bianco was born and raised into a large Italian American family in New York City. He obtained a bachelors degree in psychology from the University of Southern California and a master's degree in theology from Fordham University. Aaron has worked for the Church off and on for over twenty years. He is in a committed, loving relationship with his best friend, Joe.

All In

by Mary, with Kelly

I cannot remember a time when I did not know who and what I wanted to be. The start of my vocation was the unconditional love of my family, especially my parents. I was a strange little kid, but that never seemed to make my parents' love for me waver. When I was around four, upon meeting a person for the first time, I would look them in the eye and confidently assert, "My name is Mary but you can call me Bob." Boys seemed to have better clothes, toys, games, haircuts, names, and just generally a better deal. So I insisted on wearing boys' clothes, having my hair cut short, and I would even walk around the house in jeans with no shirt. At first it was kind of cute and quirky, but as I got older, it became awkward. I was mistaken for a boy regularly, and that started to feel somehow shameful. But this was not some sad or painful chapter in my life for two main reasons.

First, my parents taught me about an unconditionally loving God, and they modeled to me what that love looked like. Don't get me wrong, my parents—especially my mom— really disliked my disdain for all things "girly." But the resounding message of my childhood was that I was loved no matter what. I remember my mom telling me that even if I were a serial killer, she would still love me. I was simply more to them than anything I would ever do. Just by existing, I had their unending love. Second, as they gave me this living example of God's love, they were simultaneously giving me a faith tradition. I prayed at bedtime and meals, went to Mass on Sundays and Holy Days, received all my sacraments, and attended Catholic schools. They created a world around me in which the existence of a loving God was a taken-for-granted reality. God was present to me always, cared about what I cared about, what I was struggling with, what I was grateful for, and what I hoped for in life.

Over time, the feeling of love and acceptance I got from my parents, and from the God they introduced me to, instilled in me self-confidence and trust. When my instincts led me to something outside of the norm or the expected, I did not hesitate to embrace that. I wanted to be an English teacher despite the fact that I would not have as much wealth or prestige as a lawyer. Then, in college I took a required theology course and fell in love. I embraced theology as my major despite its impracticality as an educator and a woman, essentially tying myself to Catholic schools professionally because I had found my calling.

In an ironic twist, just as I was feeling so sure of my professional vocation, I was also coming out as a gay woman. I fell in love again in my early twenties—and all at once—I could imagine a whole life: doing work I love, sharing that life with a person I love, and eventually starting a family. All the pieces fit together, except that according to many in the Catholic Church, my life was at odds with what I wanted to teach. The Church that fostered my relationship with God and taught me that my life's purpose was to discover my vocation was now the main hindrance to pursuing it. Nevertheless, I had a bone-deep sense that this life I was being called to was not bad. So I pursued theological studies, planning to forge a career in Catholic education and create a family as an openly gay woman. I moved forward on an uncertain path, not knowing if anyone would ever hire me or if this vision of a life was even possible. A few years later, I met Kelly.

We had a lot in common. We were both the oldest of three sisters, had one brother, had a parent who was raised Protestant in Iowa, and had moved west as a child, and on the other side, we each had big Irish Catholic families. We went to Jesuit universities, we were surprised to find ourselves studying theology as graduate students because it was not what we had planned, and we were also certainly surprised to find *each other* in that particular setting. Not only was our common past striking, but we also shared ideas about our futures. We both felt called to teach in Catholic schools, to marriage, and to creating a family through adoption. Despite the fact that we also shared strong Catholic identities, the one fundamental difference between us was that I had been raised a Catholic and she a Presbyterian. She converted to Catholicism in college, and that conversion in the context of her Jesuit education (and a pretty spectacular Italian piazza) gave language and a spiritual home to her sense of vocation.

When I asked Kelly to think about the role of vocation in her life, she expressed that her experience of pursuing her vocation as a religious studies teacher in Catholic schools, marrying the person of her choosing, and then becoming a parent has largely been an experience of overcoming fear, of following a call despite a constant perceived threat of job loss or social rejection. My sense of vocation preceded my awareness of being gay, and it actually helped me to move through that discovery with some confidence despite trepidation. Her sense of herself as gay and her understanding of vocation emerged simultaneously and are inextricably woven together. She sees the primary work of her vocation as searching for the freedom to be who she is and to live with integrity.

Both of us spend much spiritual energy resisting giving tacit credence to the surface-level judgments that our life choices are wrong. All Catholics—in the pews or in collars— struggle to make decisions of conscience in light of Scripture and Tradition. It is not the role of the Church to exclude people based on a human assessment of sinfulness. To do so is hubris and rejects the example of God's unconditional love as modeled by Jesus. To be clear, our ongoing and deep discernment has led us to believe our marriage is not sinful. But LGBTQ Catholics are made to feel like their "sin" is grounds for exclusion, not exclusion from the Church, but from pursuing an earnestly arrived-at vocation. The Church can best support our vocation by simply getting out of the way.

Since that support was not forthcoming, we supported each other as we forged a marriage and careers despite fear and insecurity. We were married in a nondenominational chapel by a female Mennonite pastor, but it was a Catholic wedding because it was a sacrament we two deeply Catholic women bestowed on each other. And when the time felt right, we decided to start our family by pursuing adoption through the foster care system. As foster-to-adopt parents, we agreed to take children into our care without any guarantee that they would stay. We were trained to understand that our role was to agree to take in children who needed care, to support and fully embrace them as our children, and be ready to adopt them, while simultaneously assisting in the efforts to reunite them with their biological families. Our job, in essence, was to be "all in."

About a year and a half after we signed up for training, we got a call about two little girls who needed placement immediately. We knew little beyond their ages and had no assurance of their need for adoption, but when I heard their names, I knew that they were the ones. But actually, like all parents, I knew *nothing*—nothing tangible at least. Not whether they would stay or go; whether they would be in our lives for two days, a few months, or forever; what kind of personalities they would have; whether they would be permanently damaged; or if I could handle any of it. I knew nothing, except that I was *in*.

Throughout that first year, we really did not know whether they were going to stay or go. Their birth mom resurfaced and entered rehab, we took our youngest to weekly visits, we waited to see if any member of the birth family wanted them, and we fretted about and showed up to countless court dates for months and then years, only to have their cases further delayed and to gain no more certainty about our situation. All the while we cared for them as they learned to crawl, walk, talk, dance, laugh, to trust us, to call us Mommy and Mama, and they became loved by a huge extended family that embraced them completely. Throughout that emotionally tumultuous time, well-meaning people in our lives would lament the delays, unable to understand how the court could not see that they belonged with us. "Those girls are ours!" they would say. But I was always really clear that that claim was not true. They were not ours. But we were theirs. I had control over that. I could simply be theirs and let go of attachment to outcomes. This experience of knowing our place in their lives so profoundly gave us new insight into vocation.

Being gifted with the experience of caring for and loving children has blown my understanding of God wide open. I have been rendered a puddle of mush by this palpable experience of a God whose love for us is like the love I have experienced for these children. I know now that the God whose love has authored my life, who is so tangible to me in my children, is not *my* God. But I am God's. That lived truth in my life humbles me deeply. The only way I know how to respond to it is to be grateful and live a life that reflects my gratitude, despite whatever imperfect or messy outcomes might come of it in this world. This is what vocation means to me now.

Mary, PhD, thirty-eight, is a high school teacher with a BA, MA, and PhD in theology with a focus on ethics. She has been married to Kelly, also a high school teacher with a BA and MTS, for eight years. They live, work, and worship in communities they love and who love them and their now three adopted children.

Questions

1. Dr. Michele Dillon notes that American Catholics' acceptance of those in same-sex relationships has shifted where LGBTQ Catholics choose to worship, with many now electing to worship in traditional Catholic parishes rather than gay-specific Catholic liturgies. What do you think about worshipping alongside LGBTQ Catholics? Is your parish doing anything for LGBTQ Catholics?

2. Do you have experiences with LGBTQ Catholics? Are they involved or estranged from the Church? Or somewhere in-between?

3. What are the challenges LGBTQ Catholics face in the Church and larger world? What are some pastoral initiatives Catholics can extend to the LGBTQ community? How might we respond to LGBTQ Catholics' parents, siblings, partners, and children?

Going, Going, and Some Are Gone

MARGINAL AND FORMER YOUNG ADULT CATHOLICS

by Maureen K. Day

Of all the subsets of young adult Catholics in this book, one of the largest populations dwells within the following pages: the marginally and formerly Catholic. I have complete confidence that the reader personally knows at least one, if not several, young adults who have drifted from Catholicism. Some of these may have switched to another faith, others may be simply unaffiliated, and some may have already come back to Catholicism. To shift from our immediate world and look at national Pew Research data from 2014, nearly one-third of Americans were raised Catholic.[1] Yet only 59 percent of those raised Catholic continue to identify as Catholic; this is a substantial decrease since 2007, when 68 percent of those raised Catholic continued to identify as such as adults. This significant rate of attrition means

---

1. Pew Research Center, "America's Changing Religious Landscape," May 12, 2015, http://www.pewforum.org/2015/05/12/americas-changing-religious-landscape/.

an astounding 13 percent of *the whole U.S. population* are former Catholics, constituting the second largest "religious" group in the United States! It is true that many traditions are losing adherents, but no other religious group in this Pew survey was losing members as quickly as Catholicism, which loses more than six adherents for every convert gained.

According to Church teaching, there is no formal way to renounce one's Catholicism. However, it is clear that Catholics leave the Church in practice, and they do so in a variety of ways.[2] Some struggle with a particular teaching or set of teachings and eventually exit; some of these return when they are able to reconcile or navigate this tension (and some do not). Others get caught up in emerging adulthood and, in filling their schedules, religion is relegated to the back burner and often forgotten; some return when they reconsider their priorities with marriage or the birth of a child (and some do not). Some encounter a new faith and worship in a different context; some of these will return when their circumstances change (and some will not). Some stay; some leave and return; some leave, never to return.

Specifically, amongst all those raised Catholic, 52 percent leave at some point.[3] About half of these leave religion altogether, one-fourth identify as evangelical Protestants, one-eighth affiliate with mainline Protestantism, and the remainder join smaller religious groups.[4] This number is slightly higher than past defection rates, with a 1978 survey finding that 42 percent of Catholics leave for two years or

---

2. Kaya Oakes, *The Nones Are Alright: A New Generation of Believers, Seekers, and Those in Between* (Maryknoll, NY: Orbis Books, 2015).

3. Caryle Murphy, "Half of U.S. Adults Raised Catholic Have Left the Church at Some Point," Pew Research Center, September 15, 2015, http://www.pewresearch.org/fact-tank/2015/09/15/half-of-u-s-adults-raised-catholic-have-left-the-church-at-some-point/.

4. Pew Research Center, "America's Changing Religious Landscape."

more, typically in their teens or early twenties.[5] Sociologist Dean Hoge reported that the majority of those who left Catholicism eventually returned. However, at present only about one in five return and another one in five linger on the fringes as "culturally Catholic"—meaning they have some sort of self-identified tie to Catholicism; the majority now remain outside of Catholicism.[6] This is corroborated elsewhere; in a recent longitudinal study, of the forty-one teens who self-identified as Catholic or were raised Catholic, just twelve could be considered significantly tethered to their faith only five years later.[7] These numbers are too small to be taken as nationally representative, but they warrant a serious pause.

Christian Smith and his team of researchers analyzed data from the National Study of Youth and Religion to understand the faith lives of contemporary teens and young adults. Gathering data over three waves, this study examines the shifts and stabilities among a nationally representative group of youth using survey and interview data. Smith's team focuses only on the Catholic respondents in their *Young Catholic America*, providing an in-depth look at eighteen- to twenty-three-year-old Catholics.[8] Comparing historical patterns of Catholic and Protestant church attendance reveals that adherents show a dramatic decline in attendance in the teen years. However, by their mid-thirties, Protestants have rebounded to higher levels of attendance than their Catholic counterparts.[9] This signals that even if young adults are

5. Dean R. Hoge, *Converts, Dropouts, Returnees: A Story of Religious Change among Catholics* (New York: Pilgrim Press, 1981), 10.

6. Murphy, "Half of U.S. Adults Raised Catholic Have Left."

7. Christian Smith, Kyle Longest, Jonathan Hill, and Kari Christoffersen, *Young Catholic America: Emerging Adults in, Out of, and Gone from the Church* (New York: Oxford University Press, 2014), 89.

8. Smith, Longest, Hill, and Christoffersen, *Young Catholic America*.

9. Smith, Longest, Hill, and Christoffersen, *Young Catholic America*, 58.

leaving the religions of their childhood across the board, Catholicism will feel it most strongly in the long run.

There were some bright spots in the Smith team's data. For one, no matter how distant the interviewed emerging adults were from Catholicism, many had fond memories of their parish priests and few harbored any hostility toward the Church.[10] Also, most Catholic young adults' religiosity is not very different from the religiosity of their teen years, which is to admit that most were not especially religious then either.[11] The study also revealed three factors that strongly correlate with high young adult religiosity: having relationships as teens with adults—from parents to youth ministers—who have a strong faith life; internalizing Catholic beliefs as teens; and regularly practicing one's faith as a teen.

There are many implications in this data, and I will discuss two here. To begin with, this overall young adult religious atrophy is not something that "happens." It is the cumulative result of years of inadequate faith formation. The number of cracks that can occur in this broad offering of faith formation are many. Focusing just on the Smith team's data, first, one's parents might not have had the time, awareness, or personal convictions to have been strong first teachers in the faith, which resulted in Catholic beliefs and practices worn lightly rather than a more intense socialization. Second, one's parish might not have networked these youth with other adults who could have served as mentors in their parents' stead. Third, this faith formation might not have presented material in a way so that it was truly internalized and incorporated into one's belief systems. In this case, when emerging adulthood brings a more critical lens to the world, immature notions of God that were passively accepted rather then systematically explained and regularly

---

10. Smith, Longest, Hill, and Christoffersen, *Young Catholic America*, 113–14.

11. Smith, Longest, Hill, and Christoffersen, *Young Catholic America*, 161.

developed are abandoned. Finally, religious practices that were relevant to youth were either not regularly available or were not presented in a way that made the religious meaning apparent (e.g., service as a good deed rather than an act of compassionate and just charity). Two of the three contributors that follow discuss or hint at inadequate faith formation in their youth. Faith formation programs must seal the cracks in their youth programs if they want vibrant communities with young adults.

A second implication is an optimistic twist of the data. There are many who began their lives as Catholics and as such are more equipped to *re*enter Catholicism as adults than their non-Catholic counterparts. These 13 percent of Americans who were raised Catholic but no longer identify as such provide a ready opportunity to grow the Church. This growth should not be viewed solely in terms of numbers, but also as a qualitative boon. These returning Catholics can share their experiences in leaving and coming back—the struggles, questions, and tensions these involved—to help illuminate the meaning of Catholicity and faith more broadly. In sum, the data has implications for both youth programming and the evangelization of young adults.

Given this information, how can the Church respond? The data on the importance of youth programming yields a straightforward directive: put resources into youth faith formation. Cultivating relationships and instilling beliefs and practices will have long-term effects, helping to decrease the staggering rate of attrition among Catholic young adults. However, beyond the preventative, a looming question remains: How do we reach those young adults who have left Catholicism or are teetering on the brink of leaving? The answer lies in a theme that recurs throughout many of the essays in this volume: listen to us. Repeatedly, many of the contributors within this book have asked the Church to avail itself to their young adult experiences, believing the Church is either out of step or needs to speak more boldly given their reality. Whether they want parish-sponsored young adult groups so that they may cultivate faith-based relationships with peers or they want more active engagement in society, they want to see the relevance of the faith to their lives and the relevance of their lives to the faith.

The upcoming synod provides one such occasion for the Church to listen to young adult Catholics. Dioceses and parishes should conduct their own local synods to discover what the most pressing issues are among their young adults. Rather than having only the most active Catholics, however, the Church would do better to include those who are marginalized or have left altogether. Pope Francis made this very point at an April 8, 2017, prayer vigil in preparation for World Youth Day:

> Some people say: "Let's hold the Synod for young Catholics, for those belonging to Catholic groups; that way it will be better." No! The Synod is meant to be the Synod for and of all young people. Young people are its protagonists. "But even young people who consider themselves agnostics?" Yes! "Even young people whose faith is lukewarm?" Yes! "Even young people who no longer go to Church?" Yes! "Even young people who—I don't know if there are any here, maybe one or two—consider themselves atheists?" Yes! This is the Synod of young people and we want to listen to one another….All of us need to listen to you!

Pope Francis has explicitly urged us to include even a-religious young adults as we consider the most effective ways to minister to young people. In listening to those who are estranged from Catholicism, the Church will learn much.

For in this learning, the Church can better accompany young adults who are in a variety of places on their faith journey. The young adults in this section of the book represent those who hold their Catholicism in different degrees and ways. Ash O'Conor feels strongly Catholic, but simultaneously feels marginalized by her Church as a lesbian who seeks ordination. Edward Kelinsky seems to have simply drifted from the Church after seventeen years of Catholic education because he grounds his beliefs in reason and has little patience for leaps of faith. Patrick Burns was raised Catholic and is now an agnostic. These voices tell different stories, offering the Church a chance to learn new ways to accompany even marginal and former young adult Catholics.

Maureen K. Day, PhD, is the Assistant Professor of Religion and Society at the Franciscan School of Theology in Oceanside, California, and Research Fellow at the Center for Church Management at Villanova University. Committed to young adult ministry, Maureen is a member of the Alliance for Campus Ministry, an advisory group to the USCCB's Secretariat on Catholic Education. Her writings on American Catholic life appear in both Catholic and academic publications, including serving as editor of this collection as well as authoring a forthcoming book on American Catholic civic engagement (NYU Press). She has provided her expertise on families and young adults to the Church at both the diocesan and national level, recently assisting with the San Diego Synod on the Family as well as with the data analysis of the 2017 National Study of Catholic Campus Ministry in collaboration with the USCCB's Secretariat on Catholic Education.

Expansive Love

by Ash O'Conor

A door opens to me. I go in and am faced with a
hundred closed doors.

—Antonio Porchia

With trepidation and exuberance, I walked through the
open doors of the university Catholic church after years
of absence. The hardship of accepting my identity and
discerning my vocation throttled me into a search for God.
Through what can only be described as the Holy Spirit, my
eyes were opened to God's unconditional love. In my final
year of college, I could hear God shouting, "Do you finally
get it? This is how I created you. You are my beloved."
Yet, just as soon as I stepped through open doors into the
expansive sanctuary, I encountered many closed doors in the
form of exclusionary doctrine. Authority in the institutional
Church is too often grounded in status instead of God's
tenderheartedness. Discriminatory doctrine promulgated
by the Church engenders the heartless marginalization of
women and LGBTQ people.

My love of Catholicism is rooted in the sacrality of the
liturgy, its rich history, and the beauty of Catholic social

teaching. Yet the essential parts of my identity are sources of exclusion from my beloved faith. I am a woman. I am a lesbian. I am called to priesthood. I am a marginal Catholic because the center of the institutional Church pushes me to the edges, contests my needs for pastoral care, and dismisses my call to leadership. And it is deeply hurtful.

A painful experience of this marginalization occurred on the evening following the mass shooting in Orlando, Florida, on June 12, 2016. Like many that morning, I woke up to the news of the deadliest mass shooting in United States history; my newsfeed replete with the tragic news that forty-nine people were murdered. It was also the deadliest incident against LGBTQ people in the United States. The victims of this attack were young, LGBTQ, and predominantly Latino/a. In tears, I watched Vice President Joe Biden address the country that morning, saying, "They were our brothers and our sisters; our friends, neighbors, and loved ones....May God give strength to the families, friends, and all those who grieve today, with broken hearts, but unbound resolve." Brokenhearted, I looked forward to attending Mass that evening to grieve with my faith community.

I longed for my pastor to voice his resolve to combat hatred and offer words to ease my grief. During Mass, there was no mention of the shooting; a national tragedy that impacted many in the congregation was overlooked in the sacred space where I sought support. In response to why he did not acknowledge the shooting, the priest answered with a terse, "Well...it just happened this morning." I was marred by his reply. The shooting killed dozens of the most marginalized in American society, and my parish, a diverse Catholic church called to be an advocate for the marginalized, did not respond. This is just one of many personal examples that I could offer of the division that exists between the institutional Church and LGBTQ people. This disparity is in desperate need of reconciliation. Reconciliation must first take place in the form of a public confession by clergy that the Church has hurt many believers by its lack of compassion, perpetuation of discrimination, and tactlessness in training insensitive clergy. Does the Church realize that this discrimination impedes the faithful from feeling loved by the God whose image they bear? I strike a harsh tone because this reaches beyond issues of power, but is, in fact, about the value of human life.

The institutional Church actively stands in the way of God's blessings for humanity. If I cannot voice the fullness of my identity to my congregation and pastor, then I cannot be fully human. Christianity was conceived and continues to evangelize through personal testimony. Yet heteronormative testimonies are preached while stories of diverse identities are sequestered outside of church walls. Sharing testimony on the basis of being a woman or an LGBTQ person often incites reprimand, shutting another door on God's beloved people. Women and LGBTQ people provide prophetic witnesses to God's love and must be allowed to voice that witness in church, where they are *listened* to by the congregation and clergy. Without compassionate listening, the marginalized cannot access the love of God proclaimed by the Church.

Despite closed doors, my love of the Catholic faith compels me to forge a place in the Church. As God revealed to Moses at the burning bush, I am who I am. I yearn to be accepted by the Church for all of who I am. Acceptance is essential for LGBTQ people *and* parishioners who do not identify as LGBTQ because every Catholic must know that Christ's love is boundless. Everyone has a closet—an experience that is difficult to share—whether it be divorce, addiction, poverty, abuse, or shame. God calls us to come out of our closets, to kick down closed doors, into the healing and expansive arms of Christ. Instead of a bulwark of hierarchy, the Church can be an institution guided by Christ's unconditional love.

My vision of a loving Church sustains my vocation in Catholic education. I am a secondary school theology teacher and campus minister. In my ministry, I am forced to navigate between telling the truth about who I am and hiding what might give the bishop cause to fire me. I am a source of spiritual authority and pastoral care at my Catholic school, yet I personally count among the most marginalized in the Church. My marginalization is further apparent in the fact that I must use a pseudonym to publish this essay. I cannot reveal my real name for fear that I could be fired for voicing my pain caused by the institutional Church.

My ministry involves a daily voicing of how much God loves my students exactly as they are. My students who fall outside the confines of what is acceptable by the Church need affirmation that they are essential members of the Body of Christ. I agree with Carl Rogers when he spoke of the power of personal testimony, leading him "to believe that what is most personal and unique in each one of us is probably the very element which would, if it were shared or expressed, speak most deeply to others." If I cannot speak of my own experience as a woman and lesbian in my ministerial setting, how can other women and LGBTQ people see a place for themselves in the Church?

Jesus slipped into flesh to be one of us so that *we may have life and have it abundantly*, not a heavily regulated life on the margins. Jesus is the ultimate example of radical love, dissolving societal boundaries to embrace the marginalized. Jesus still does this today, acting through the marginalized to expand the center's notion of love.

Last semester, my senior theology class examined the Beatitudes. I asked the students to write the Beatitudes in modern language. If Jesus were in front of us today, who would he call blessed? This is what they had to say:

> *Blessed are...*
> *all people of color,*
> *the feminists who fight oppression,*
> *those who accept change,*
> *those who face discrimination because of*
> *their sexual orientation,*
> *the questioning and confused,*
> *those who listen,*
> *those who face injustice because of their race,*
> *gender, or their courage to stand on their own*
> *for what they believe,*
> *the tired: tired of excuses, tired of being let*
> *down, tired of history repeating itself.*

I say to you, my reader, whether lay or religious, the work necessary to restore the blessedness of *all* people is not radical or new. The Church has always possessed expansive love, beginning with the prophets and apostles. Pope Francis is imbuing the Church with compassion, but the clergy and laity must drive this movement of belovedness. The Church must make institutional decisions based on the truth that St. Paul knew two thousand years ago: We are one Body in Christ.

The marginalized will continue to be marginalized if we are denied a voice, a listening ear, and freedom from retaliation as we eradicate systemic discrimination. The love proclaimed by the Church is conditional if it places restrictions on who is acceptable. The Church necessarily contests the value of all human life when it does not manifest God's unconditional love.

The Church must publicly confess that Catholic doctrine and clergy have lacked compassion and perpetuated discrimination. Women and LGBTQ people are prophetic witnesses to God's love, whose voices must be heard inside church walls. Finally, women and LGBTQ people possess the agency and the solutions to end institutional marginalization if clergy have the courage to be responsive to the needs of God's people.

Reader, you have heard my story but you do not know my name, and this causes me pain. I maintain hope that the institutional Church will open its closed doors and allow the marginalized to finally speak their blessed names without fear.

Ash O'Conor is in her late twenties. She has a master's degree in theology. Ash is a campus minister and theology teacher at a Catholic high school in California.

My Marginal Catholic Identity

by Edward Kelinsky

I am a member of a very Catholic family. As I write this, I realize how odd it is that Catholics self-segregate themselves into various strengths of belief. Honestly, I don't know members of any other religion who have to delineate themselves from "very" to "raised." It's weird for me to give myself a label in this way, but I would say I am a marginal Catholic. In numerous ways, I respect and agree with many of the decisions made and positions taken in the Catholic Church by serving those on the edge of society, notably under the influence of Pope Francis. Yet, I also vehemently disagree with other Church teachings, such as not allowing same-sex marriage, female priests, contraception, and others.

My grandmother was one of my first examples of what it means to be Catholic. When she was a child and young adult, my grandmother seriously considered becoming a nun and used to kneel on broken pottery when she prayed. Yes, a pre–Vatican II type Catholic (no, she is not crazy and is a wonderful mother and incredible grandmother). She and my grandfather met at a Catholic university, raised seven children, and taught marriage and baptism classes well into their golden years. They celebrated their sixty-second anniversary together last summer before my grandfather passed away in December. In short, my grandparents had an old-school view of Catholicism, one that guided most of my perceptions of what Catholicism entailed: Things are right or wrong, and one could either believe in Church teachings and attend Mass weekly, or he or she should not call themselves Catholic. Simple and effective!

Growing up, my brother and I attended Mass with my family weekly and learned biblical stories from my family and the newest *VeggieTales* videos. We hit all the typical Catholic milestones, from making our first communion in grade school to confirmation in high school. All this in addition to attending Catholic school every year from kindergarten until I graduated college. As I grew up, my studies and understanding of Catholicism grew and matured. As a child, it was easy for me to understand the simplistic and straightforward stories from the Bible that my grandma told me. I said the blessing before meals and enjoyed being an altar server. As someone who actually understood and practiced Church teaching, I was in the vast minority even throughout my time in a Catholic elementary and middle school.

The crucible of my religious self-identity took place primarily in high school and college; it is worth noting that these eight years of my Catholic education took place at Jesuit institutions. For those who are unaware, Jesuits are an order of priests founded by St. Ignatius of Loyola in the hope of reconverting Protestants back to Catholicism. The Jesuits are known for being liberal, educated, and elevating reason above all else, which was a style of Catholicism I could truly get behind. Their critics, however, might call them narcissistic and too liberal: Pope Francis is the first Jesuit ever selected to be pope, and reactions to his remarks are a good indication of how divisive Ignatian thought can be.

VOCATION THROUGH IDENTITY AND PRACTICE

Like most children raised in a religious environment, my earlier years were spent listening to stories and never truly understanding the nuances of faith and belief. In high school, I found that the Jesuits' specific brand of theology really struck a chord with me. Through my participation in immersions and community service, I came to believe in a more progressive style of Catholicism characterized by service and a well-rounded education that includes self-reflection and honest self-evaluation. Students of Jesuit education are asked to view their own gifts and talents in relation to the needs of the world, and then apply these talents in a way that elevates the common good.

This application of faith could not have come at a better time in my own spiritual journey. I began to question some of the simplistic answers I was given as a child when I examined doctrines of the Church. At the same time, my high school's theology classes began to teach me to review Church teachings and search for a higher level of understanding, rather than simply recite Church beliefs or mindlessly enact any practice. During my first year of high school, I took a Scripture class that was one of the most formative religion courses of my life. Within the first month, the teacher, a deacon in his parish, gave us a challenging reflection. He stated, "God is eternal, so God exists outside time; therefore, everything that has happened, is happening now, or will ever happen is all taking place at once. So, what is the point of prayer? It can't change or influence any outcomes, as all God's decisions have been made."

This sort of critical thought is just one example of how my thinking about my Catholic faith changed. While I sharpened my analytical thinking skills on the school's debate team, I began to look for inconsistencies within Church teaching in order to gain a deeper understanding of the religion. Even from a young age, I learned that not everything in Catholicism could be explained rationally, as it relied on *faith.* Transubstantiation? Faith. Immaculate conception? Faith. However, I wanted to understand and be able to rationalize as much of the faith as I could—my Jesuit education had taught me that faith without understanding is meaningless. Still, I could not help but think that the Church's positions on social issues were perplexing at best and contradictory at worst. If life begins at the moment of conception, then why should Catholics who are not ready or willing to have a baby avoid contraception? If homosexuals are unable to wed because they cannot procreate, then why should women who have gone through menopause be able to? If non-Catholics can go to heaven as long as they are good people (as stated by Pope Benedict XVI, a conservative pope by many standards), then why practice any faith at all? These were just a few of the questions I wrestled with, finding no satisfying conclusion.

Rather than give up my faith, I doubled down on involvement in the Church, hoping that my service could somehow fill the hollow space I felt when I tried to truly believe in the spiritual aspects of Mass. Even if I felt or heard nothing when I prayed, maybe I could get to a deeper level of spirituality by working hard enough at it and doing all the right things young religious people do. So I joined my church's youth group, went on immersions, led retreats, and played music at Mass. I became extremely concerned with working hard at being a student and avoiding drinking or doing drugs—mostly because the thought made me uncomfortable. My friends in high school were mostly of the same mentality, and I felt comfortable and happy with the life I knew. While I didn't think of myself as exceedingly religious, religion became a part of who I was and how others perceived me. I even decided on a Catholic university where I knew there would be groups for religious students, where I could find a place to fit in.

Things came to a head during my freshman year. Even though I tried attending Mass weekly (as I had before), the ability to skip out without disappointing my family felt…freeing? My childhood sense of Catholicism would have chided my absences as lazy and a desire to avoid the sacrifice that faith necessitates. However, it felt good that I didn't have to feign that I was a "good Catholic" when I had this spiritual and rational dissonance. My attendance dwindled to about once per month, and by the time summer rolled around, I spent its entirety not attending Mass.

Reflecting upon my faith journey and where I have landed now, it is hard to pinpoint one exact moment or big idea that moved me from "Catholic" to "non-practicing." I think lots of rituals do have an important purpose, and I still try to use them in my daily life. For example, I resolved my conundrum of prayer's purpose by reframing it as a time for meditation; for me, prayer is an opportunity to clear my mind and allow myself the ability to focus on my goals and needs, especially surrounding how to "do the right thing" given the challenges present in my life at the time. I think that the Church is steadily moving away from being old-fashioned and, in some areas, toward being a groundbreakingly progressive institution. How many political figures advocate for open borders, pressure first world nations to adopt and ratify environmental protection measures, and literally wash the feet of the imprisoned?

I think the common thread uniting nonpracticing, marginal, and former Catholics is that we are never satisfied without reasonable answers. I continue to search for spiritual and religious practices that can make me a better, more holistic and loving person, in whatever form that medium might be. Who knows, maybe someday this will mean a return to Catholicism. For me, this would require a change in some foundational Church teachings, like allowing contraceptives, homosexual marriage, and female priests. Moreover, it would need to be more flexible in its teachings and embrace the ambiguity that comes with nonabsolutist religious practices. While global figures like Pope Francis are a good start, I think it would take an act of God for me to return to Catholicism (pun intended). I would need to feel some sort of spiritual awakening that could help me join faith and rationality together, bridging the gap between the two. Until then, I can only keep asking deeper questions of myself and remaining open to where I need to be.

Eddie Kelinsky, twenty-three, was born and raised in sunny Southern California, a third-generation resident of Pasadena. After finishing high school, he moved to Northern California to attain a dual BS in political science and environmental studies. He currently works at his alma mater and enjoys cooking, watching television, and traveling the world.

Being Left

FROM CATHOLIC TO AGNOSTIC

by Patrick Burns

I hold what the political establishment would deem very "liberal" views. I have a prolabor outlook and support unions. I consider myself a feminist. I am concerned with social issues such as racial injustice, the rights of immigrants, and LGBTQ rights. I support social services for the poor, higher taxes for wealthy citizens, and generally believe the government should play an active role in improving the lives of marginalized groups at the expense of the powerful. I am not a pacifist, but strongly believe that the world would be a better place if war and military intervention were reduced.

To categorize me on the Catholic spectrum as "marginal" is a significant understatement. I am probably what most would describe as an "agnostic"—I neither believe in nor deny the existence of God. I do not have faith in a Christian God, at least as I have understood the conception of it. I believe Jesus existed and was an extraordinary human being, but a mortal or a prophet, possibly the most powerful prophet the world has ever seen. As for moral issues, I believe that contraceptives should be distributed widely, even to teenagers. I believe homosexual people should have the same rights as heterosexual people. I believe women should be eligible for the priesthood and have the same rights as men in the Church's hierarchy. I hold pro-choice views and do not believe people who have had abortions have committed sins. My stance on issues of life is more complicated—I do not support the death penalty, for example, but also think euthanasia should be legal. All that said, I strongly believe in the Church's message about the redistribution of wealth and taking care of the less fortunate. As a citizen and marginal Catholic, I also retain an interest in the affairs of the Church. I try to follow changes to the Church's platform and leadership, but my role with respect to the Church is mostly that of an engaged outside observer.

My remaining connections to the Catholic Church are twofold. First, my aunt and uncle are very involved in their community church group and invite me to church events. I enjoy interacting at the events with many Catholic people, and at times I have engaged in Catholic traditions. Second, many of the charity groups that I am involved with are Catholic ones, such as a local political action group. Also, I perform a limited amount of pro bono work, representing undocumented immigrants. That pro bono work mostly comes through the Catholic Legal Immigration Network, a generally pro-immigration organization that advances the rights of immigrants.

I was raised in the Catholic Church. I was baptized at an early age and received first communion and confirmation. I never confessed to a priest. I remember going to Sunday school, but not frequently. As a teenager, my parents took me to Mass every Sunday until I started high school. From there, my participation and interest dropped off significantly. I was married in the Catholic Church (but am divorced now), although at the time I was not a very engaged or active Catholic.

I recall feeling conflicted about the Catholic Church at an early age. On the one hand, my ancestors were Catholic and I had many friends with whom I went to church. I also was drawn to the teachings and words of Jesus Christ as spelled out in many verses of the Bible. On the other hand, I had a great appetite for history and was disappointed to learn about the violent and oppressive history of the Catholic Church, such as the Inquisition, the Church's views on slavery in the Americas, or Pope Pius's support for the Nazi party. That negative history, as well as the fact that I never developed any kind of faith or belief in a Catholic God, is what drew me away from the religion. In high school, and especially in college, I began to study other religions. My interest was limited to studying the religions; I never practiced any. By the time I left college, I had developed the view that Catholicism, and Christianity in general, influenced many undesirable views and negative outcomes, and I did not want to be an active member of those religions.

Despite my problems with Catholicism, I am attracted to the social and political goals and views of the Church. I am drawn to pursuing racial and social justice and the Church's emphasis on advocating for and helping the less fortunate. Of the various Christian branches, I find Catholicism to be much more in line with the words of Jesus Christ. Although I do not believe Jesus Christ is Godlike, I am attracted to his message and teachings about cherishing the poor, taking care of family, and putting the needs of others before your own.

I like that Catholics are more prolabor than what I know of other branches of Christianity. Catholic groups are highly engaged with labor strikes and workers' rights initiatives. When I was a union organizer, liberal Catholic political action groups would often support our goals. I also am attracted to the pro-immigration views of the Church, and appreciate that Catholics tend to support the rights of immigrants. A lot of my experience working with immigrants on pro bono cases involves interacting with other Catholic lawyers. And though I would wager that we hold very different views on faith in God, and other aspects of Christianity, I really appreciate that those lawyers make a tremendous personal sacrifice. They could earn more money and have greater job security, but choose to advocate for refugees who have come to the United States as victims of oppression.

In short, macro-level issues attract me to the Catholic Church. I am in favor of the Church's approach to solving the larger issues in our society such as poverty, homelessness, immigration, and labor, and appreciate that many of the Catholics I know do valuable charitable work. What I find unattractive about the Catholic Church are its prohibitions against individual-level "sins" and its decrees of morality. I admit it is possible that I hold a distorted view of the Church's position on individual moral issues, and I understand not all Catholics believe in many of these prohibitions and doctrines. But I have heard plenty of Catholic leaders decry certain sexual behaviors that I find completely acceptable: impure thoughts, premarital sex, masturbation, and so forth. Aside from my own personal disagreement as to the virtue of those acts, I have no interest in an organized religion reinforcing negative views about sexual behavior. For those within the religion, I have no problem with how they live their own lives, but I do not think prominent Catholic leaders should be preaching about sexual moral issues.

The other part of the Catholic Church I find unattractive is its paramount teaching that one can only achieve salvation through faith in God. To be fair, I do not believe in salvation at all. But to the extent salvation exists, I do not understand why the way one lives one's life is not more important than devotion to a deity that nobody could possibly know with certainty exists. I realize that at some point a religion may not be a religion if there is no teaching about connecting to God and having faith in a deity, but the Catholic Church holds up faith as an indispensable quality.

I am also not attracted to Catholic prayer and worship. I do not enjoy the fact that Mass every week is virtually the same, except for possibly a few different words in the priest's sermon. I do not feel better by engaging in the ritualistic aspects of Mass, such as taking the Eucharist and reciting the same prayers over and over again. I understand that many of these rituals are central to Catholics' belief in the holy sacrifice of Mass, but I do not understand why Mass cannot incorporate what I view as the positive aspects of the Church, like the social welfare and political directives. Some biblical readings touch on these issues, but it is not enough to make me interested in attending Mass regularly.

I also have a distaste for Catholic organization and hierarchy, beginning with the idea of the supremacy of the pope and equating the pope with the Holy Father. I find the Catholic Church hierarchy to be very authoritarian and, as an outside observer, it constantly feels as if the Catholic Church is wielding a tremendous power in secret. I do not like that, even if my perception is overblown. In addition, the pope and the cardinals seem to be much more conservative, rigid, and traditional than many of the Church's members. This rigid hierarchy and failure of leadership is partly to blame for some of the Church's major scandals that have turned me away from it, such as the covering up of widespread instances of sexual abuse committed by priests in the past few decades. This covering up of terrible acts explicitly contradicts core tenets of the teachings of Jesus.

Finally, I must mention what I consider the biggest failure of the contemporary Catholic Church: inequality toward women. The teachings of Catholicism have the potential for feminism to exist, and yet the Church is overtly antiwoman. Since everything flows from ordination in the Catholic hierarchy, the inability for women to be ordained as priests prevents them from being a means to salvation. I also disagree with the Church's positions on sexual health issues that disproportionately affect women, such as deeming abortion to be a grave sin and suppressing the availability of contraceptives. At the very least, it is not good that there are so few female voices with the ability to make decisions within Catholic leadership. I believe this is a total failure of the Catholic Church and is part of why I find the Catholic hierarchy so unappealing. This absence of voices leads to official views that are drastically out of touch with those of its members.

Patrick Burns is a thirty-three-year-old lawyer living in San Francisco. He grew up in Sacramento, California, and has lived across California throughout his life, save a two-year stint in New Mexico. Patrick has a BA and MA in political science, as well as a JD to practice law. Previously, he spent time working as a union organizer, teaching assistant, high school teacher, and reporter.

Questions

1. Dr. Maureen Day discusses the scope of marginal and former Catholics in the United States, and offers some ideas for prevention and others for outreach. What can your parish do or improve in these respects? What can you do personally to contribute to either effort?

2. Do you have marginal or former Catholics in your life? Do they feel active marginalization from the Church (like Ash O'Conor), are they loosely tethered (like Edward Kelinsky), or do they have strong disagreements on issues of faith or morals that they cannot reconcile (like Patrick Burns)? What sort of personalized approach might you take for each of these authors to invite them from the periphery of Catholicism more closely to the center? That is, what sort of pastoral needs do each have?

3. Authentic, deep listening—as a sincere human act—can be hard to do. This is compounded by practical difficulties when those whom we want to listen to are "over it" or do not feel that speaking is worth their time, as may be the case for many marginal or former Catholics. How can you and your local Catholic community create opportunities to listen to the stories of marginal and former Catholics? What are some forums or projects that might help build authentic relationships between you and marginal or former Catholics?

PART 3

Vocation—Ecclesial Leadership

Young Adult Sisters in the United States

by Jeana Visel, OSB

Young women becoming sisters in the United States today enter in a time of profound transition. Presently, congregations of women religious in the United States may belong to one of two leadership conferences. These began as one national conference in 1956, when the Conference of Major Superiors of Women was founded. In the years following, this conference actively engaged the renewal agenda of Vatican II. Issues of social justice became particularly important, and many communities modified or discarded a habit. In 1971, the conference was renamed the Leadership Conference of Women Religious (LCWR).[1] About the same time, a smaller group broke off from LCWR. Calling themselves the Consortium Perfectae Caritatis, the sisters of this group shared a concern that LCWR had deviated from authentic Church teaching regarding the essentials of religious life. This second group has continued, and in 1992, the superiors of its eighty U.S. communities

---

1. Leadership Conference of Women Religious, "LCWR History," accessed April 30, 2017, https://lcwr.org/about/history.

petitioned Rome and were granted recognition as a second leadership conference, the Council of Major Superiors of Women Religious (CMSWR).[2]

At the time of the split between the two conferences, the LCWR represented most of the apostolic congregations of women religious, with 648 members from 370 communities.[3] Today, the conference still represents nearly 80 percent of the religious sisters in the United States.[4] However, data from the Center for Applied Research in the Apostolate (CARA) indicates that the new growth in religious communities is primarily among those belonging to the CMSWR. These communities tend to maintain more traditional elements of religious life than those of LCWR. While many communities of LCWR are on the decline and may soon die out, a number of those in the CMSWR are growing quickly. Given all this, a young woman joining religious life today may have a very different experience depending on which community she enters.

In studying the data from the CARA survey on those entering religious life in 2016, it becomes clear that the number of young women joining communities belonging to CMSWR outnumbers those joining communities belonging to LCWR or independent contemplative communities. For this study, CARA contacted major superiors of 759 religious congregations, provinces, or monasteries identified by LCWR, CMSWR, the Conference of Major Superiors of Men (CMSM), and the United States bishops (reporting independent contemplative monasteries of women), receiving responses

---

2. Council of Major Superiors of Women Religious, "Who We Are," accessed April 13, 2018, https://cmswr.org/about/who-we-are/.

3. LCWR, "LCWR History."

4. Leadership Conference of Women Religious, "About LCWR," accessed April 30, 2017, https://lcwr.org/about.

from 80 percent of inquiries.[5] The CMSWR reported 144 new
women, the LCWR reported 66 new women, and the contemplative women's communities reported twenty new women.
Of note, 70 percent of superiors reported that no one entered
their institute in 2016 and another 14 percent reported only
one new entrant. Including both men's and women's communities, a mere seven congregations reported receiving ten
or more new members (7). Clearly, much of the new growth
in religious life is concentrated within a limited number of
communities.

Of the 230 new women reported by superiors, 156 of
these individuals responded to the survey, representing 73
religious congregations, provinces, or monasteries (8). Most
of the women entering religious life are young adults, with
95 percent of respondents being forty-five or younger and
82 percent being thirty-five or younger. While the youngest
was eighteen and the eldest sixty-five, the median age was
twenty-six and the average age was twenty-nine (8). Most of
these women first considered a religious vocation at about
age eighteen (20). Thus, the survey responses of women
entering religious life today, for the most part, were colored
by their experiences as young adults. Who are these young
women, and what do they say they are looking for?

For starters, this is a diverse group. While 82 percent
of them were born in the United States, respondents represent thirty-three different countries of origin, with Vietnam
and Mexico being the most common birthplace of those
born abroad (9). In terms of racial diversity, just over one in
five are non-white (10). Most have been Catholic since birth,

---

5. Center for Applied Research in the Apostolate, "Women and Men Entering
Religious Life: The Entrance Class of 2016," ed. Mary Gautier and Bibiana Ngundo
(national survey report, Georgetown University, Washington, DC, February 2017),
7, http://cara.georgetown.edu/2016EntranceClass.pdf. Further references to this
study will be given parenthetically by page number.

coming from families in which both parents are Catholic (11). Most have siblings, and many come from families with at least three children (13). Levels of education range widely, but three-fourths have completed at least an undergraduate degree (14). Many of these women attended a Catholic school in their youth, and sixteen percent have been home-schooled for at least part of their education (15). Most have had some experience with retreats, volunteer work, or high school or college campus ministry (18), and were likely to have been involved in liturgical ministry, faith formation, or music ministry at some point (19).

Respondents noted elements of religious life that attracted them to this vocation. They were "somewhat" or "very much" drawn to religious life by a desire for prayer and spiritual growth, as well as by a sense of call to religious life (23). A majority also felt drawn by a desire to be of service, to be part of a community, and to be more committed to the Church (23). A sense of call to the life was notably stronger for women than for men, while men tended to feel a stronger desire to be committed the Church (24). In terms of what drew new entrants to their particular religious institutes, the spirituality, community life, example of the members, prayer life, and mission of the institute all were "somewhat" or "very much" factors for over 90 percent of respondents. Other factors that at least "somewhat" attracted 80 percent of the respondents include welcome encouragement from current members, the institute's fidelity to the Church, and the community's particular ministries. The life and work of the institute founder and a personal invitation also played significant roles in attracting these young adults (25).

Women became familiar with their religious congregations through their own internet searches, through the recommendation of a friend or advisor, by some interaction at an institute where the members served, and a number of "other" options, with retreats being prominent (27–29). Women more than men indicated that contact with institute members, "Come and See" experiences, and visits to the motherhouse were very helpful to their discernment (31).

When it came time to decide to enter their religious institute, more than nine in ten of all respondents indicated that the community life and lifestyle of the members were "somewhat" or "very much" influences on their decision. More than four in five respondents were "somewhat" or "very much" influenced by the prayer life/styles and type of ministry engaged by the members. Over three-fourths of respondents were influenced by the congregation's practice regarding a habit. Other significant factors affecting the decision to enter included geographic location, age of the members, having an international presence, institute size, and racial/ethnic background of the members (32). Women were more influenced than men by community prayer practices and practice regarding the habit (33). Among the women who responded, 86 percent reported that members of their community wear a habit, while 14 percent indicated that they do not. Across the communities represented that offer the option of wearing a habit, the majority require it to be worn in most or all circumstances; a smaller portion require it only at certain times, or allow it as an option (37). Women's communities are far more likely than men's to require a habit all or most of time (38).

Among the prayer practices ranked most important to them, a vast majority of women indicated that private personal prayer, daily Eucharist, Liturgy of the Hours, or eucharistic adoration were "somewhat" or "very" important. Other devotional prayer (such as the Rosary), faith sharing, common meditation, and nonliturgical common prayer all were similarly ranked "somewhat" or "very" important by most respondents. Women more than men were likely to rank eucharistic adoration, other devotional prayers, faith sharing, common meditation, and nonliturgical common prayer as "very important" (34–35). New sisters value praying and living with other community members, eating together, sharing leisure time, and working together. Over 90 percent of respondents ranked these as "somewhat" or "very" important; no less than 64 percent of respondents ranked each of these as "very" important (36). Clearly, common life matters for these new sisters.

Most women rank their religious community highly, indicating that it is doing a "good" if not "excellent" job in many areas, including opportunities for personal and spiritual growth, commitment to ministry, faithfulness to prayer and spiritual growth, welcome and support of newer members, focus on mission, opportunities for ongoing formation, and fidelity to the Church and its teaching (39, 41–42). More than nine in ten respondents also ranked their religious institute as "good" or "excellent" in their efforts to promote social justice, relationships with one another, response to the needs of the time, quality of community life, sense of identity as religious and as community members, educational opportunities, communal prayer experiences, formation programs, and preparation for ministry (40).

Open-ended questions also allowed respondents to describe with great honesty what drew them to their congregation, and the human and spiritual challenges they face as they become incorporated into community life (43–51, 71–117). While the survey shows some notable prevailing trends among young women entering religious life, these responses also demonstrate the profoundly personal experience of transitioning from independence to a level of interdependence in the rarified environment of initial formation in religious life.

Those entering religious life today need courage. Although the life itself brings its own challenges, looking ahead, members of shrinking communities may find themselves collaborating and perhaps "refounding" their congregations with renewed or transformed vision. If current trends continue, sisters in more traditional, growing communities will soon become the "new normal." Those communities with clear identities and practices currently flourish as countercultural signs of Christianity. However, in the face of an increasingly secular world, these more traditional sisters will need to continue to find creative ways to evangelize and remain engaged with the culture. Their joy and contentment with the life will certainly help.

Sr. Jeana Visel, OSB, joined the Sisters of St. Benedict of Ferdinand, Indiana, in 2003. After teaching high school theology for several years, she pursued further studies at St. John's School of Theology-Seminary in Collegeville, Minnesota, and Catholic University of America. She is Dean of School of Theology programs and Director of the Graduate Theology program at St. Meinrad Seminary and School of Theology. Her most recent book is Icons in the Western Church: Toward a More Sacramental Encounter *(Liturgical Press, 2016).*

Take the Leap of Faith and Jump!

by Clare Bass

I am a young adult Catholic sister. While it is rare to hear that these days, there are many young adult Catholic sisters around the nation and world, and we are alive and kicking! I did not always know I wanted to be a sister or even think I could ever be one. I was born and raised Catholic in a devoted family. My family gave me a strong foundation of love and faith from which to grow. I am so grateful for their love and support in my life. They were my first teachers about what it means to "find your vocation." I am a firm believer that your vocation is tied into your deepest passion(s) and finding your vocation is part of reaching your God-given potential. My mother and grandmother both exemplified this throughout their lives and careers. They each balanced careers and motherhood, and their passion for both aspects emanated from their lives. If you saw them in action on the job, you could tell that something special was there; that it was not ever just about the money, that it was always more about service and helping others. As I grew up, I knew that I wanted to find a career and vocation that I loved as much as they did. As time went on, I became aware of what I was passionate about and what I was not thrilled about.

I knew Catholic sisters growing up as I had a few Irish Sisters of Mercy as teachers and a Daughter of Charity was our superintendent of education. Although I loved and admired them growing up, I did not ever think I would become one of them! I attended a Catholic elementary school and high school, and I was always active in campus ministry in high school and in college. In college I discovered that I got to make my own plans for my life, so I planned a career path and focused on all those things that follow college. I kept praying about my life and brought it all to God. I would get hints that I should consider being a religious sister, but I was so very quick to dismiss them. I laugh now at my denial, but at the time it was no laughing matter. I thought there was no way I could ever do such a thing. On to graduate school I went. Now things were really getting serious! I was more mature than when I was an undergraduate; and at the time, I thought it was the end of my school days, and I really felt I needed to figure out some sort of life plan. So I went about making my own plans: establish a career in politics and government, eventually get married, raise a family. But in my heart, I felt something was missing. I kept trying to figure out what that missing piece was and would adjust my plans to see if that feeling would go away; it didn't. Yet, at the same time that I was praying about my growing confusion, my courage was growing, too. I knew I had to be honest with myself and really look at religious life as a serious option.

As I earnestly began discerning religious life, the peace that filled my heart remained unexplainable. It is "beyond words" because you have to experience it to be able to know it and understand it. Discernment is an involved process, and like any other major decision, not everything happens overnight. Rather, there is an unfolding that happens in God's time, which grows your patience and your self. I went on to find out that other young adult women were being called to religious life and were still joining communities. I found out that there are thousands of communities to choose from. I learned that formation takes awhile and is a set process. I saw that communities of vowed women religious are so full of life and love and, importantly, again I saw that same notion of what it means to "find your vocation," just as my grandmother and mother had.

Life became more vivid for me as I began this new adventure, because love was so present and so were the fruits of the Holy Spirit. I formally began the process of formation with the Sisters of St. Joseph of Carondelet in St. Louis. There, I opened up my heart and mind more than ever before because it became no longer just my *personal* discernment; when I formally joined community, I entered into *communal* discernment.

I learned early on in formation that all relationships are a two-way street, and so I had to clearly communicate with my directors and leadership and vice versa. These past seven years have been the most profound years of my life, and I am not looking back. They have been filled with love, joy, sadness, disappointment, laughter, happiness, and everything in between. It was a major decision for me when I asked to profess first vows with the community. While I was asking to profess vows of chastity, poverty, and obedience for only three years, which is the standard length of time for first profession, for me it might as well had been for life.

Embracing your vocation is also about embracing the mystery of love, of which God is the source, and this Love is shared with each of us. Life is about finding that place within yourself where you can totally share your love with others. How did I ever end up on this particular path in life? Why do some couples end up getting married? How does anyone last fifty years or more in *any* vocation? When we share our stories and get to know one another, we inspire, motivate, and learn from each other. In the end, however, it really is about embracing the mystery of love and faith. I decided take the leap of faith and jump! I do not have all the answers of why it works, but I have also decided it's worth it, it is worth everything I have to offer. And this makes all the difference in the world.

The first thing that comes to mind when I think of the Church and my age-group is that we need to be heard. We need a space within the Church where we can deeply share matters of faith and spirituality. We need a space where true dialogue—that promotes understanding and honesty and not discussion that is adversarial—can occur. After college, it is hard to find a place within the Church, as most of parish life is geared toward families. As far as vocations go, I think the Church and society heavily promote marriage as the best and only option for life. There is more to love than just the romantic aspect, and we do not do a good job of teaching this. Specifically, I would feel more supported if we began to promote and really focus on the integral human development expressed in our Catholic social teaching. We need to look at all aspects of life—including actions and teachings—as a whole Church to evaluate whether we are truly promoting the development of the whole self. It is only from the place of wholeness that each of us can find our vocations. American Catholics will not accept blindly the teachings of the hierarchy and, for my generation especially, I think this means openly discussing the challenges the Catholic Church collectively faces with honesty and integrity. We will not stand for anything less.

As a Catholic sister, I think it is way past due to expand women's leadership within the Church. What would help me in living out my vocation is for us to move beyond the old expectations of religious sisters from the past. I am not "better than" or "higher than" anyone and neither is anyone else. We are all called by God to be loving and compassionate, and to follow the gospel mission of Jesus. We are all called to fully live out the vows we make, whether personal or public, communally or individually. We are all called to work for justice and to promote the common good.

Beyond all the issues, we do have a sacred and rich faith tradition that I want to share with our future generations. My community of women religious is one of those sacred treasures that I want to share. I want to keep inviting women and men to religious life and the priesthood. But it will be hard to invite if no one is around. Quality pastoral care will address the issues with courage and honesty. True dialogue will then be able to take place. The Holy Spirit will steadfastly guide us and our pilgrim journey will continue. Let us put our trust in God so that we can keep sharing the good news of the gospel, so that we might have a conversion of hearts, and so that one day in the future, we can bring about the reign of God on earth.

Sr. Clare Bass, CSJ, is a thirty-four-year-old Sister of St. Joseph of Carondelet under temporary profession. She is passionate about working for social justice and the common good and being a sister in community. She is studying to become a social worker.

The Long Call

by Mara D. Rutten

When I was in my novitiate, we were asked to come up with an image of how we saw God. My classmates came up with many profound and beautiful images: "father," "beloved," "shelter from the storm." All lovely, and all true. But what came to my mind was "alumni association."

I moved a lot after college. Each time I would lose touch with family members and friends, but even as the number of birthday and Christmas cards dwindled each year, my alma mater never failed to find me. God was like that. "Can you give more?" he'd ask. No matter how many times I said, "no," "not now," "I can't," and "maybe next time," he never gave up.

I was the recipient of what I've termed "the long call." Unlike the call stories in the Bible, like those of Moses, Mary, or Paul, there was no one defining moment. They all benefitted from an audible, even physical, offer to take up God's specific plan for them. Set my people free. Bear my son. Stop persecuting my Church. Each a clear command. Even in the more subtle approaches, like in Joseph's dreams, God's instructions were too vivid to ignore.

My call, on the other hand? No burning bushes. No angels. No lightning bolts. Instead it was a buildup of small moments and unmomentous signs that only revealed themselves in retrospect. It was a restlessness that would not abate. It was a still, small voice that pushed me forward, even as I pushed back.

I'm considered a late vocation because I didn't begin the process until my late thirties (I'm now forty-five, but am considered a "young sister" in religious circles, where the average age is mid-seventies). But my story starts much earlier, when I was eight, and four American churchwomen were murdered in El Salvador.

I had never given much thought to martyrdom. It was something I associated with lions' dens. I didn't realize that such injustice and persecution still existed in our world, and I didn't know that following Jesus's commands to feed the hungry, clothe the naked, heal the sick, and visit the prisoner—seemingly so banal—were so revolutionary. I didn't know that people in my time died for it. It was the most beautiful thing I had ever heard, to love that deeply. I wanted to do that.

I had no idea how. I didn't know what I wanted to do when I grew up, except that I wanted to "make a difference." I pursued academia, then public service. I put down roots in the community, was active in my parish, and gave money to various charities and causes. Whenever I thought that I'd finally found my way, I'd get that same restless feeling. The better my life got professionally, personally, financially, even romantically, there was that call again. I could almost see God on the other end, a wry smile on his face, as he asked, "Now?" Because I had long suspected that I might best serve God and the poor in religious life.

It wasn't that I was saying no to God about this so much as I was saying, "Make me another offer." My role models were modern martyrs, and that was a lot to live up to. I may have been good at a lot of things, but I didn't feel I was good enough to deserve the same kind of call these women had. In the rural county where I grew up, there were no Catholic schools, and we had only one priest and no sisters. My only other points of reference for what nuns were like was summer Bible school and *The Sound of Music*. Evidently you had to love children and play the guitar, and I never could master barre chords.

I had a hundred excuses about why I couldn't do it, most of them modern variations on standard biblical dodges. Moses may have been slow of tongue, but mine was razor sharp. Amos was a lowly sheepherder, but I had a PhD and too much educational debt. Jeremiah may have been too young, but I'd been putting it off for so long that I was getting too old. Jonah just up and ran off. I tried that, but God had seen it all before and was onto me.

It was another murder that caused me to take stock of my life and finally stop making excuses. I worked in law enforcement when my city experienced a mass shooting. For nearly two weeks, my office worked twenty-four hours a day. At the time, I was volunteering overnight at a homeless shelter because it was the only ministry I could fit into my work schedule. As our working hours kept changing, I canceled at the shelter three times with little warning. While sympathetic, life went on and the women needed to have someone dependable. I had to give it up.

That's where God found me, so vulnerable that I was able to be honest with him and myself for the first time since I was eight. I had told everyone, God included, that my life was about service; but in reality, it had been self-serving. I served an idea of myself that was comfortable championing the poor, but didn't spend much time getting to know them. The shelter was the only place in which I stopped talking about "the homeless" and was really present to them. I had been relegating the real moments of my life, the ones I most valued, to my spare time, as if my vocation—the call to serve the poor I'd first felt as a child—was a hobby.

"We've been doing things your way for awhile," God whispered. "How's that working out?" I knew it wasn't. I had everything; I was living a good, Christian life. But I needed the shelter, that contact, that commitment. "Now?" he whispered, again. This time, the answer was yes.

Answering Jesus's call to drop everything and follow him was a little more difficult in the twenty-first century than I had anticipated, and I felt real empathy for the rich, young man who couldn't do it. With a mortgage worth more than my house and grad school debt, it took me a little over a year to raise enough money to be able to pursue a vow of poverty (the irony is not lost on me). I sold everything from my house to the hangers in my closet. My friends and family hosted yard sales, and my parish held a spaghetti dinner. I even ran a marathon that my church sponsored.

Many of my friends have since asked why I entered religious life instead of becoming a lay missioner or working for an NGO. I can only explain it like this: We each have a primary person at the center of our lives who guides our decisions. For most people, this is a spouse, child, parent, or even a friend. But for me, that primary person is God as manifested in the poor and marginalized. This is whom I have chosen to wholly commit my life to.

I am now under first vows with the Maryknoll Sisters of St. Dominic, serving as a missionary sister in Cambodia. Although I didn't know it all those years ago, this is the congregation that lost two of the women in El Salvador that first sparked my vocation. From them I've learned not only to stand up for the poor but to journey with them, to offer the unconditional love of God to each person we meet. These tough ladies have given me a lot of advice for being a missionary sister: pray constantly, love unconditionally, and learn to fix an outboard motor!

I don't regret how my journey unfolded because it made me who I am. But part of the reason I am a late vocation didn't stem from my hesitation. On more than one occasion over the years, I looked into religious life, but the second question vocation directors always asked me was about student loans. It often felt to me that if this was the main reason that I couldn't pursue religious life—money—then maybe I wasn't being called after all. I'm not the only one: a December 2015 *Global Sisters Report* by Dawn Araujo-Hawkins stated that 34 percent of congregations had aspirants decline to apply because of student debt.

Prayer leads to action, and when the Church prays for vocations, it also needs to take action. With the decline in numbers of those interested in religious life, we cannot afford to discourage these young people. Several foundations have considered the problem, and every vicar for religious and every vocation director should know about them. Dioceses can offer grants as part of their charitable works. Some congregations will consider helping aspirants on a case-by-case basis, and this should be considered, for if a congregation could use an aspirant's skills, should she be rejected because she didn't wait to go to school until after she took vows?

The Church also needs to remind the faithful that we are all, by virtue of our baptismal promises, called to serve, even if we aren't all called to live in a religious community. I was lucky that my parish understood this. I had a wonderful, supportive community who pledged to my marathon, threw a spaghetti supper, donated items for me to sell, and opened their homes when mine sold. They weren't just sending me to religious life; they were participating in mission with me. I've hung my marathon medal on my wall in Cambodia for just this purpose: to remind myself that sometimes the journey can feel impossibly long, but with perseverance, and lots of support, you will find your way.

Sr. Mara D. Rutten, MM, PhD, is a forty-five-year-old Maryknoll Sister of St. Dominic. Originally from Minnesota, she received her PhD in American Indian history from Arizona State University before pursuing a career with the federal government. She now works with migrants, refugees, and victims of human trafficking in Cambodia.

Growing in Relationship with God and Others

by Karla Felix-Rivera, VDMF

Like many prophets' journeys, my vocation story includes grace-filled times of fervently seeking to unfold God's will and moments of trying to convince God that consecration was not for me. With the following words, my hope is to express one thing: my vocation is an ongoing relationship with my Creator.

I grew up in Tequila, Jalisco, Mexico, and quickly became my grandmother's shadow. As a child, following her around included frequent visits to a monastery and our town Church. I still remember standing before the monastery's wooden front door waiting for one of the nuns to open so we could enter the ever-so-mysterious cloister. My grandmother explained how consecrated women were holier, closer to God, and merited our respect. Not surprisingly, I grew up seeing consecrated life in "us" versus "them" terms: "us" the normal people in the world and "them" the consecrated women who gave their lives to God because they couldn't find husbands. Visiting the blessed sacrament at random moments during the day allowed me to learn small prayers while my grandmother repeated elaborate grown-up

335

prayers. My first theological reflection took place around the age of five or six while repeating my only memorized prayer: *Niñito Jesús, eres niño como yo, por eso te quiero y te doy mi corazón* (Little child, Jesus, you are a child like me, that's why I love you and give you my heart). Staring at the tabernacle while pondering about the consequences of Jesus being a little child led me to ask God two questions: "How do you fit inside that box?" and "Are you comfortable in there?" The answer I received was twofold: Jesus was indeed cramped up and my visits made him happy since he couldn't get out. This response told me that God is someone real, is present in my physical space, and welcomes my company.

My family moved to the San Francisco Bay Area when I was seven years old, and I studied with the Carmelite and the Salesian sisters prior to entering Mercy High School in Burlingame. In the sixth grade, I joined the school choir and was introduced to "The Wedding Banquet" song. The song contains creative excuses to get out of the celebration. One after another, the man lists reasons, from family to work, as to why he cannot come to the wedding feast. Somehow, I felt Jesus's disappointment when his party didn't work out as intended. Touching God's sorrow brought me to tell God, "If you invite me to an exciting project, I won't make excuses." I entered high school in 1993 without forgetting that I had promised God that I would be open to divine invitations.

I discovered boyfriends, sneaking out to parties, and late-night bonfires on the beach at the same time I perceived the call to become a consecrated woman. My mother literally forced me to attend a teenager's retreat offered by the Verbum Dei Missionary Fraternity when I was in high school. I tried to convince her that retreats were for nonchurchgoing, problematic individuals. In my estimation, I did not qualify for retreats. As expected, my mother had the last word and I was dropped off at the missionaries' retreat center. When the time came to say goodbye, I asked one of the missionaries a question that changed my life, "What do missionaries do?" The question was important because these were young women who seemed like they were smart and talented enough to pursue careers and have families of their own; that they didn't was bewildering. She responded spontaneously, "We nurture our friendship with God and help others relate with God." Her response demanded an applause and I replied, "Good for *you*, keep up the good work!" I was unable to forget her words and eventually found myself in a spiritual crisis since my relationship with God was a dry and boring monologue. I knew God existed, but I didn't know how to perceive God's thoughts, feelings, desires, and actions. Curiosity seized me and I began attending a simple weekly prayer group guided by the Verbum Dei missionaries.

I slowly began to practice a contemplative approach that involved meditating on Scripture; this method of prayer is at the heart of the Verbum Dei Missionary spirituality. The more I took time for this type of prayer, the more my personal emptiness, questions, and need for a fulfilled life became apparent. I discovered that prayer required self-disclosure, stillness, and openness. Although I was still under eighteen years old, I attended retreats and activities with married couples, priests, and single and consecrated persons. Eventually, I was part of retreat leadership teams composed of consecrated and nonconsecrated individuals. The "us" versus "them" mentality shattered, and I was awestruck when I first heard that I was "consecrated" in baptism and that all baptized persons had a place in the missionary life of the Church.

Attending Mercy High School made me value education and political engagement. As a result, I was involved in political campaigning and wanted to pursue a career in teaching political science to shape the minds of future voters. During a conference given by one of my political heroes, I was dev-astated when his proposed programs seem contradictory to what I had learned regarding God's vision for humanity. My disappointment led to the realization that evangelization had political consequences. It was simple: God's unconditional love meant compassion, equality, and justice over violence, racism, divisions, and greed. Unexpectedly, I related with Moses as he stood before the burning bush hearing God call him to a full-time "job" as a prophet in the world. What I had intuited became obvious: God was calling me to pursue a missionary life in the Verbum Dei Missionary Fraternity.

Perhaps I was distracted, but I had not realized that consecrated missionaries professed the evangelical vows of poverty, chastity, and obedience. The thought of living a vowed life petrified me. I wanted to follow Christ, help others grow in their relationship with God, and transform the world by preaching the gospel. Yet *those* archaic vows seemed incompatible with my personality and modernity. After a period of lengthy arguments with God and even get-ting a tattoo to feel I had a claim over my life, I realized how the vowed life is a path to inner freedom. After years of for-mation, temporal profession, and theological studies, I pro-fessed perpetual vows in 2007.

I entered my community seventeen years ago, and I have developed deep friendships and experienced painful losses. A few consider me a blessing and others deem me a head-ache. Already having professed perpetual vows, I once hope-lessly fell in love and had to rediscover, redefine, and renew my choice as a consecrated missionary woman. Challenged in serving on my provincial's formation and leadership teams, today I find peace remembering that no member in my insti-tute has it all figured out. Over the years, my ministry has included preaching to uninterested teenagers, dedicated catechists, semiatheist university students, married couples, and hardworking bishops.

My life is not without troubles, and pain has helped me discover what is at the core of my vocation: the experience of unconditionally belonging to God, especially when I find myself broken and empty-handed. Among several experiences over the years, one stands out: the day the doctor called to inform me that my back injury was severe and the chances of recovery were unknown. I remember going to the chapel with tears running down my face. Since I was unable to kneel or sit due to pain, I leaned against the wall as feelings of sadness, grief, fear, and uncertainty invaded my whole being. I was suddenly a deflated "superwoman" who had nothing to offer. "God, I'm really sad." God's response was powerful, "Me, too." In that instant, I felt incredible joy and fulfillment. It became clear that consecration was about sharing every intimate experience of life with my Creator, and I understood that the only thing God expected from me was that I trust that God is unconditionally loving me when I am powerless, weak, and unsuccessful. After years of recovery, I returned to rollerblading at the San Francisco Marina and recently discovered snowshoeing.

Missionary women need support from the Church community since our mission is essential to the future of the Church. In my personal experience, a full-time dedication to prayer and ministry of the Word—which unfolds in preaching, teaching, and providing formations—requires much preparation. The degrees I've obtained have prepared me in important ways, but the real preparation ultimately requires long hours of meditation, contemplation, and study. Belonging to a relatively new and small institute is challenging. One of the biggest challenges is remaining faithful to my charism and not getting distracted by looking for paid work that is not related to my charism. It is hard to find financial support for spiritual programs, and as a Church community, we need to support small communities that provide much-needed ministries. Obtaining a canon law degree has allowed me to work in the Church as a woman in diocesan tribunals as a "Defender of the Bond" and judge as well as a professor in the permanent diaconate program in my home diocese. I've also been offered opportunities to guide retreats and give workshops that have never been given by a woman. While I am thankful for the opportunities, it is disheartening to see how our Church still needs to grow in trusting and *requesting* women to participate in the life of the Church.

My personal journey and work with married couples and young adults have led me to strongly encourage vocational discernment as a necessary tool for all individuals. Because there are many states of life in the Church (vowed, married, ordained, and single life), vocational programs cannot be limited to those who express interest in consecrated life or ordained ministry. We must promote prayer as that sacred relationship with our Creator through which our personal paths of life are discovered. Further, we must present all states of life as equal journeys toward holiness, happiness, and discipleship. Otherwise, consecrated life will continue being viewed as that "other," holier, and isolated path of life reserved for a "weird" few.

Sr. Karla Felix-Rivera, VDMF, JCD, is a thirty-eight-year-old member of the Verbum Dei Missionary Fraternity and lives in California. She completed a BA in philosophy at the University of San Francisco, an MDiv at the Jesuit School of Theology at Berkeley, and a canon law licentiate at the Catholic University of America.

Questions

1. Sr. Jeana Visel provides us with the scope of women entering religious life in the United States today. There are not only fewer women, but there are shifts in the motivations and theological visions of these women. What do you believe has contributed to the decline in vocations and what is fueling these shifts? What does this mean for the future of the Church?

2. The essayists share a common theme of actively resisting when they initially discerned a call to religious life that is not present in the men's stories (or at least not to the same degree). Why do you think this might be?

3. Two challenges that emerge from some of these women's stories are (1) financial difficulties facing women religious (either as an obstacle to religious life or for their community broadly) and (2) a reluctance or unwillingness to include women in important leadership roles (see Coleman's excursus for more on this). First, what sort of financial responsibility should Catholics and Catholic institutions offer women's religious communities? Second, why do women, even women as well educated, highly trained, and committed as these, experience such resistance when serving the Church?

Seminarians and Priests

ORDAINED LEADERSHIP IN THE TWENTY-FIRST CENTURY

by Mary L. Gautier

Parish-connected Catholics are gradually realizing that the large numbers of priests and sisters that provided the bulk of the pastoral work force for the last fifty years have been diminishing in recent years. This decline has been a contributing factor in many dioceses around the country in decisions to merge and close parishes, and share a pastor among more than one parish. It has also been a contributing factor in the rapid increase in the numbers of permanent deacons and lay ecclesial ministers being added to the pastoral workforce. Some are beginning to question whether religious vocations are becoming a relic of the past among contemporary Catholics.

The reality is that young men continue to respond to a call from God by committing themselves to a lifelong religious vocation. The number of Catholic men enrolled in postgraduate level formation for priestly ministry has been steady at about 3,500 each year for the last twenty years, producing roughly 500 ordinations per year. This is still too few new priests to compensate for the numbers of older priests who are retiring or dying each year. A few hundred new ordinations hardly make a dent in the demand for priests in areas of the country where the Catholic population is increasing rapidly. Yet it does provide evidence against the trope that lifelong religious commitment is anathema to young Catholics. This précis explores data on seminarians and newly ordained priests from recent studies by the Center for Applied Research in the Apostolate (CARA) at Georgetown University. The analysis herein will describe their numbers, their demographic characteristics, and what has motivated and encouraged them to become priests.

A CARA survey in 2012 found that 13 percent of never-married Catholic men ages fourteen and older had considered priesthood at some point in their lives. This proportion corresponds to nearly 1.5 million eligible Catholic men who have considered priesthood as a vocation. More than half of them first considered a vocation when they were teens, but a fifth began thinking about priesthood when they were children. What factors influence the likelihood that a young man will consider priesthood?

The study found that men who attend a Catholic high school are six times as likely to have considered a vocation as those who did not. Those who were active in a parish youth group during their elementary school years are more than five times as likely as to have considered a vocation than those who were not active in such a group. Men who had been encouraged to consider a vocation by another person were more than twice as likely as those who were not encouraged—and each additional person who encouraged a vocation increased the likelihood of that person considering a vocation! Having a friend or a relative who is a clergy or a religious also increases the likelihood of considering a vocation. Finally, those who attended a World Youth Day or a Catholic Youth Conference were more than four times as likely to say that they had considered becoming a priest as those who did not.

Considering a vocation is not the same as following through with a vocation, but other CARA studies of the men who have responded to the call to ordination in recent years find corresponding characteristics among recent ordinands. New priests in 2017 say that they first considered a vocation to priesthood at age sixteen, on average. About half of these ordinands attended a Catholic elementary school, and four in ten attended a Catholic high school. This is more than double the proportion among the U.S. adult Catholic population as a whole who have attended a Catholic high school. Half of these new priests had participated in a parish youth group, too, which was another contributing factor noted in the previous study.

Four in five of the men ordained in 2017 said that someone in their life had encouraged them to consider a vocation to priesthood. In fact, they report an average of four different people who had encouraged their vocation. Most commonly, these encouragers included their parish priest, a friend, a parent, or a parishioner. A third of these men had a relative who is a priest or a religious, too. Finally, 15 percent of these men had participated in a World Youth Day and 7 percent had participated in a National Catholic Youth Conference before they entered the seminary.

Another CARA research study on seminaries, from its annual Catholic Ministry Formation Directory database, also describes some of the demographic characteristics of those who are answering the call to the priesthood today. In particular, the data show that men in the final four years of seminary formation (known as theologate level) are trending slightly younger than in years past. While less than half of these men were in their twenties in the early part of the

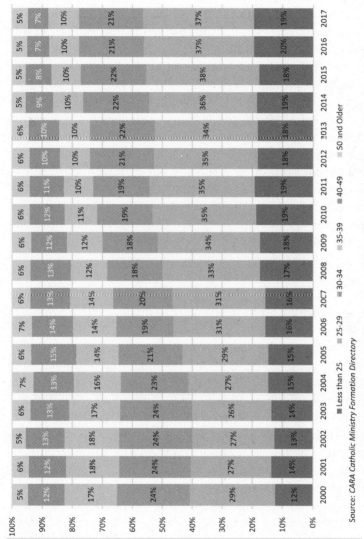

Figure 1. Age Distribution of Theologate Enrollment in U.S. Seminaries, 2000–2017

Source: CARA *Catholic Ministry Formation Directory*

Legend: Less than 25 ▪ 25-29 ▪ 30-34 ▪ 35-39 ▪ 40-49 ▪ 50 and Older

twenty-first century, by 2009 more than half of the men studying at the theologate level were in their twenties. During the same period, the proportion of seminarians in their late thirties and older declined, from a third of all seminarians in 2000 to just over a fifth in 2017.

In terms of their race and ethnic background, the men studying for priesthood now and those recently ordained are more similar to the overall Catholic population than they are to the priests that preceded them in ministry. About seven in ten men in theologates are Caucasian, about one in ten are Hispanic/Latino, another one in ten are Asian/Pacific Islander, and the other tenth are African American, Native American, or some other race or ethnicity. This compares to less than six in ten adult Catholics nationally who are Caucasian, about a third who are Hispanic/Latino, 4 percent who are Asian/Pacific Islander, and another 4 percent who are some other race or ethnicity. In contrast, more than nine in ten Catholic priests in the United States are Caucasian, and just 3 percent are Hispanic/Latino, 3 percent are Asian/Pacific Islander, and 2 percent are African American or some other race or ethnicity.

Another factor that contributes to increasing the ethnic diversity of these seminarians is the fact that about a fifth of seminarians are foreign born, most commonly from Mexico, Vietnam, Colombia, Nigeria, the Philippines, and Poland. In fact, a quarter of the men ordained to priesthood in 2017 were born outside the United States. These men increase the ethnic diversity of the priesthood and provide cultural richness that contributes to the multicultural reality that is Catholic parish life today.

These studies can tell us a great deal about who these seminarians and new priests are, in terms of their characteristics, experiences, and backgrounds. The studies do not shed any light, though, on how these men will function as priests. What sort of priesthood do they anticipate? Will they be "shepherds living with the smell of the sheep," as Pope Francis called on them to be during his homily at the Chrism Mass in St. Peter's Basilica on March 28, 2013? These men grew up during the papacies of St. John Paul and Benedict XVI, and their vocational call was influenced by the words and leadership styles of these two popes. Some anecdotes suggest that this younger generation of priests may have a different understanding of priestly identity and church leadership than that of the generation before them.

To test that hypothesis, the late sociologist Dean Hoge constructed a scale of priestly identity he called the "cultic model index" from priests' responses to a set of five statements having to do with aspects of priestly identity. Hoge's research concluded that these younger priests tend to place more emphasis on maintaining a distinctive priestly identity, with a clear distinction between priests and laity—a "cultic" model of priesthood as distinguished from a "servant-leader" model of priesthood that was more common among older generations of priests.

CARA replicated that index in its 2009 national survey of priests and then divided priests by age group to see whether this distinction still holds. CARA divided all priests in the sample into four roughly equal-sized groups according to their responses on the "cultic model index" and then separated them by decade of age.

Priests in their seventies are approximately evenly distributed across the index, from more progressive "servant-leader" type priests to more traditionalist "cultic" type priests. Priests in their fifties and sixties tend to be a bit more on the progressive end of the index and priests in their thirties and forties tend to be more on the traditionalist end of the index. But does this apparent difference in attitude about priestly identity translate into a different style of church leadership?

Figure 2. Model of Priesthood by Age of Priest

	More Progressive ... More Traditionalist			
30s	9%	23%	31%	37%
40s	14	32	18	36
50s	22	32	24	22
60s	33	34	19	14
70s and older	22	28	26	24
All priests	24	31	23	23

After all, regardless of their attitude about what it means to be a priest, these men will still be ministering with permanent deacons and lay ecclesial ministers in parishes large and small. In the majority of parishes, these ministers outnumber active priests. CARA asked priests nationally about their attitudes toward collaboration in ministry and found that two in three or more, regardless of age group, agree that the Church should move faster in empowering laypersons in ministry. Similar proportions of priests, across all age groups, agree that the Church should allow women greater participation in all lay ministries. More than two in three recently ordained priests agree that there should be more discussion in the Church about collaboration with deacons, lay ministers, and international priests.

Young men today continue to be influenced by the secular and the religious culture around them as they listen for, and respond to, a call to priestly vocations. There is much that we can do, as Catholics, to nurture and support that call, from earliest childhood, through seminary formation, and even into the early years of priestly ministry. If we as a Church desire happy, healthy, holy priests, we need to pay attention to the factors that influence, strengthen, and support priestly vocations.

Mary L. Gautier, PhD, is a Senior Research Associate at CARA, the Center for Applied Research in the Apostolate at Georgetown University. She has a PhD in sociology from Louisiana State University. Before coming to CARA in 1998, Mary taught sociology at Louisiana State University and Texas Christian University, and served as a lay pastoral associate at St. George Parish in Baton Rouge, Louisiana, for six years. At CARA, Mary specializes in Catholic demographic trends in the United States, manages CARA databases on Church information, and conducts demographic projects and computer-aided mapping. She also edits The CARA Report, *a quarterly research publication, and other CARA publications. She is coauthor of nine books on Catholicism in the United States, most recently* Catholic Parishes of the 21st Century *(Oxford University Press, 2017).*

The Life of a Young Parish Priest

by Carlos Medina, OSA

I wasn't always a priest. In fact, I was ordained to the presbyterate less than a year ago in June 2016. Ten years prior to that, I was a twenty-year-old college student, listening to a parish mission appeal at St. Francis Catholic Church in the Oakland Diocese that had a profound effect on me. The missionary priest who preached the appeal asked for prayers and financial support for his mission in Egypt, but I felt that through him God was calling me to be part of God's mission. At the time, the only way I could conceive of becoming a part of God's mission was to become a priest. Since I desired to live in a community, I visited a few religious orders, and eventually found in the Order of St. Augustine the kind of community life I longed for.

What I found most attractive about the Order of St. Augustine was the fraternal love among the friars despite the great diversity of personalities and points of view. When St. Augustine wrote our rule of life, he had already experienced living in community with men who had entered from various socioeconomic levels. He knew the struggles of living with men from different backgrounds. Yet after his conversion, and for the remainder of his life, St. Augustine lived in common with other men to help him seek God and better know himself. The Augustinian charism is to place the search for God above all else—which every human heart longs for—in the context of community life. Like Augustine, I felt I could continue growing to become who God was calling me to be, accompanied by other friars in the same quest for God.

As I was being formed during my first three years as an Augustinian friar, I felt increasing certainty that God was, indeed, calling me to dedicate my life to God's mission. This calling, for me, meant living a consecrated life as an Augustinian friar. Still, I questioned whether I was called to be a priest. We have friars who are not ordained and remain brothers as well as friars who are ordained, so I continued to wonder whether or not my call within religious community included sacramental ministry to God's people.

It was through the people I served that I received Christ's confirmation that he had called me to the priesthood. First, I had been visiting patients in a hospital and in nursing homes in supervised ministry for almost two years. During this time several patients told me I would be a great priest, and I felt myself wishing I was a priest already so that I could absolve their sins.

A second confirmation of my priestly calling occurred during my ministry with a community of Catholic refugees from Burma during a year of pastoral formation in San Diego. It started when a Burmese refugee asked me to start a Burmese Catholic group. I knew several Protestant and Buddhist refugees from Burma in San Diego, but I did not know any Catholics. The man said he had heard there were Catholics who had been going to Protestant churches because they did not have a group or know where the parish was. I reluctantly agreed, unsure of how to begin, but trusting in the guidance and aid of the Holy Spirit. One by one, individuals and families joined our group, which gradually grew to about a dozen families. As they came in, I helped them register at the parish and provided catechetical instruction and sacramental preparation. I very much enjoyed calling forth the gifts of several equipped people and seeing the small community grow in that year. This taught me that one of the functions of a priest is to govern by way of calling forth the gifts of others, collaborating with them to build up the local church. As I was working with this small Catholic community of Burmese refugees, they asked for me to be ordained so that I could also preside at special moments of religious significance, such as weddings. Through these confirming experiences during my formation, I felt that God was calling me to be ordained to the priesthood.

I am now the assistant pastor in a parish with a significant Hispanic population and a K–8 Catholic school under our spiritual care. Since I am an Augustinian, each day I take part in common morning and evening prayer with several other friars, as well as dinner and social time. Because I also maintain close ties with the Burmese refugees in the area, my particular vocation within the priesthood remains engaged in both local and global concerns.

Most people, including myself, associate the priesthood with the Eucharist. I see a connection between celebrating the death and life of Christ at the table of the Lord and celebrating special occasions around a meal in the homes of these refugees. The former is eucharistic in the typical, liturgical sense of giving praise and thanks to God the Father through the true presence of Christ at the altar, and the latter opens my eyes to the realities of the suffering of working, poor families who struggle with rent, food, and healthcare. As a priest, I pray Christ uses my presence to convey to these families that the same Christ who is present at the altar is also with them in their daily lives. As an Augustinian, I see a strong connection between communion with God and communion with others different from myself. Part of this servant leadership also involves collaborating with other clergy and community leaders in the area to create more inclusive spiritual and social spaces for a multitude of communities. From planning liturgies to bringing in a law clinic so that immigrants may know their rights, I help coordinate the various gifts of many people in the parish, the parish school, and the community at large, so that we may be the visible Body of Christ in our corner of San Diego.

I also encourage the distinctly Mexican Catholicism of our families by helping parents prepare for *quinceañeras*—the Mass of thanksgiving for the fifteen years of a daughter's life—which is a cherished tradition in Mexico. I schedule an hour of family catechism, facilitate a faith sharing experience with the parents and daughter centered on the sacraments of initiation, and plant a seed in the young woman to finish high school and attend college. I've seen strong fathers tear up when I've reminded their daughter of the deep love parents have for their children.

Being a parish priest, I also exercise the privilege of hearing confessions and absolving sins on a regular basis. Confession allows me to observe the spiritual progress of people who come regularly, as well as to welcome back people who have been away from the Church for many years. In both cases, I am a witness to the power of God's providential guidance that urges us always closer to himself. In confession, I use the listening skills I learned through my supervised ministry in the hospital and nursing homes. The deep listening, along with years of spiritual reading and the inspiration of the Holy Spirit, have led to some moments of providing minor spiritual counseling, which the penitents have told me is quite helpful. From welcoming the penitent at the beginning to the absolving of sins at the end, confession is a sacramental sign of God's infinite mercy.

I have felt very encouraged as a young adult priest in my parish. I am always in need of prayers, and I am truly grateful for the many people who pray for me. The ongoing gestures of appreciation I have received also mean a lot to me. I am very grateful for the older priests who have offered their wisdom, and especially thankful to our pastor for granting me autonomy in several areas. I am truly blessed to find much support in my religious order, and I hope that older diocesan priests also reach out to young diocesan priests and offer themselves as mentors and friends.

Looking back on my own journey to the priesthood, I heard the call through the testimony of a priest who shared with enthusiasm his own missionary vocation, and that call was confirmed through families and individuals who asked me to consider the priesthood. In an age of declining priestly vocations, I would love to see priests more frequently sharing their personal witness of the ways the priesthood animates their life, and I also request that families and individuals continue to ask young men to consider the priesthood.

Fr. Carlos Medina, OSA, is a thirty-year-old Augustinian priest. He was born in Colombia and immigrated with his family to California when he was thirteen years old. After graduating from college, he entered the Augustinian novitiate and was ordained to the priesthood in June of 2016. He is the Associate Pastor at St. Patrick's Catholic Church in San Diego, California.

The Quiet Obviousness of God

by Keith Maczkiewicz, SJ

When I recount the story of my vocation to religious life in the Society of Jesus (the Jesuits), I usually remark that there are three versions. All three versions are true, of course, but all three stories do not necessarily say everything there is to say. The first version is for people who ask, but do not really want to know: "It's a long story," I'll say, giving them a chance to back away. The second version is for people who want to know, but cannot make the time or space for it: "I entered the Jesuits because I knew happy Jesuits," I tell them; this seems to satisfy. The third version—the longest and most detailed—is infrequently heard, save for groups considering religious life, faith sharing gatherings with my Jesuit brothers, or with my close friends or family members.

I have these different versions to protect, or rather to hold sacred what I have seen as the common thread that runs through the whole of my story, and what some might easily misinterpret or miss: *the quiet obviousness of God*. There have been no lightning bolts in my vocational journey, no hack-neyed forks in the road that caused dramatic hand wringing, no booming voice from a cloud with pronouncements about my future. Rather, my vocation to the Jesuits was gradual, born of my experiences of and interactions with others and God, and a growing understanding that what I most deeply desired at any moment in time had broad and lasting implications for the future.

As a first-year college student unconcerned with matters of faith, I found myself in Boston, a little homesick and unsure of my chosen major and path in life. Inexplicably and unexpectedly I found that the only stable and familiar place for me was in an aged and relatively empty neighborhood parish; it was the only place I felt I could be myself. This was among the few things I learned that first year of college—that perhaps my faith mattered to me after all. I decided to transfer, searching for a Catholic university closer to home where I might practice a faith whose hold on me I did not completely understand.

A few months later, now enrolled at a Catholic and Jesuit university, I found myself drawn to campus ministry groups and activities, and unsure why. I was leaning into something, even if I could not say what it was or why it had become important to me. During my senior year, a young Jesuit chaplain said to me—in passing—"You should think about this, the Jesuits." I was dating someone at the time and dismissed it, but his invitation—simple, quiet, and flattering—remained in the back of my mind as I graduated and embarked on two years of postgraduate service, a choice that I never would have considered when I first transferred. But something happened to me and *in* me during these formative years of college; in some mysterious way, I was being drawn out of myself, filled with a desire to be for and with others.

So for the following two years, I worked in a Catholic high school and lived in a community with other volunteer teachers. I was the campus minister at the school, a position I basically fell into when there were no other teaching jobs available there. My experiences in college were enough to get me an interview, and I jumped at the opportunity presented to me; I wanted to do this work. My level of excitement betrayed what were only hidden, unnamed desires until that point, desires that were suddenly given a chance to surface and that I was able to embrace openly for the first time. Still, I wondered, *Where was this new development—built upon my past—leading?* I could not be sure.

What I was sure of was that at the end of two years in the high school, newly single and with a graduate degree in hand, I was still hearing the voice of that young priest telling me to think about life in the Jesuits. I was not ready to make any sort of commitment, as I felt unprepared and unworthy: *Who am I? I don't know enough and I certainly don't pray enough.* Still, I decided to move a little closer to this possibility, to work for and with the Jesuits to see if there was more than just an attraction there, and so I began working in the campus ministry office at one of the Jesuit universities on the East Coast. My boss for those two years was the same Jesuit chaplain from my undergrad days, and now he was pitching a new idea at me, this time as colleagues: "What are you waiting for?"

His question was not without merit.

So, in the two years I worked there, I began seriously contemplating life as a religious and future priest. I looked back on my experiences and my interactions and, with time, space, and perspective, I could see where God was in all of it. I began to realize that God was leading me, slowly and gradually, to each next place or step—from college to college, from faith community to faith community, from interest to new interest, from job to job. These movements were always the next apparently obvious thing: small linear steps, always ahead from what had come before, seamlessly, quietly. The obviousness of it all was borne of my desires, even desires I could not always express well or completely. But God was in the desires I was uncovering and wrestling with, even as I remained unsure of what they were about. If I was sure God was there, what *was* I waiting for?

For too long I thought I needed to prepare myself somehow, to present myself in some way. But the purpose of formation in religious life is to be formed, not to take some shortcut around it. I realized in my application to the Society of Jesus that all I needed to be "ready" was the knowledge that God had led me and that God had met me, with promises for more in the future. Even a conditional yes to this loving God was all that I needed to take the next step, for God would do much of the rest. My experiences told me that God always had been active in my life—quietly, and in retrospect, obviously.

In the almost ten years I have spent in formation with the Jesuits, I have had many more experiences—experiments, we call them—to sift through, to find where God has been present and active. As a religious, I have benefitted greatly from the help of spiritual directors and superiors who have guided me (and goaded me) along the path, along the Way. Indeed, I have been privileged to have the structures of the Society of Jesus and the rich spiritual tradition of our founder, St. Ignatius Loyola, to help me in my discernment these many years. Still, I wonder if there is more the wider Church could have done to help me as a future priest grow into my vocation as a religious, serving the needs of the Church. Allow me to offer a few practical suggestions.

Perhaps it is cliché, but a richer liturgical experience—including thoughtful and well-prepared preaching—would have served me well. A celebration of the Eucharist that invites the community to "remember well," conscious of our communal history and tradition—what T.S. Eliot called the "pastness of the past, and of its presence"—would go a long way in helping to form the community as a whole, as well as each individual member, in understanding their experiences and in locating God within these. The liturgy stands at the crossroads of time, where "now" and "then" are intimately tied up in one another. What I have discovered, though, is that our desires mirror this dynamic; what I deeply desire today has implications for the future and where I am headed, for I move toward that which I love and most deeply want. When the liturgy is celebrated poorly, it is devoid of this great and mysterious dynamic. Instead of forming us to remember well what God has done, is doing, and still promises to do, poor liturgy too often gives us a sort of spiritual amnesia, leading us to forget whose we are, where we have been, and where we are going. A recovery of the best of our anamnetic tradition would be a boon to vocational discernment in all areas of the Church's life.

Second, the Church ought to find ways to inculcate joy in all of its works and ways of proceeding. For me, joy and laughter have been a barometer of sorts. As a novice, I quickly realized that religious life devoid of joy would be deadly for me, and I started to keep track of how much laughter was in my life. *When I stop laughing*, I thought, *that's when I will start thinking about leaving the Jesuits*. Ten years on, much laughter remains in my life, with friends and family, with the people of God, and with my Jesuit brothers. The joyful example of Pope Francis is, of course, helpful here, but the application of joy in the pastoral care practices of the Church might prove elusive. Still, perhaps there is nothing greater to focus on, for joy is a true sign of the Holy Spirit's presence and action. Why did I join the Jesuits? I often tell people it is because I knew happy Jesuits. There were more significant reasons, of course, but the outward signs of joy that I noticed is where my discernment began, while the inward gifts and effects of the joy I have received are, to a large extent, why I remain and why I am able to minister to others.

Keith Maczkiewicz, SJ, thirty-five, a native of New York State, joined the Jesuits in the summer of 2008 and has ministered primarily in campus ministry in high schools and colleges. In August 2015, he began his theology studies at the Jesuit School of Theology in Berkeley, California, and he will be ordained to the priesthood in June 2018.

A Church for the Poor

by Ryan Thornton, OFM

Before I was ordained a priest, I served as a hospital chaplain.
The hospital was in Guatemala, providing care for the very
poor of the country. One day I was listening to a young
couple as they cradled their year-old girl who had a cleft lip
and palate. They were from one of the poorest regions in the
state, and they had saved up for months in order to get to the
hospital. However, they hadn't known that their daughter's
surgery would require multiple trips, and now they weren't
sure how they would be able to afford another one. It was a
conversation that changed me and that I have thought about
many times since. I had done the currency conversion in my
head for the amount of money they were talking about, and
it seemed wrong that there should be a world where so many
people could not afford to pay so little for so much. I never
looked at $20 the same way again.

The occasion was not the first when such a theme had
presented itself in my life; in fact, it was a defining moment
in my vocation as a Franciscan, a member of the Order of
Friars Minor. When I was in college, I felt called to be a
priest, and so I started by entering the diocesan seminary.
While I was there my job was to be one of the assistant sac-
ristans. On this particular day, the cardinal archbishop was

coming for some meetings and wanted to join the seminarians at the evening Mass. But the archbishop made it clear that this was to be a regular liturgy as the seminary would normally have—no incense, no special procession, he wasn't even going to wear his miter or use his crozier.

So in the afternoon, as I was getting things ready for Mass, the head sacristan came and asked me, "Which chalice are you going to use tonight for the cardinal?" Now, there was actually a closet full of chalices, and I pointed to a simple silver one saying, "Since the archbishop has said that he just wants a regular liturgy, I thought that this would be a good choice." In reply, the head sacristan said to me, "What about the Pius XII chalice?" As you might guess, the Pius XII chalice was a chalice given to the seminary by Pope Pius XII at its foundation; it was gold, jewel-encrusted, and very valuable. So I told the head sacristan, "That does not seem to be what the archbishop is going for in terms of the liturgy." He then told me, "Think about it some more, and then do it."

And I did think about it some more, and I thought that I was right, so I put out the silver chalice. About fifteen minutes before Mass, the head sacristan came running into the sacristy and asked me, "Who told you to put out that chalice?" I said, "I don't understand what you mean by 'who.'" "Did the archbishop tell you to put it out?" "No." "Did the rector tell you to put it out?" "No." "Did anyone at the seminary tell you to put it out?" "No." "Then why didn't you put out the Pius XII chalice?" "Well," I explained, "you said to think about it some more, and I did. I thought that it would be great for the cardinal to use the silver chalice as a sign of solidarity for all those parishes that do not have a Pius XII chalice." The head sacristan then stared at me right in the eyes and said, "Look, the cardinal pays for this seminary; so when the cardinal comes, the cardinal gets what is best."

In that moment, I realized that we had totally different views of the Church. He really thought the cardinal was like a feudal lord who from his private largess generously bequeathed funds for the seminary. By contrast, it seemed to me—and still does—that the archbishop was but the steward of the monies entrusted to him by the people of God. And it was on that day that I began to search for a place within the Church that was comfortable with being poor.

I was not searching for some idol of poverty to worship, but for the place of the one who said, "Go, sell your possessions...then come, follow me" (Matt 19:21). Such is what I found amongst the friars, brothers of St. Francis and followers of Christ. Franciscan poverty is multidimensional: it involves a material simplicity, but it extends to and includes the much more difficult goal, humility. And I assure you that it is far harder to give up one's will to God than it is to forgo houses or family or lands (cf. Matt 19:29).

Of lessons in humility, I can name many. I can tell you about being a happy parish priest, only to be sent to do additional studies. I can tell you about finding oneself in a gospel parable, seated at a table with dignitaries only to be moved to the lowest place because someone more important had arrived (cf. Luke 14:9). And I can tell you about working in the Tenderloin of San Francisco, inviting the homeless to a free lunch in our dining room only to be cursed at so badly that if the insults were written here verbatim, they could not be published.

These things are humbling, but there are the moments too when God presents us with the choice of humility, and we must decide whether we will accept it like he did (see Phil 2:8). It was Holy Thursday, and I was walking along the River Liffey in Dublin on my way to dinner before Mass. About a block ahead, a bus swerved and slammed on the brakes, shrieking to a stop. Thinking it was a simple fender bender, I crossed the road and continued going toward where it had happened since it was on my way. As I got closer, there was a crowd of people standing around the bus—none of them doing anything, all of them gawking. There, underneath the bus, was a man who had gotten hit.

Everyone was just standing in a circle, doing absolutely nothing. When I approached, I went up to the man and discovered that he was still alive. Someone called a nearby policeman who gave the fellow a once-over and then went to take witness statements, leaving him where he was, under the bus. Then the paramedics came—without an ambulance—chided the fellow for trying to kill himself, and then ignored him so that he was left only to talk to me. And finally, the crowds dispersed, the ambulance arrived, and the man was taken away.

It strikes me as no coincidence that this happened on Holy Thursday, the traditional anniversary of the institution of the priesthood. In fact, it was the first Holy Thursday that I celebrated as a priest, and I believe that God brought me there, to Dublin, on that day, at that time, along that very street to show me what it means to be a priest. The priest, at least the Franciscan priest, is the one who does not walk away, but stays.

The priest is the symbol of the One who is with us in good times and in bad, in sorrows and in joys, in hardships and in triumphs, the One who is with us always even until the end of the age. It is so much easier, though, to enjoy just the good times, so much more pleasant to go to the reception instead of the funeral, so much more relaxing to dine with the rich than to break bread with the poor. And that is why the priest must start with them. It was the insight of St. Francis of Assisi that there is not some sanctity exclusive to poverty, but that if you can make it there, you can make it anywhere.

It would seem to follow then that our systems of formation for priests—religious and diocesan—should facilitate such encounters after the example of our Lord, who became poor so that we might become rich (see 2 Cor 8:9). Indeed, it is hard to learn the meaning of poverty by reading a book, and it is hard to understand what is to be poor if we have never met someone who is. It is not always easy, it is not always graceful, and yet it is always grace filled.

This engagement with the poor is something that is to be done by every Christian; it is a ministry for all, though not all need serve in the exact same way (cf. 1 Cor 12:4–6). Once at our dining room in the Tenderloin, a lay volunteer asked me why I was in the line to bring food to the tables instead of mingling with the guests as usual. When I told her that I thought I should try serving the food, too, and let someone else have a chance to do the talking, she turned to me and said quite earnestly, "Please, Father, let me do that. Because what you do—with them—I can't do that." Her perspective was completely eye-opening for me, and from the tone of her voice I imagined the struggle she must have faced in coming and serving; but serve she did, week after week. And there we should all be   at the edge of what we think we can han dle, but where we know we should be because our Lord has told us He will be there, too (see Matt 25:35–45).

Pope Francis once put it this way, "I prefer a Church which is bruised, hurting and dirty because it has been out on the streets, rather than a Church which is unhealthy from being confined and from clinging to its own security" (*Evangelii Gaudium* 49). All I can say is, "Me too." It is my hope and prayer that we are a Church for the rich and for the poor.

Fr. Ryan Thornton, OFM, graduated from Harvard University in 2006, made solemn vows as a Franciscan in 2014, and was ordained a priest in 2015. He served as parochial vicar at Sts. Simon and Jude Parish in Huntington Beach, California, and is currently studying economic philosophy in Paris at L'École des hautes études en sciences sociales. He is thirty-three.

Questions

1. Similar to the shifts among vocations to women's religious life, Dr. Mary Gautier outlines overall declines in priestly vocations as well as pastoral and theological shifts. What factors, in your estimation, have contributed to the decline in vocations, and what, if anything, can Catholics do to mitigate them? What are the strengths and drawbacks to both the cultic and the servant leader notions of priesthood?

2. The essayists appear to diverge from the cultic conception of the priesthood common among young priests and seminarians, and share a conception of the priesthood as one of servant leadership. We glimpse a more cultic model from another priest within Thornton's story about the chalice. What do these attitudinal shifts among priests mean for priestly relationships across the generations? What sorts of qualities do you hope for in a priest?

3. These men ask for different things from the Church to support their and others' vocations: joy, community encouragement, richer liturgies, and an embrace of poverty and humility. While these seem to have little in common, they are distinctly Catholic responses to contemporary American problems, respectively: stress and worry, isolation, elevation of the rational over

---

Questions

the affective, and an unyielding pursuit of wealth and ambition. Likewise, what sort of problems do you, your community, and your parish encounter and what are distinctly Catholic responses? What problems are unique to young adults that might have Catholic responses?

Shifting Ministries

AN EXCURSUS ON TODAY'S PRIESTS AND ECCLESIAL COLLABORATION

by John Coleman, SJ

I am eighty years old and have been a priest for fifty years. I am obviously aware of how very much my cohort of young seminarians and priests is strongly different from that of current young adult seminarians and priests. Just look at some comparative statistics. When I was ordained, there were 59,192 priests in the United States; 37,272 were diocesan priests and 21,290 were religious congregation priests. Today, there are only 37,192 priests; 25,760 of these are diocesan and 11,432 are religious congregation priests. When I was ordained, the average age of U.S. priests was early thirties; now it is in the sixties. There were nearly nine hundred ordinations the year I was ordained. In 2016, there were only 548. In 1970, there were 6,602 graduate seminarians. In 2016, that was nearly halved to 3,520.

In 1970, there were 160,931 religious sisters. In 2016, the number was 47,170. Similarly, the 11,623 religious brothers in 1970 has fallen to 4,119 in 2016. Parishes without a resident priest have swelled from 571 in 1970 to 3,499 in

2016. In 2016, there were also 379 parishes where a bishop had entrusted the pastoral care of the parish to a deacon or some other person (e.g., a religious sister). All this while the Catholic population in the United States has risen from 51 million to 74.2 million. One positive ministerial shift, however, between 1970 and 2016 involved the growing number of permanent deacons—who now number 18,173—and lay ecclesial ministers in parish ministry, who number 39,651.[1]

Not only have there been numerical shifts among priests, but attitudinal shifts as well. Some of these have important implications for ecclesial leadership more broadly. An indispensable resource for doing a systematic comparison of younger priests with older cohorts of priests is the 2009 CARA study of American priests, *Same Call, Different Men.* Although several years have now passed since 2009, studies of the ordinands in 2010, 2015, and 2016 show that these recent ordinands look largely like the young priests in the 2009 survey.[2]

Younger priests are more likely than older priests to see their role as cultic leaders rather than servant leaders, with a greater emphasis on being an "alter Christus" and a man set apart from the laity. This may partially explain why they are also less likely to emphasize the need for and role of lay leadership in parishes. Eighty-three percent of pre–Vatican II priests, 78 percent of Vatican II priests, 76 percent of post–Vatican II priests, and only 65 percent of millennial priests said that an open discussion on "collaborating with

1. CARA (Center for Applied Research in the Apostolate), "Frequently Requested Church Statistics," accessed April 16, 2018, http.//cara.georgetown.edu/ frequently -requested- church-statistics.

2. Mary Gautier, Paul Perl, and Stephen Fichter, *Same Call, Different Men: The Evolution of the Priesthood since Vatican II* (Collegeville, MN: Liturgical Press, 2012); see also Mary Gautier, Mary Bendyma, and Melissa Cidada, *The Class of 2010: Survey of Ordinands to the Priesthood* (Washington, DC: Center for Applied Research in the Apostolate, 2010).

lay ecclesial ministers" was "somewhat" or "very" important. Similarly, 81 percent of Pre–Vatican II priests, 72 percent of Vatican II priests, 72 percent of post–Vatican II priests, and only 64 percent of millennial priests said an open discussion was "somewhat" or "very" important on collaborating with deacons. Further, 76 percent of pre–Vatican II priests, 65 percent of Vatican II priests, 63 percent of post–Vatican II priests, and only 56 percent of millennial priests thought it was "somewhat" or "very" important to have an open discussion about working with lay administrators in parishes to be run by lay administrators. Overall, younger priests seemed less keen on issues of collaboration.[3]

Similar divides between older and younger priests were shown in questions about the priesthood and the Church today. Eighty-four percent of pre–Vatican II priests, 89 percent of Vatican II priests, 82 percent of post–Vatican II priests, and only 65 percent of millennials either "somewhat" or "strongly" agree that the Catholic Church should allow women greater participation in all lay ministries. Eighty-eight percent of pre–Vatican II priests, 90 percent of Vatican II priests, 76 percent of post–Vatican II priests, and only 62 percent of millennials agreed either "somewhat" or "strongly" that parish life would be aided by an increase in full-time professional lay ecclesial ministers. Again, 84 percent of pre–Vatican II priests, 86 percent of Vatican II priests, 75 percent of post–Vatican II priests, and only 65 percent of millennials agreed somewhat or strongly that the Catholic Church needs to move faster in empowering laypersons in ministry. Millennials were more likely to agree that "ordination confers on the priest a new status or a permanent character which makes him essentially different from the laity within the church." They agreed 88 percent as opposed to

3. Gautier, Perl, Fichter, *Same Call, Different Men*, 83.

agreement by 77 percent of post–Vatican II priests, 61 percent of Vatican II priests, and 75 percent of pre–Vatican II
priests. They also were more likely to agree that "it is essential to uphold the distinction between priests and laity in the
church." They agreed 79 percent compared to 67 percent of
post–Vatican II priests, 55 percent of Vatican II priests, and
66 percent of pre–Vatican II priests. To the question, "I would
be happy to attend primarily to the sacramental life and let
the laity assume responsibility for most other functions,"
66 percent of pre–Vatican II priests agreed, 68 percent of
Vatican II priests also agreed, 61 percent of post–Vatican II
priests agreed, but only 55 percent of the millennials agreed.[4]

This theological and pastoral conservatism among
younger priests and seminarians is all the more notable
because the general religious climate in the United States
would not have suggested it. Phillip Brown, the rector at Theological College, sees some ambiguity in the new younger seminarians and offers a caveat. "We see a lot of young people…
who have experienced what they perceived or experienced
as chaos in the life around them and society around them.
Many of them have been looking for a more orderly or safe
kind of life that they see that the tradition of the church represents." Brown says that is not inherently a bad thing. "But to
the extent that it might represent a kind of retrenchment and
unwillingness to engage the world, rather to see yourself as
against the world around you, that is not a good thing. That's
not what the Gospel is about, that's not what the Christian
faith is about, that's not what the church is about."[5]

Other voices have criticized young priests and seminarians because they are more traditional, conservative, or

---

4. Gautier, Perl, Fichter, *Same Call, Different Men*, 87.
5. Maureen Pao, "At U.S. Seminaries, a Rise in Millennials Answering God's
Call," *NPR*, September 23, 2015, 2, http://www.npr.org/2015/09/23/442243849/at-us
-seminaries-a-rise-in-millennials-answering-gods-call.

legalistic than much of their flock. One diocesan official, who is the director of the Office of Worship in his diocese, stated the following:

> The last several years, I have increasingly found it difficult to engage in a positive and constructive way with many of our newly ordained priests.... While I can handle the criticisms (the type of censer we use or the style of vestments, etcetera), lay ministers in parishes are having more difficulty coping. I often receive calls in my office from lay ministers and parishioners regarding actions by these men. The issues include rigidity, unwillingness to receive people where they are, offending messages during homilies, confusing interpretations of rubrics, very lengthy processes of purifying vessels at the altar and making changes to parish practices. My encouraging lay ministers and the faithful to speak with the priest about these issues doesn't seem to work. They are afraid or unwilling because of a perceived lack of openness on the part of the priest, or a very real fear of being fired for speaking up."[6]

Another diocesan official had this to say:

> What some individuals are taught in seminary may be "de-formative"—perpetuating a strident clericalism. Too often, we place the ministry of priests and the ministry of others (deacons, laity) in a zero-sum relationship: one can be promoted

---

6. Anthony Ruff, "Pastoral Difficulties with Recently Ordained Priests," Pray Tell blog, January 26, 2015, 1–2, http://www.praytellblog.com/index.php/2015/01/26/pastoral-difficulties-with-recently-ordained-priests/.

only at the expense of the others. Such an attitude is nonsense, yet still gets play....If we are promoting clericalism in seminary (and deacon formation programs) or an anti-clerical attitude (in deacon and lay ministry formation programs), then we need to take a hard look at ourselves.... While seminarians are exposed to a great deal of philosophy and theology, what is needed is the experience of putting such learning into practice. Ideally, the assigning of new priests to be tutored by a more experienced priest ought to help bridge the gap between theory and praxis. Unfortunately, that is not always the case. Effective mentoring requires that mentors be properly formed in the liturgy (both intellectually and spiritually), have the skills to mentor constructively and take the time to do so. Sadly, such is rarely the case....The selection and formation of seminarians, a willingness to discern whether or not a given candidate has the proper dispositions to be a good priest..., preparation of effective mentors for those newly ordained: all of these are important issues that need to be addressed.[7]

Responding to this blog, a deacon notes, "Let me say there are two categories of the recently ordained: (1) second career, older men with maturity and life experience and (2) those in their mid twenties [*sic*] who have not fully matured. The first seem more willing and able to smell like the sheep while the latter often seem intent upon bringing back a Church they never really lived in. In either case, our only

---

7. Ruff, "Pastoral Difficulties with Recently Ordained Priests," 3–4.

response is to love them, lead them to places they perhaps do not want to go, and by all means pray for them."[8]

Especially since the age of priests is steeply rising (the median age was thirty-four in 1970 and by 2009 it was sixty-four), collaboration with younger lay ministers is important for the life of a parish. Things younger priests used to do (e.g., minister to teenagers and young adults) is harder for an aging priesthood. But there is a relatively significant number of younger lay ministers to be found in parishes who can help with these tasks. In parishes, about one in five parishioners are eighteen to thirty-nine years old and some 21 percent are under eighteen, calling for some younger ministerial care. Among lay ecclesial ministers in parishes, 7 percent are under thirty years of age and 11 percent are in their thirties.[9] However, the previous data demonstrates the difficulties some may have in collaborating with younger priests; younger priests are less likely than older priests to accept women in ministry, or to agree that parish life would be aided by an increase in full-time professional lay ecclesial ministers, or that the Catholic Church needs to move faster in empowering laypersons in ministry.

In the end, however, as the deacon cited earlier put it, whatever we think of current seminarians and young priests, even if we disagree with some of their stances, "our only response is to love them, lead them to places they perhaps do not want to go, and by all means pray for them." Let us do the same for all those whose vocation is to minister to the faithful.

---

8. Ruff, "Pastoral Difficulties with Recently Ordained Priests," 8.

9. Mark Gray, Mary Gautier, and Melissa Cidade, "Emerging Models of Pastoral Leadership: The Changing Face of U.S. Catholic Parishes" (study, National Association of Lay Ministry, Washington, DC, 2011), 61, https://nalm.org/wp -content/uploads/2016/05/Changing-Face-of-US-Catholic-Parishes.pdf.

Fr. John A. Coleman, SJ, PhD, is a Pastoral Associate at St. Ignatius parish, San Francisco. John holds a PhD in sociology and was, for many years, a professor at the Graduate Theological Union, Berkeley, and later at Loyola Marymount University, Los Angeles. John has written or edited sixteen books, dealing either with sociology of religion or social ethics.

Young Adults Answering "Yes" to the Call of Lay Ecclesial Ministry

by Mark Erdosy

"What am I going to do with my life? I have no idea where I'm going or what I should do?" asks a twentysomething young adult sitting in my office. With a little more prodding, the young adult confesses, "You know, I think I'm being called to ministry full-time. I just don't know whether that is as a pastoral associate, youth minister, or religious educator." The conversation continues for several more minutes when she suddenly asks, "Wait, are there people my age who are full-time lay ministers in the Church?" Yes, about 15 percent of the more than 39,600 lay ecclesial ministers in the United States are considered young adults (eighteen to thirty-five).[1] Young adults answer the call to "come, follow me" by collaborating with the ordained as pastoral associates, parish catechetical leaders, youth ministry and young adult

---

1. CARA (Center for Applied Research in the Apostolate), "Frequently Requested Church Statistics," accessed April 16, 2018, http://cara.georgetown.edu/ frequently -requested- church-statistics.

ministers, school principals, and directors of liturgy or pastoral music.

The pathway into lay ecclesial ministry is as varied as the number of people who serve in it. There is no one quintessential pathway. There are many. Reading call stories in Scripture or biographies of saints, or listening to priests, religious, or lay ecclesial ministers reveals very quickly that people responding to a personal call come from every walk of life. What unites them is their "yes," albeit in very different ways. In this précis, I will briefly talk about the meaning of *vocation.* Second, I will summarize what lay ecclesial ministry is and how these ministers serve the Church. Third, I will name a few national organizations supporting lay ecclesial ministers.

"GOD, WHAT DO YOU WANT ME TO DO WITH MY LIFE?"

"God, what do you want me to do with my life?" asks St. Francis of Assisi as he stands or kneels before the cross in the dilapidated pilgrim's church down the hill from Assisi. He hears the unmistakable voice of God command him, "Francis, go rebuild my house which you see is fallen into ruin." Like St. Francis of Assisi and so many others before and after him, the call to discipleship is personal, communal, and has vocational implications. As Kathleen Cahalan says in her book *Introducing the Practice of Ministry,* "God initiates a call and invites a response, one that is both loving and kind as well as relentlessly demanding."[2]

The word *vocation* comes from the Latin word *vocare,* which means "to call" or "to summon."[3] All throughout

---

2. Kathleen Cahalan, *Introducing the Practice of Ministry* (Collegeville, MN: Liturgical Press, 2010), 27.

3. Cahalan, *Introducing the Practice of Ministry,* 27.

Scripture we see God interacting with humans through calls. God calls each of these people in a personal way. How we respond depends upon who we are as individuals. Sometimes it takes humans longer to recognize in themselves what God saw at the moment of their conception. Our calling is the way in which we respond to God using all of our gifts, talents, and charisms. The basic call is the same for all the followers of Christ, namely, "that all Christians in any state or walk of life are called to the fullness of Christian life and the perfection of love, and by this holiness a more human manner of life is fostered also in earthly society."[4] We have been called to be stewards of these gifts and to make a return for the Lord, using them to build the kingdom of heaven here on earth.

Historically in the Roman Catholic tradition, if a person had a vocation, it meant a divine calling to priesthood or religious life. Today, it is common for laypersons to describe hearing an unmistakable call to their state in life (married or single) and profession. In fact, lay ecclesial ministers report having heard a call to ministry, and more than a third of young adult lay ecclesial ministers said they wanted to be of greater service to the Church.[5]

WHO IS A LAY ECCLESIAL MINISTER?

The U.S. Catholic Bishops defined the term *lay ecclesial minister* in a 2005 statement, *Co-Workers in the Vineyard*

---

4. Second Vatican Council, Dogmatic Constitution on the Church (*Lumen Gentium*) (*LG*), no. 40, in *Vatican Council II: The Conciliar and Post Conciliar Documents New Revised Edition*, ed. *Austin Flannery* (Collegeville, MN: The Liturgical Press, 1992), 397.

5. CARA, "Lay Ecclesial Ministers in the United States" (study review, Georgetown University, Washington, DC, 2015), 16, https://cara.georgetown.edu/lemsummit.pdf.

Answering "Yes" to the Call of Lay Ecclesial Ministry

of the Lord: A Resource for Guiding the Development of Lay Ecclesial Ministry. **Lay ecclesial minister** is a generic term that encompasses and describes several growing and developing roles within the Christian community.[6] For example, lay ecclesial ministers are persons who serve as pastoral associates, parish catechetical leaders, youth ministers, school principals, and directors of liturgy or pastoral music.[7] The ministry is *lay* because it is service done by laypersons. The sacraments of initiation—baptism, Eucharist, and confirmation—are the sacramental basis for lay ecclesial ministry. The ministry is *ecclesial* because it has a place with the community of the Church, whose communion and mission it serves, and because it is submitted to the discernment, authorization, and supervision of the hierarchy. And finally, it is *ministry* because it is a participation in the threefold ministry of Christ, who is Priest, Prophet, and King.[8]

In order to be a lay ecclesial minister, one must receive authorization from competent Church authority to serve in ecclesial ministry.[9] Unfortunately, there is no uniform authorization process for lay ecclesial ministers. Each diocese establishes their own requirements for education, formation, and ministerial specific experiences. Some include graduate level theology courses, certificate programs, and the acquiring of certain skills suitable to ministry. Likewise, each diocese has their own methods of recognizing lay ecclesial ministers. For example, in some dioceses lay ecclesial ministers are appointed to a position by a diocesan bishop or, in some cases, by a pastor in parish ministry. Still others

---

6. CARA, "Lay Ecclesial Ministers in the United States," 11.
7. USCCB, *Co-Workers in the Vineyard of the Lord: A Resource for Guiding the Development of Lay Ecclesial Ministry* (*CWVL*) (Washington, DC: USCCB, 2005), 9.
8. USCCB, *Co-Workers in the Vineyard*, 11.
9. USCCB, *Co-Workers in the Vineyard*, 54.

may hold a public ceremony or liturgy for the conferral of an office. For instance, the Archdiocese of Chicago will hold a commissioning ceremony for their newly approved lay ecclesial ministers. This public ritual emphasizes the relationship between the diocesan bishop and the lay ecclesial ministers.

PATHWAYS INTO LAY ECCLESIAL MINISTRY

The pathways into ministry are as varied as the people responding yes to the invitation to serve. The good news is that young adults interested in lay ecclesial ministry have a number of different types of lay ecclesial ministry formation programs from which to select. There are certificate and degree types of programs. According to the Center for the Applied Research in the Apostolate 2017 report, "Many lay ecclesial ministry formation programs can be classified as either exclusively diocesan-based or academic-based, but several are the result of collaboration between a diocese and an academic institution." In these cases, often the diocese assumes responsibility for the human, spiritual, and pastoral formation, while the academic institution is responsible for the intellectual formation. Currently, 101 active programs are sponsored or cosponsored by a diocese, 53 are sponsored or cosponsored by a Catholic college or university, and 15 are sponsored or cosponsored by a seminary or school of theology.

Nearly 30 percent of students in lay ecclesial ministry formation programs would be considered young adults (eighteen to thirty-nine). Young adults comprise 41 percent of students enrolled in degree programs. This is consistent with one of the findings reported in *Their Chips Are All In: A Closer Examination of the Current Reality,* a report developed by the National Association for Lay Ministry and the National Catholic Young Adult Ministry Association from the Emerging Models of Pastoral Leadership program in 2012.

Most young adults are responding to a vocational call by first receiving a degree in theology or pastoral studies before acquiring their first ministry job. Hispanics make up more than half (53 percent) of participants in lay ecclesial ministry formation programs.

Our education and formation continue even after receiving graduate degrees and certificates. Those for whom we have been called to serve will shape us if we see with the eyes of our hearts. Having a good sense of humor, a robust prayer life, active sacramental life, daily theological reflection or examen, spiritual direction, and reading theological and spiritual books are helpful for any lay ecclesial minister or someone discerning ministry.

Ways of Support

After this the Lord appointed seventy others and sent them on ahead of him in pairs to every town and place where he himself intended to go.

—Luke 10:1

How and where do lay ecclesial ministers find ways of support? Some are at the local level, meaning parish. Still others exist at the diocesan level. For example, it is commonplace within dioceses to have organizations for pastoral associates, catechetical leaders, youth ministers, music ministers, campus ministers, and so forth. These diocesan offices and organizations offer support, networking opportunities with peers, and educational and spiritual resources. Asking a parish priest or lay ecclesial minister, or perusing a diocesan website would be helpful.

There are a number of national organizations that serve their membership and the larger Church in the United States.

I will only highlight a few.[10] The National Association for Lay Ministry is a collaborative organization that brings together Catholic lay, religious, and ordained ministers from a variety of ministerial contexts. For catechists and others who participate in the teaching mission of the Church, they can find support through the National Conference for Catechetical Leadership. The National Association of Pastoral Musicians connects liturgists and musicians with a variety of resources both spiritual and practical. Campus ministers can find formation, ways to network, and other resources through the Catholic Campus Ministry Association. The National Federation for Catholic Youth Ministry provides support for those who minister to youth, and the National Association of Church Personnel Administrators helps its members to see the spiritual foundations to the work they do in keeping their organizations faithful to Catholic teaching. Each of these organizations provides support, resources, and accountability for lay ecclesial ministers.

CONCLUSION

The rise of lay ecclesial ministers since the end of Vatican II has been a boon to the Church. In the words of the late Cardinal George, "The life and ministry of lay ecclesial ministers strengthens the church's mission by complementing the life and ministry of ordained priests."[11] Throughout history, God has and continues to call ordinary individuals

10. For more information regarding the national organizations, see chap. 6, "Professional Organizations of Ministers," in Zeni Fox, *New Ecclesial Ministry: Lay Professionals Serving the Church*, rev. and exp. ed. (Franklin, WI: Sheed & Ward, 2002).

11. Francis Cardinal George, "Developing Lay Ecclesial Ministry," in *In the Name of the Church: Vocation and Authorization of Lay Ecclesial Ministry*, ed. William J. Cahoy (Collegeville, MN: Liturgical Press, 2012), 150.

to do extraordinary things. All God needs is our unequivocal "yes." As my former student Liam said to a group of prospective students, "God doesn't call the equipped. God equips the called." "With the help of lay ecclesial ministers, the gifts of Christ are more easily shared."[12]

Mark Erdosy, MTS, serves as the Executive Director of the San Damiano Scholars Program for Church Leadership at Marian University-Indianapolis. He has been active in parish ministry, serving as a youth minister, college campus minister, and pastoral associate. He has also served on diocesan organizations as well as national organizations such as the Catholic Campus Ministry Association, National Federation for Catholic Youth Ministry, and the National Association for Lay Ministry. He currently serves on the board for NALM. Mark earned his master's in theological studies from St. Meinrad School of Theology in 1995.

---

12. George, "Developing Lay Ecclesial Ministry," 160.

Embrace the Journey

WALKING WITH JESUS AS A LAY ECCLESIAL MINISTER

by Rosie Chinea Shawver

Be who God meant you to be and you will set the world on fire.

—St. Catherine of Siena

I often pray to St. Catherine for perseverance and the boldness that I need as a wife, mother, and professional lay ecclesial minister (LEM) in the Church. When I pray and reflect upon my life, I believe that I am joyfully "setting the world on fire."

Vocational discernment toward marriage was not a straight or easy path. My parents have been a good example of marriage, and so from a young age, I wanted to be married. This year they will be celebrating forty-one years of marriage! I have vivid memories of witnessing my parents' joys and struggles in marriage. Faith is an important component in their relationship. Growing up, we would go to Mass as a family. My parents were part of the parish's pastoral council and Engaged Encounter groups. My mom's full-time job was in social justice work at the local Catholic hospital. She provided healthcare to migrant farm workers, helped young pregnant mothers learn about healthy habits during pregnancy, and taught the community about AIDS through theatre in the late 1980s. She taught me that faith and action are integral in one's faith life. Growing up, it was the domestic church, not the institutional Church, that shaped me to be a faithful Catholic today.

Listening and remaining patient for God to reveal himself to me in his time was where I struggled. My first crush on a boy was when I was nine years old. I started to date when I was a twenty-three-year-old graduate student!

When I was an undergraduate at the University of California, San Diego (UCSD), something unpredictable happened in my life. During my freshman year, I struggled with roommate issues, grades, and homesickness. A friend kept on inviting me to come to church with her. I had stopped going to church some time in high school and did not desire to go back. Since my friend kept nagging me, I told her I would go. To my surprise, the first time I stepped through the doors at the Catholic Community at UCSD I was drawn into it. Ultimately, through my experience of authentic community, deeper friendships with others striving for gospel values, and the consistent reception of the sacraments, I fell in love with Christ.

Falling in love with Christ meant that I desired to know everything about him. I spent hours in adoration, praying the Rosary, going to daily Mass, reading spiritual books, and contemplating Scripture. Because of my deep love of Christ that was developing, I felt that God was calling me to enter religious life. However, it was difficult to discern something that felt inaccessible. I did have a spiritual director but, due to the lack of sisters around me, the discernment always felt inadequate no matter how hard I tried.

This is an area of growth for the Church. How do we bring religious sisters into the everyday lives of Catholic college students in universities? The need for college-aged women to interact with religious sisters is mutually crucial. If we hope to increase the number of women who are even willing to *consider* a vocation to religious life, we must get more religious women on college campuses. With the dynamic staff at my current place of employment, we have initiated a project with the Hilton Foundation, in which we are attempting to create a national model for bringing religious sisters to college campuses so that young women can experience the joyful lives of religious sisters, which in turn will invite students to begin to contemplate the idea of religious life.

After three years of discernment, I felt as if God was not opening the door to religious life. By that point I knew that God was calling me into college campus ministry full-time as a professional LEM. I pursued a masters in divinity so that I could inflame the fire of his love on college campuses.

As I continued to run toward Christ through my pursuit of the master's degree at the Jesuit School of Theology (JST), I learned a lot about theology and ministry. What was missing in my studies was the administration side of ministry, such as fundraising and nonprofit management. Also missing were more candid discussions about the collaboration between priests and laity. It would be beneficial if laity were trained alongside priests universally so that these crucial conversations could happen on an even playing field, rather than after a priest has hired a professional LEM and they discover an unhealthy power dynamic. Another hurdle is the sheer cost of pursuing a master's in divinity and the disparity between one's educational debt and the salary one earns working in the Church.

As a professional LEM in the Church for eleven years, there are several areas of ministerial professionalism, such as annual retreats, certification, and training, that need to improve.

Most religious, clergy, and deacons have an annual retreat paid for by their employer or religious community. In my experience, professional LEMs do not have this built into their contracts. It would be incredible just to offer professional LEMs a yearly paid retreat as part of a national standard.

Certification and training for clergy, deacons, religious, and professional LEMs is a big need in our Church. Besides the aforementioned need for training in administration, con tinuing education in theology, lay presiding/homiletics, hospitality, and so forth should be required. As stated in canon law, "Persons who devote themselves permanently or temporarily to some special service of the Church are obliged to acquire appropriate formation which is required to fulfill their function properly" (no. 231). In my experience, this is especially necessary when LEMs change ministries or clergy, religious, or deacons are assigned to new ministries.

Currently there are five organizations approved by the United States Catholic Conference of Bishops to offer certification for different ministerial groups in our Church. The Catholic Campus Ministry Association (CCMA), one of the groups to which I belong, offers certification to its ministers. As a professional committed to a career in college campus ministry, I desire the professionalization of this ministry. Providing educational and ministerial standards for college campus ministers and understanding the ministerial benchmarks to strive for in college campus ministry is important if we are serious about helping to shape the future of our Church through young adult leaders. However, the value that is placed on certification is low. In most dioceses, being a certified campus minister does not help you get a job or increase your salary, providing little to no incentive for certification. If we are serious about the souls of our young people, we must also be serious about the training and certification of the ministers who are ministering to them.

Pope Francis has focused his pontificate on discernment and accompaniment. Because of my experiences, I feel equipped to journey with people in their walk with Christ. However, I am humble enough to recognize that any skill needs to be refined. Right now is the time to train and refine the skills of all professional ministers in the arts of discernment and accompaniment. The ministry of discernment and accompaniment should not, however, remain solely in the hands of professional ministers in the Church. These are skills that all Christians need. Like the apostles, we must learn to master the skills ourselves so that we can pass them to others who are not professional ministers so that they may do the same through intentional discipleship.

We also need more accessible training to train new spiritual directors. At minimum, each diocese should have a list of trained spiritual directors that is updated yearly so that parishioners can have access to spiritual accompaniment. People grow in faith together in relationship with others and God, not through programs. If we desire our Church to thrive, we need to become master artists of accompaniment.

As described earlier, I was impatient with God when it came to discerning my life. However, with advice from a friend to continue to run toward Christ while pursing my passions, I met my future husband on a trip to South America sponsored by the Maryknoll and CCMA. We met and there was an instant connection. Because of our shared value of dating with the intention to find our future spouse, our conversations went deep quickly.

Within six months we were engaged and started our marriage preparation. We met with our parish priest, took the FOCCUS premarital test, met with a sponsor couple to discuss things such as finances and communication, went on an Engaged Encounter retreat, and took our own personal retreat to prepare for the sacrament of holy matrimony. We also both had (and continue to have) monthly spiritual direction. Most engaged couples grumble at Catholic marriage preparation. I believe that because of our relationship with Christ and the conversations we had early on in our relationship, our friendship is built on solid ground. Where the Church can help support young married couples is through the certification of more Catholic marriage and family counselors, and linking them to Catholic parishes at a reduced rate.

Our vocational lives are not stagnant, rather they are alive and something that we are constantly navigating. Through the power of the Spirit, while living our vocations as his disciples, we grow closer to Christ. I find peace and joy in knowing that I am living my vocations as wife, mother, and campus minister for the greater glory of God and pray for the grace to continue to seek his will as I continue to strive for holiness and bringing others closer to him.

Rosie Chinea Shawver, MDiv, is thirty-six years old and began her work experience at Annunciation House, a home for immigrants in Texas. She then earned her master's in divinity at the Jesuit School of Theology. At twenty-six, she became Director of Campus Ministry at the University of New Mexico. She is currently Director of Campus Ministry at the USC Caruso Catholic Center in Los Angeles.

Nudged by the Spirit

Discerning Lay Ecclesial Ministry

by Karen Chambers

"What do you want to be when you grow up?" An animal trainer. A veterinarian. A zookeeper. I had a few different answers throughout my childhood, but I always knew two things: (1) I was going to work with animals and (2) I was *not* going to be a teacher. My mother was a teacher. In fact, she was *my* teacher for three years; all my middle school math skills come from her. Determined not to show me any favors, I had to call her Mrs. Chambers while at school, and if I forgot to write down my math homework, I had to call a friend to get it because "other kids don't have the advantage to ask their mom." Now, here I am all these years later as a lay minister: a theology teacher and director of campus ministry at a Catholic high school. So how did I get here? How did I discern what would come to be my vocation?

Some may call it luck, some may say coincidence, but I believe it to be the nudge of the Holy Spirit. After graduation from an all-girls Catholic high school where my interest in my spiritual life had been piqued—but not admittedly acted upon much—a suite mate of mine in my first year of college asked if I was Catholic and if I would like to go to church with her. Honestly, it hadn't really occurred to me that I could/ should go to church while in college, but I figured "Why not?" We took advantage of the "Pizza, Pepsi, and a Priest" promotion, where students could invite a priest over for dinner, and he would bring the pizza and Pepsi. It was a great way to not only bring church home, but to see the priest as a regular person—not the holier-than-thou figure we sometimes imagine. That priest ended up taking a big risk on me, the shy girl, and asked me to be a student minister. I jumped at the chance, having no idea just how much that experience would change my life. I not only found a faith that felt like *mine* and *real*, but I started to question if the one thing I was always so sure of—a future career with animals—was really the path I should continue on, the path where I could make the most impact and receive the most fulfillment. It was near the end of my junior year when I first voiced aloud that I might not want to work with animals anymore—I might want to work with people instead—and do something that more directly puts my faith in action.

I believe we are all nudged by the Spirit throughout our lives. Discernment is when we tune into those nudges. The Catholic faith is rich in discernment techniques, and college students (whether knowingly or not) are in dire need of help when it comes to discernment. Too many times, though, students don't know how to find the Newman Center or campus ministry office, or they don't even think to look for it. Once students do arrive, however, it is imperative that they all feel welcome and feel like it is a place they can call "home." My experience changed me so much because I realized I felt at home with God. God was not some distant or remote God. God was close. God was with me and within reach. God was home.

By the time senior year came to a close, I still did not have a clue what I wanted to do with my life other than something that would allow me to put my faith in action. I did a year of service with Boys Hope Girls Hope at a girls' group home in Pittsburgh. As one of the most challenging, rewarding, and best years of my life, it convinced me I was on the right path; I was listening to those nudges by the Holy Spirit. While in Pittsburgh, I began to apply to master of divinity programs.

I entered my program certain that I would discover my vocation. In my mind, *vocation* had always meant one of two things, either your state in life (married, single, ordained, religious) or your career. I thought there was one career/vocation we are each meant to do and that the metaphorical light bulb would turn on by the time we entered the "real world" so that we would know exactly what that one thing is. However, after three years in the MDiv program at the Jesuit School of Theology in Berkeley, I still did not know what career path I wanted to take. What I did discover during that time, though, is a new definition of *vocation*. I began to realize that *career* and *vocation* are not synonyms. I could know my vocation and still not know my career. I could become the person God calls me to be through various avenues.

During my third and final year in the program, one of the Jesuits in my class told me he thought I would be good at a Cristo Rey school. I nicely explained to him that I would never be a teacher. He nicely explained to me that maybe I should "get over it" and then continued to tell me about the Cristo Rey Network. So here I am today, teaching and ministering in a Cristo Rey high school, and I couldn't be more fulfilled. I now teach my students about vocation. I teach them to look around and become aware of the world's needs, look inside and see what makes them content and happy, then reflect on what their gifts are, what they're actually good at. Where those three things meet—the world's needs, their joys, and their talents—*that*, I tell them, is where they'll find their vocation. I warn them, though, that a vocation is not just a job. I may think of teaching and campus ministry as my vocation, but those are really the vehicles through which I live out my vocation. I could also live out my vocation through a number of other careers. I am grateful, though, for the choices I made. I find that I can most directly and concretely live out my vocation through lay ecclesial ministry. I have the privilege of being able to explicitly discuss and teach the faith in a way that not only inspires my students to put their faith in action, but reinspires me to do the same. A student once asked me, with genuine interest and curiosity, "Ms. Chambers, you always tell us to go out and make the world a better place. But what are *you* doing to make the world better?" It is moments like that that hold me accountable to the active faith I teach my students. Of course, part of my answer was, "I show up each day, trying to inspire some of you to do it!" The path I took to discover how I would live out my vocation—whatever path any of us take—requires lots of discernment. However, through focusing in on those nudges of the Holy Spirit, by finding those paths and choices that bring us consolation, we can trust that God will lead us by the right path. And even if we stray (sometimes on purpose, sometimes accidently), we can, as Thomas Merton tells us in *Thoughts in Solitude*, "believe that the desire to please [God] does in fact please [God]."

What is my vocation then? I would say I am called to help adolescents discover and know that they are God's beloved—and to be aware of the benefits and responsibilities that come with that. As a director of campus ministry, my job entails everything from planning retreats to simply sitting with a student while he shares the struggles and triumphs of his journey. I do not take for granted the privilege I have of hearing our students' stories and walking with them on their journeys. Before each retreat, student leaders share their personal stories, and we work together to help them prepare a powerful talk that will inspire the other students to share their own stories of suffering, joy, and healing. Additionally, one of the courses I currently teach is called "The Paschal Mystery: Suffering and Death." Throughout the semester, students continuously reflect on their own experiences of suffering to apply the theological concepts covered in the course, and to ultimately, with God's help, turn stories of pain and suffering into stories of grace—just as Jesus transformed the suffering of the cross into the hope and joy of the resurrection. Whether I'm watching a student having a transformative experience at retreat, or hearing a student say he has regained his faith in God because he learned in class that God didn't actually want him to suffer, or seeing the weight lifted off a student after a reconciliation service, I know that I am living out my vocation. I try to accompany my students in the way Pope Francis has called us to—with love and mercy.

That being said, as a young ministering adult, there can also sometimes be frustrations. It can be hard to watch a really good kid make a really bad choice. Collaboration can be complicated when there are competing theologies—perhaps both legitimate theologies—within the Church. Unfortunately, there are still times when the gifts a woman—specifically a young woman—can bring to ministry and more are not recognized, or worse, are even challenged. To clarify, this can be an issue among both clergy and laity; there are many lay Catholics who do not see the ministerial worth of the laity. In addition, the Church has the responsibility to ensure the clergy are trained to collaborate with laity (and vice versa). I look back with gratitude for everyone—both clergy and laity alike—who showed me such great support along my journey. Fortunately, I have had more than enough support to counter the few negative experiences I've had with those who do not believe that a young woman has a place in formal ministry. Sometimes, though, even those clergy who are very supportive fail to understand the needs of laity, whether financial, familial, or otherwise. Whether through my own experiences or those of friends in ministry, I have observed that clergy don't always understand the full scale of our other responsibilities, and so needs are not always met. That being said, I know there are also responsibilities of clergy that we lay folks don't always fully grasp. Open and constant communication is so vital. Even with these frustrations, though, it has been ingrained in me to "find God in all things," and I try to do so every day. I find God in my students—both the "perfect" student and the one who makes me want to tear my hair out. I find God in my colleagues who support me and challenge me to always become better. I find God in those times of frustration, nudging me to respond in the best way possible. The answers are not always clear; in fact, they are rarely clear. However, that is the life of a young, ministering adult. We continue to reflect, discern, and act—abiding in faith and trust.

Karen Chambers, MDiv, is a thirty-six-year-old single woman working as Director of Campus Ministry and theology teacher at an all-boys Catholic high school that is part of the Cristo Rey Network. She earned her MDiv from the Jesuit School of Theology and her MA in education from Loyola Marymount University.

Coming of Age Catholic

THRESHOLDS OF YOUNG ADULT LEADERSHIP IN THE TWENTY-FIRST-CENTURY CHURCH

by Rebecca M. Freeman

As the generations of the Church have come and gone, each one has had an impact on not only styles of religiosity, but navigating the tensions that have moved the Church into the future. Young adults are a paradox in the pews, holding the old and new, one foot in the Apple-Uber-Frappuccino-Snapchat secular world and one foot in the patron-saint-donning, frankincense-burning, worship-music-listening world of Catholic culture. And sometimes these two areas feel at odds with one another. Often we see the world through media-influenced lenses, interpreting events in a way that can drive wedges between us or that are filled with immense hope and offer chances to connect (sometimes they offer both of these simultaneously!). It is a time for young adults, like myself, to discover how complex we can be and how our unique individuality is lived out within the context of community, in both the religious and secular communities we inhabit. These worlds have much to offer one another and I, as a young adult, am the nexus between these worlds.

As a young adult lay minister in the Church today, there are many areas of focus worth addressing, but for me, the areas of inclusive formation, community building, and commissioning are key areas worth exploring. While I do not claim to speak for the experience of all young adults, I do speak from my own experience and the stories of those around me. In 2017–18, we have first- and second-generation immigrant youth or "Dreamers," often being the first in their families to graduate from college. We have extremely diverse college populations including international and global exchange programs. We have parental identities shifting among those who come to parenthood somewhat unexpectedly, perhaps even as single parents or unmarried couples living with one another. We have young people of color and allies taking to the streets and media to organize entire movements such as Black Lives Matter. We have young adults, both men and now women, in active duty combat. We have the hipsters, artists, techies, and conservative traditionalists all coming into the pews, many who haven't sat there in some time. The millennial generation has the potential for being the leaders of faith in the next century in the American Catholic Church. There is also the chance to miss this generation. It is most wise for the Church to tune into our experiences at this crossroads.

In this era, there is so much being explored in terms of identities that affect participation and formation in faith. A major community that is often overlooked or stigmatized in parish life is the LGBTQ community. For instance, during a session on faith and religion led by the LGBTQ college student group, some straight members of religious communities and faith-based clubs joined in a dialogue. Students used red, green, or yellow cards to name how strongly they associated with a particular situation or question such as, "I feel comfortable in my place of worship." One of the most enlightening experiences of this meeting for me was witnessing and hearing just how many Catholic students there were who called themselves "former Catholics." One young woman in particular explained, with tears in her eyes, just how much she loved being a lector and how special her confirmation was, but how she experienced discomfort and shaming when she "came out." While many students had painful and frustrating experiences, no one that evening made me feel isolated or blamed, and they thanked me for being a part of the dialogue. In the aftermath of hate crimes and the Florida nightclub massacre, there is much in the way of compassionate dialogue and healing that needs to occur between the Church and the LGBTQ community.

This highlights a key issue in young adult formation within parish life today: We have a great deal of diversity in our experiences and identities. We can view this diversity as a challenge or an opportunity; as a lay minister, I encourage churches to do the latter. Like the LGBTQ group did, we should open a dialogue to expand our thinking and extend a greater mercy and care to one another rather than marginalizing others because of their differences. As young adults are exposed to the world around them, especially in regard to justice and human rights, they will connect their abstract positions to real, living people. This helps us move beyond positions and categories to a more nuanced understanding of issues and perspectives. People can come to demonize a *person* because of strong *conviction*. Fostering an inclusive community begins with love and conversation, which may increase young adult Mass attendance while it also provides a unique formation opportunity. Justice issues and Catholic social teaching often are embraced by young people in the Church. Therefore, dialogue connects the Church with the pastoral needs of our world today and plugs young adults into this conversation and implementation in a way that will also bring them closer to their faith.

In terms of formation, it can be difficult to engage with Church life after college graduation, sometimes even high school graduation. Often, young adults are making major geographical moves, perhaps for the first time in their lives, and it can be hard to dial into a new parish. Sometimes in overly curriculum-based young adult programs, the focus isn't always organic or honoring of the fact that young adults are indeed adults. Rather than selecting topics that seem to stem from a defensive posture such as "Apologetics of the Catholic Faith in a Protestant World" or "How to Make the Argument against Abortion," I wonder what "Learning to Listen" would look like. What kind of fruit would grow from "Learning to Discern the Spirit and Instill Mindfulness into Hectic, Over-Technologized Lifestyles"? What kind of Church could we be in if we ministered to the whole brilliant spectrum of Catholics who came to us looking to satisfy *their* longing, rather than using a cookie cutter model that assumed *we* knew the needs of every person?

Fellowship and community based formation are the pillars to young adult engagement, getting to the core of what is really relevant for young people in the Church today. Rather than topics for young women constantly focusing on themes of chastity and modesty, perhaps extending such topics equally to their male counterparts would be more equitable. Offering a self-defense class through the parish would be an embodied way to connect a spiritual practice of honoring the temple of the Spirit with the physical practice of knowing how to protect oneself and others. As a young female leader in the Church, my chastity and modesty hinge less on the length of my skirt and much more on the normalized assumptions and slut shaming of society that often justifies violent behavior yet overlooks where it comes from. Thus, as a young woman in the Church, I hope for more opportunities to expand the conversation on what is coming up for young women in this country and how the Church can be a place of strength and an opportunity for leadership. As a Church, we have the power to take on the complexities of identities, issues, and challenges and move with them—this is essentially what we have done for centuries in theological debate, discussion, and the discernment of the Spirit, and young adults can and should play a major part in this.

Countless people and events within Catholicism have influenced my faith life: teachers, confirmation sponsors, godparents, parents, professed religious, families, and opportunities I have had to serve. Yet I first learned chaplaincy was a vocation in which I could serve as a layperson from a secular college chaplain from the United Church of Christ. This vocation to chaplaincy was then supported by the deacon of the local parish who helped me discern my graduate theological education. How would it affect vocations to lay ministry if Church leaders prayed for young adults not simply to discern vocations for priestly and religious life, but also lay ecclesial ministry? Perhaps a Mass of commissioning or some process of acknowledgment of these lay ministries, whether directly in the parish or outside, would be reaffirming and rekindling for the young adult community. Or even an annual retreat offered in discernment of involvement in religious life, lay ministry, and life more broadly. Exposure to these roles and encouragement from the faith community would be a beneficial way to tap into the energy and vigor of the young adult community.

Young adults have come of age and stand at a unique threshold of spiritual life. We believe that Christ himself was probably around thirty years old when he broke into his public ministry. Mary was raising the son of God in her twenties after giving birth to him as a teenager. St. Francis of Assisi was a troubadour turned disciple in his youth. Thus, the Church has the responsibility of not only guiding and forming the young adult community, but also encouraging resilience and courage to face new possibilities and challenges with the wellspring of faith. In encouraging leadership and involvement, as well as grassroots formation and dialogue, young adults will guide the future of the Church, navigating tension and conflict with compassion and opening wide the doors of radical spiritual love to our communities.

Rebecca Freeman, MDiv, is twenty-six years old and has a bachelor of arts in child life in hospitals and the community from Mills College and a master of divinity from the Franciscan School of Theology. She is a certified Child Life Specialist and is currently working on clinical pastoral education in pursuit of professional hospital chaplaincy certification.

Questions

1. In his excursus, Dr. John Coleman, SJ, outlines the potential problems lay ministers may have in collaborating with young priests and seminarians. The two lay ministers mention this same problem (they note that they have also had positive experiences of collaboration). What do you think drives some priests' difficulties with collaborating? What would help both lay Catholics and clergy move past this?

2. In his précis, Mark Erdosy discusses the lack of awareness many Catholics have of lay ecclesial ministry. Do you have full-time lay ecclesial ministers at your parish, campus, or other Catholic institution? Does the parish know that these ministers have received special, graduate-level training in ministry? In what ways, if any, did you welcome or recognize these people when they began ministry in your community? What sort of support do you offer them, and what are the challenges they face as lay ministers?

3. These ministers and other lay ministers in the this volume discuss the financial hardships of an expensive graduate degree (the master of divinity is a three-year, full-time degree) coupled with a fairly low-paying ministerial

salary. Is this simply a tragic reality or should the Church find ways to pay these ministers a wage that reflects the value of their work and training? What are some creative ways you might encourage fellow parishioners to give more of their treasure to sponsor such an initiative?